GILBERTO GERENA VALENTÍN:

MY LIFE AS A COMMUNITY ACTIVIST, LABOR ORGANIZER, AND PROGRESSIVE POLITICIAN IN NEW YORK CITY

GILBERTO GERENA VALENTÍN:

MY LIFE AS A COMMUNITY ACTIVIST, LABOR ORGANIZER, AND PROGRESSIVE POLITICIAN IN NEW YORK CITY

GILBERTO GERENA VALENTÍN

Edited by Carlos Rodríguez-Fraticelli
Translated by Andrew Hurley
with an Introduction by José E. Cruz

Originally published in Spanish by the Center for Puerto Rican Studies as *Soy Gilberto Gerena Valentín: memorias de un puertorriqueño en Nueva York*, copyright © 2013 by Center for Puerto Rican Studies.

Library of Congress Cataloging-in-Publication Data

Gerena Valentín, Gilberto, 1918-
  [Soy Gilberto Gerena Valentín. English]
  Gilberto Gerena Valentín : my life as a community activist, labor organizer, and progressive politician in New York City / Gilberto Gerena Valentín ; edited by Carlos Rodríguez-Fraticelli ; translated by Andrew Hurley with an Introduction by José E. Cruz.
      pages cm
  Translation of the author's Soy Gilberto Gerena Valentín.
  Includes bibliographical references and index.
  ISBN 978-1-878483-74-4 (pbk. : alk. paper) -- ISBN 978-1-878483-76-8 (ebook)
1. Gerena Valentín, Gilberto, 1918- 2. Puerto Ricans--New York (State)--New York--Politics and government--20th century. 3. Puerto Ricans--New York (State)--New York--Social conditions--20th century. 4. Community development--New York (State)--New York--History--20th century. 5. Community activists--New York (State)--New York--Biography. 6. New York (N.Y.)--Biography. I. Rodríguez-Fraticelli, Carlos, 1952- II. Hunter College. Centro de Estudios Puertorriqueños, issuing body. III. Title.

  F128.54.G47A3 2013b
  974.7'043092--dc23
  [B]

2013037032

Published by
Center for Puerto Rican Studies
Hunter College, CUNY
695 Park Avenue, E-1429
New York, NY 10065
centrops@hunter.cuny.edu
http://centropr.hunter.cuny.edu

Art Direction: Kenneth J. Kaiser
Printed in the United States of America on acid-free paper.

Cover photograph: On the soapbox, in front of New York City's Board of Education headquarters (110 Livngston Street, Brooklyn), during the 1964 school boicot. Author's collection. All photographs, unless otherwise indicated, are from the author's collection. All are reprinted by permission.

TABLE OF CONTENTS

DEDICATION

I dedicate this book to the thousands and thousands of Puerto Ricans who, like me, driven by hunger and a government that exploited their exodus in order to renegotiate the colonial status that still exists today, were forced to leave their homeland during the thirties.

I dedicate it, as well, to the thousands of Puerto Ricans across the United States who struggled so that the dignity of our people might be recognized and respected.

Finally, I dedicate it to my three daughters, Isa, Marielia, and Gilmari, to my deceased son José Gilberto (Joey), and to Taita; to Donald, whom I love like a son, and his wife Shelly; and to my wife Silita, who loves me and takes care of me. I will live for over a hundred years loving them and respecting them.

I would also like to thank Silita Tirado Colón and Marie Vélez Arocho for their help in matters of style and for other assistance in working the manuscript into final shape.

Gilberto Gerena Valentín

EDITOR'S NOTE

CARLOS RODRÍGUEZ FRATICELLI

I first met Gilberto Gerena Valentín in the late eighties. At that time, I was working at the Center for Puerto Rican Studies (CPRS), where I was part of a collaborative research project on the history of Puerto Rican community organizations in New York City. As part of that project, I went down to Puerto Rico to interview Gerena Valentín, who had returned to the island in 1985 after almost a half-century living in the United States. The interview opened my eyes to a part of the Puerto Rican community's history in New York that I knew nothing about. At that time, aside from the *Memoirs of Bernardo Vega: A Contribution to the History of the Puerto Rican Community in New York* (edited by César Andreu Iglesias, 1984 [originally published in Spanish in 1977]) and Virginia Sánchez Korrol's seminal study *From Colonia to Community: The History of Puerto Ricans in New York City 1917–1948* (1977), very little had been written about the historical evolution of that community. In the postwar years, there was nothing at all—a desert. The idea of writing a history of that period began to intrigue me. In 1990, after living for fifteen years in the United States, I returned to Puerto Rico, like many of those who had migrated both earlier and later than I had, and although I continued doing research on the subject, other professional priorities and interests claimed my time, and the project never materialized.

Two summers ago, Edwin Meléndez, director of the CPRS, contacted me to ask whether I'd be interested in editing the autobiography of Gilberto Gerena Valentín. He told me where the project stood thus far and how urgent it was that it be completed soon, and I agreed to look into the possibility of taking it on. He sent me the material. The story that I saw was extraordinary. It was at that point that I really began to see the greatness of this Puerto Rican that people talked about so much in New York City but wrote about so little. Still, I had to turn the project down. The manuscript was little more than a series of scattered texts that Gerena Valentín had written over the years, mostly after his return to the island. In among the rich and seductive stew of facts and insights there were countless repetitions and not a few historical lacunae. Which, of course, was understandable. Gerena Valentín was—and still is today, at the age of 97—a man of action, a person dedicated body and soul to two struggles: the struggle for social justice and the struggle for Puerto Rican independence. He was so active, so dynamic that at various stages of his life he seemed to have developed the ability to be in several places at the same time.

But that was just the point: My work would be not just editing and stylistic polishing, but doing active research, in order to present to readers the necessary basic historical background to the extraordinary anecdotes that Gerena Valentín narrated. I would, in a word, have to contextualize the anecdotes. I would also have to connect the stories, in order to give the final book a sense of coherence and continuity. As I was in the process of writing a book of my own and didn't feel I could give Gerena Valentín's text the time it deserved, I turned the project down. At that, Meléndez proposed a complementary project: writing a biographical essay on Gerena Valentín, to be published by the CPRS. As part of that effort, I would do a series of videotaped interviews of Gerena Valentín, who lived up in the mountains in central Puerto Rico, in the city of Lares, in Barrio Espino. These interviews would be archived at the CPRS for the use of scholars. This idea seemed more feasible, and I agreed.

Little did I know that I was walking into a trap I wouldn't be able to get out of. I was first drawn in and then enthralled by my regular visits to the home of don Gilberto and his loving wife Sila Tirado—the way I was treated there, the stories don Gilberto told. . . . . After several visits, Meléndez again asked me to consider editing the text. By then, my respect and admiration for this remarkable figure persuaded me that I had to do it. I was dealing here with a key figure in the development of the Puerto Rican community, especially from the forties through the seventies. Union organizer, community organizer, political activist, and general in the war for the civil-rights recognition of his community, Gerena Valentín had played an active part in the founding and development of all the major Puerto Rican organizations in the postwar period, including the Congreso de Pueblos, the Puerto Rican Day Parade, the National Association for Puerto Rican Civil Rights, the Puerto Rican Folklore Festival, and the Puerto Rican Community Development Project. During this period he was also a member of the New York City Human Rights Commission and a New York City councilman; he worked closely, especially during the difficult McCarthy years, with leftist political organizations such as the Communist Party of the United States, the American Labor Party, and the World Council of Peace. Gerena Valentín was also a pioneer in the creation of coalitions with the principal African-American civil rights organizations, playing a central role in the mobilization of Puerto Ricans for the famed marches on Washington in 1963 and 1968 and in the New York City school boycott of 1964, the largest in the nation's history.

So I made a counterproposal. I was willing to take on the job if I could be given license to reorganize the information as I thought necessary, and in at least rough chronological order. In exchange, I promised to show don Gilberto the text for his approval. That way, the autobiographical aspect of the project would be maintained. Meléndez thought my proposal made sense, so we discussed it with don Gilberto, who agreed to it, with the clear and unwavering understanding that he would have complete control over what was finally published. It was, after all, as he constantly reminded me, his memoirs, not mine.

With that agreement we started editing the memoirs. I would prepare the chapters and don Gilberto would look them over to add new facts or recollections or to take out any parts that were, in his opinion, irrelevant, unnecessary, or incorrect. On occasion I would discover information that I thought was important but didn't appear in his manuscripts. Some of this information has not been included because don Gilberto thought it wasn't relevant or wasn't part of his recollection of the events; much of it was accepted. My drafts of the chapters were revised at least twice for his approval. Before we sent the final manuscript to the copyeditor, don Gilberto had another look at it. Once the copyediting had been done, we sent the manuscript to don Gilberto one last time, for his final approval. The text that readers have before them now is faithful to his recollection of all the events he recounts.

I wish to express my deepest gratitude to Edwin Meléndez for convincing me to take on this project, and to the Shelly and Donald Rubin Foundation for its funding of the project. Without that support, I would not have had the great satisfaction of coming to know an extraordinary human being who merits recognition and respect by all Puerto Ricans, especially those in the diaspora that he helped to grow and prosper. My thanks go, too, to doña Sila, not just for her many kindnesses to me personally and for her reception of me and those who came with me into her home, but also for her loving care of that tamarind tree-made man named Gilberto Gerena Valentín. Finally, my gratitude to don Gilberto for being what he is: an exemplary human being.

INTRODUCTION

THE MAKING OF GILBERTO GERENA VALENTÍN: LABOR POLITICS, MILITARY SERVICE, AND POLITICAL ACTIVISM

JOSÉ E. CRUZ

When Gilberto Gerena Valentín arrived in New York, in October 1937, he left behind, reluctanctly, an island in shambles. The period between 1929 and 1938 in Puerto Rico has been described by historians César Ayala and Rafael Bernabe as "the most turbulent" in its twentieth century history (Ayala and Bernabe 2007: 95). The sugar industry had been in crisis for a decade before the Great Depression, chronic poverty was acute, unemployment led workers to make greater demands for relief, and low wages drew thousands of others to strike. The political landscape of Puerto Rico was also registering significant changes, but economics not politics, drove many, Gerena Valentín among them, to New York City to seek occupation in the lowest but comparatively better rungs of the city's economy.

Between 1930 and 1940 the Puerto Rican population in the United States increased by 33 percent, from 52,774 to 69,967. By 1950, their numbers quadrupled to 301,375, reaching the 892,513 mark in the 1960 Census (Rivera Batiz and Santiago 1994: 11). In New York City, with a count of 61,465 people, Puerto Ricans comprised a mere 0.8 percent of the city's total population in 1940. By 1950, their numbers had grown by 300 percent to 245,880 but at 4 percent were still a small proportion of the total. During the next ten years the size of the community increased by 149 percent to 612,574 or 8 percent of the total.[1] It is from this demographic critical mass that Puerto Rican politics makes its mark in the city, with Gilberto Gerena Valentín as one of its most visible and vociferous protagonists.

Before Gerena Valentín's arrival in Brooklyn, the community had already shown signs of significant political participation, and by the end of 1937 it had helped elect Oscar García Rivera, the first Puerto Rican to obtain a seat in the New York State Assembly, to represent district 17 in East Harlem.[2] Upon arrival, Gerena Valentín, like many others, was mostly concerned with finding work and going to school. His first interest was the labor movement.

From labor organizing he went on to serve in the U.S. military during World War II. After the war, and for the rest of his life in New York, Gerena Valentín combined labor and politics as the two fundamental drives of his life in the city.

THE LABOR MOVEMENT

At the time Gerena Valentín arrived in New York, the country was beginning to experience a shift in the way labor unions were recognized, from being tolerated to being encouraged (Dubofsky and Rhea Dulles 2004: 250). With the advent of the National Industrial Recovery Act (NIRA, 1933), the National Labor Relations Act (Wagner Act, 1935), and the Fair Labor Standards Act (FLSA, 1938), workers acquired three sets of legal tools that strengthened their right to organize, guaranteed minimum wages, and reduced their working hours, among other things. Unfortunately, The National Industrial Recovery Act did not last, its promise cut short in 1935 by the U.S. Supreme Court. But the Wagner and the Fair Labor Standards Act picked up where the Recovery Act left off, making the federal government an important ally of labor during the period of the New Deal.

The reaction against federal provisions favoring workers was quick and extreme. Employers leveled all kinds of charges against the Recovery Act, alleging, for example, that it would lead to a "labor dictatorship," and that through "collective bludgeoning" labor would become a force within the state more powerful than the state. Employers either refused to comply with the law or found ways around it. The law itself had no mechanism to enforce its provisions, leaving workers, in effect, with no recourse other than, at best, the strike, and at worst, violent confrontation. (Dubofsky and Rhea Dulles 2004: 252, 255–6).

Once NIRA was declared unconstitutional, the stage was set for the Wagner Act. This legislation began as an initiative of Senator Robert F. Wagner, from New York, to address certain deficiencies of NIRA. With the support of labor, the measure was adopted by the U.S. Senate a mere eleven days before NIRA was declared unconstitutional. Initially disliked by President Roosevelt, it passed the House of Representatives, and now with his favor, was signed by the President on July 5, 1935. Labor's right to organize was emphasized, and employer interference was forbidden; company unions were outlawed, and efforts on the part of employers to restrict or coerce employees from their right to organize were considered unfair labor practices. Under the law, a new National Labor Relations

Board was created and charged with encouraging and facilitating collective bargaining (Dubofsky and Rhea Dulles 2004: 259, 260).

Industrialists and their lawyers did not sit still. The Wagner Act was openly ignored and violated under the presumption that it was unconstitutional. Agents working on behalf of employers spied on workers, provoked them, and even attacked those who worked as organizers. Companies became little armies, amassing large stocks of weapons to use against workers on strike. Union leaders were routinely branded as subversives or communist agitators, and the police collaborated with employers by breaking union meetings. Violations were so blatant and widespread that even conservative newspapers protested employer tactics as violations of the civil liberties of workers. Just as Gerena Valentín stepped off the boat from Puerto Rico, workers were striking left and right in response to the anti-union fervor displayed by employers. Never mind that the constitutionality of the Wagner Act was affirmed by the U.S. Supreme Court on April 12, 1937; by the end of the year the number of strikes protesting employer tactics peaked at 4,720, involving almost two million workers. About a decade after its creation, the National Labor Relations Board had fulfilled its promise to defend the right of workers to organize according to their preferences by dismantling about 2,000 company unions and by ruling in favor of about 300,000 employees in cases of employer discrimination (Dubofsky and Rhea Dulles 2004: 262–5).

As employers and workers battled over their respective rights, the Roosevelt administration continued its reform path. Ironically, in its quest to secure a minimum wage for workers, the administration had to fight the opposition of not only the National Association of Manufacturers but also of the American Federation of Labor (AFL); the AFL feared that a minimum wage would become a maximum wage. Roosevelt was adamant that "a self-supporting and self-respecting democracy," could not justify child labor, the undercutting of wages, nor excessive working hours. In his view, the way out of recession was simple: workers needed the purchasing power that would allow them to consume the products they made. Despite strong opposition, Roosevelt had his way. The Fair Labor Standards Act, passed in June 1938, established a minimum wage, a forty-four-hour week, and prohibited child labor (Dubofsky and Rhea Dulles 2004: 268–9).[3]

Dubofsky and Rhea Dulles argue that despite the strong opposition they provoked among employers, pro-labor New Deal policies were seen favorably by public opinion. The President's view was that strong unions were proof and guarantee of a strong democracy. To his mind, big business required powerful unions to keep the power of business in check. "What does the country ultimately gain," said Roosevelt to Congress in the summer of 1937, "if we encourage businessmen to enlarge the capacity of American industry to produce unless we see to it that the income of our working population actually expands sufficiently to create markets to absorb that increased production?" (2004: 269).

Unions did not seem able to avoid internal conflict as the American Federation of Labor (AFL), the major labor organization of the 1930s and '40s, split, thus giving birth to the Committee for Industrial Organization (CIO). The dispute, embodied in the persons of William Green for the AFL and John L. Lewis for the CIO, lasted from 1934 to 1955. Ironically, the conflict between the two labor giants resulted in the growth of the unionized. In 1938, the Committee changed its name to Congress of Industrial Organizations, to reflect its permanency. By then, differences between the AFL and the CIO were clear: the latter promoted racial solidarity, focused on new immigrant workers, and gave greater attention to the demands of women workers. The CIO also waged successful organizing campaigns against major companies such as General Motors and U.S. Steel, even though its militancy was strongly condemned by conservative forces. Competition from the CIO forced the AFL to organize workers wherever it could find them, skilled or not (Dubofsky and Rhea Dulles 2004: 272, 282, 289, 291).

Was it because of this incentive that Gerena Valentín was invited to be a part of the Hotel, Restaurant, and Cafeteria Employees Organizing Committee fresh off the boat from Puerto Rico? This may or may not be the case. We do know, however, that in the fight against conservative industrialists the labor movement could not afford to waste any resources. As John Lewis put it, "We have to work with what we have," and this meant using communists, socialists, and anarchists to promote industrial unionism while making sure none of these groups took control of the CIO (Dubofsky and Rhea Dulles 2004: 299).

The advent of World War II put labor's relation to the federal government in a different light. Both the AFL and the CIO were opposed to American participation in the conflict. At the same time, the CIO was relentless in its pursuit of government assistance for organized labor. John Lewis wanted representation of labor in a federal cabinet or policy-making position, but none was offered by Roosevelt. In 1940, the context of war made for very strange bedfellows: because of his isolationism, Lewis was simultaneously applauded by communists, blacks, and reactionary industrialists. He strongly supported Wendell Wilkie for president and pledged to resign if Roosevelt was re-elected. Roosevelt won, and Lewis was out as president of the CIO. His successor, Philip Murray, threw his weight behind Roosevelt's foreign policy and program of national defense.

War made unionism stronger but not by default. Unions still had to battle recalcitrant employers in just about every sector of the economy: in the automobile industry, in the shipyards, transportation, building trades, textiles, in steel and coal mining. The number of labor conflicts in 1941 was higher than ever except 1937, with 2,000,000 workers participating in a total of 4,288 strikes. Further, as a result of a 1941 strike that threatened to halt steel production, sympathy for unions in Congress, within the business community and the public, eroded; the power of unions was considered excessive and a threat to the public interest.

During World War II jobs were plentiful, but women and blacks faced resistance to their entry into high-paying jobs. The AFL and even the CIO refused to treat blacks equally. White union members were not shy about their racism, often threatening to strike if blacks were given skilled jobs. Because of the tight labor market, organizing became easier as employers preferred a unionized workforce rather than risking productivity and profits in a competition for fewer workers (Dubofsky and Rhea Dulles 2004: 313).

The postwar period was entirely different. President Truman wanted to increase wages to ensure continued economic stability. Industrial leaders did not agree. Workers in San Francisco, New York, and the Midwest either went on strike or broke negotiations with employers. By the end of 1945 almost two million workers were on strike. The seizure of the railroads by Truman in 1946 earned him the label of strikebreaker for bankers and railroads, but a bill he proposed to keep workers in line did not become a law. Still, while workers secured higher wages and unions achieved more institutional security, employers kept their managerial prerogatives virtually intact (Dubofsky and Rhea Dulles 2004: 326–34).

For employers this was not enough. When conservative and anti-labor forces in Congress passed the Taft-Harley Act in June 1947, Truman vetoed the bill, declaring that it was "shocking—bad for labor, bad for management, bad for the country." Congress overrode his veto, giving employers greater rights and powers than they had before—full freedom to express anti-union views and to refuse collective bargaining, control over wage negotiations, the right to sue unions in federal court for breach of contract, protection from secondary boycotts, and the right to require affidavits from union officers certifying that they were not members of the Communist Party. This last provision affected Gerena Valentín directly: when he refused to sign the affidavit, he was banned from the New York Hotel Trades Council for three years. Ironically, by 1954 unions achieved their membership peak of 35 percent of non-agricultural workers, and the South, where Taft-Harley had a more restrictive impact than elsewhere, saw a rapid growth of its unionized cohort (Dubofsky and Rhea Dulles 2004: 336–7, 343).

In 1952, the death of the president of the AFL, William Green, and of the CIO, Philip Murray, provided an opportunity for improving the relationship between the two labor organizations. This opportunity was taken by their respective successors, George Meany and Walter Reuther. They set up a Joint Unity Committee and after much deliberation, all in secret, on February 9, 1955, the merger of the AFL and the CIO was announced. The new organization would be driven by four goals: to organize the unorganized, to eliminate corruption, to accept members regardless of race, and to protect the labor movement from the influence of Communism (Dubofsky and Rhea Dulles 2004: 348–52). In regards to Communism, Gerena Valentín stood to the left of the AFL, even before its merger with the CIO. Otherwise, the context created by the 1955 merger fit his agenda to the letter.

In New York, the dominant labor force during the first two decades of the Twentieth-Century was the AFL. Thus, the politics of organized labor during this period reflected the business unionism of the AFL, even though it also had a streak of socialist agitation embodied in the Industrial Workers of the World union (Isaac 2002: 22). In this regard, New York was similar to other industrial states. In New York, labor also cooperated with the progressive movement (Yellowitz 1965: 17). Labor leaders were careful to distinguish between their support for the Democratic Party and support for the principles espoused by Democrats. Nevertheless, the Democratic Party was the party of labor, while the Republican Party was openly hostile to unions and to any kind of social reform in the state (Yellowitz 1965: 231, 238). During the second half of the twentieth century, the labor movement in New York lost its socialist color and, in general, it focused more on lobbying for protective legislation than on organizing. During this period, workers in the city realized that in the battle for rights they had to fight not just their employers but their union bosses as well (Davis 2003). Corruption within the New York labor movement was significant during the second half of the twentieth century. In some cases, it was impossible to purge unions from the influence of organized crime, despite aggressive efforts to do so with the tools provided by the Racketeer Influenced and Corrupt Organization Act (RICO), passed in 1970. Emblematic of this failure are the New York District Council of Carpenters and the Laborers' International Union of North America (Jacobs 2006).

Before Gerena Valentín's time in the city, organizing efforts by Jews and German immigrants along ethnic lines produced a strong segment of the labor movement that was effective both economically and politically (Michels 2005: 3, 4). Unfortunately, by the time Gerena Valentín entered the labor movement scene in New York, the features that, according to Michels, facilitated the emergence of a strong Jewish labor movement in the city were not altogether there (2005: 15). During the first decades of the twentieth century, Jews were a demographically significant minority in New York City, whereas in the late 1940s Puerto Ricans were not. Jews concentrated in the garment industry, a strategic industrial sector of the city's economy; Puerto Ricans also concentrated in the garment industry and many, like Gerena Valentín, were in the hotel, food, and services sector. However, just as the garment industry was populated by Puerto Ricans, its strategic value began to decline.[4] Furthermore, as the U.S. economy shifted from manufacturing to services during the 1950s and '60s, Puerto Ricans continued to concentrate in manufacturing jobs—but at lower rates of participation and higher unemployment (Rodríguez 1989: 86–7). Michels argues that radical intellectuals "played a crucial role in the rise and development of the Jewish labor movement." He notes that "as organizers, lecturers, journalists, educators, popular poets, and fiction writers, radical intellectuals translated day-to-day travails into a broad ideological framework and institutional structure" (Michels 2005: 10–1). In the 1940s and '50s the Puerto Rican community could not boast to having a comparable cadre of radical intellectuals. Gerena Valentín was, at best, an organic intellectual in a loosely understood Gramscian sense, and he was only one among a few. Finally, before World War II the American labor movement experienced numerous instances of class conflict; after the war, when Gerena Valentín began the extended part of his activism, the institutionalization of the labor movement made it less militant, more inward-looking, and concerned with Cold War issues.[5]

Tony Michels challenges the proposition that socialists turned the Jewish labor movement in New York City into an agent of Americanization. He argues that the path from a "Yiddish-language socialism to English-language liberalism" was not smooth and that socialism was not a "one generation-phenomenon" (2005: 19–21). But while the path may have been rocky, the destination remained the same—Jewish integration into American political life. Socialist aspirations did not disappear, but they failed to become the ideological and normative political standard. Something similar happened within the Puerto Rican community in New York. In other words, the Spanish-language nationalism of Gerena Valentín emphasized unionism and wished for radical change, but it was appealing only to the extent that it was congruent with the community's main outlook, which was liberal and integrationist (Cruz 2011: 69).

Thus, on the one hand, the context in which Gerena Valentín entered the New York City labor movement encouraged and facilitated, at least for some years, the development of strong unions. On the other, that same context included features that limited the growth, cohesion, and impact of workers as an independent force in politics. To the extent that Gerena Valentín saw labor organizing in purely economic terms—as a vehicle for the promotion of socioeconomic advancement—the political limitations of American trade unionism after World War II were irrelevant. For him politics was about something else—it was about acculturation, cultural affirmation, democratic rights, independence for Puerto Rico. And those issues fit better on the agenda of the Puerto Rican Day Parade, the Congress of Puerto Rican Hometowns, the 1964 public schools boycott, or the New York Committee of the Puerto Rican Pro Independence Party, than on the agenda of the New York Hotel Trades Council, the Food Workers Industrial Union, the International White Collars Union, the AFL or the CIO.

SERVICE IN THE U.S. MILITARY

Two years after Gerena Valentín made it to New York, world history took a turn for the worse. On September 1, 1939, Adolf Hitler invaded Poland, thus igniting World War II. In retrospect, the war seems foreordained and predictable in light of the events that preceded the 1939 invasion: Italy's invasion of Ethiopia in 1935, the German militarization of the Rhineland in 1936, and their annexation of Austria and the Czech Sudetenland[6] in 1938. Yet, the response of the American government to these acts of aggression was to pass four Neutrality Acts between 1935 and 1939.[7] The existence of war was acknowledged, President Roosevelt took steps to prepare the country for it, and military production was the last nail in the coffin of the Great Depression. But it took a direct attack to the U.S. at Pearl Harbor, on December 7, 1941, for the United States to finally recognize the seriousness of the aggressive intent of Germany, Italy, and Japan. The U.S. declared war on Japan the very next day. After Germany and Italy declared war on the United States on December 11th, the United States reciprocated (Axelrod 2007: 375, 389).

Historically, military service has been a way of gaining formal membership— as a citizen—within a given society. Participation in warfare has also been one way in which citizens accumulate social and political capital. Further, the act of warfare has been understood beyond defense or aggression, as a way of making citizens fully aware of their membership in a community larger than family, village, ethnic, or racial group (Krebs 2006: 184–8). Michael Bellesiles offers an alternative way of thinking about military service: citizens serve because they are drafted or because they have no better choice. Those who join may justify and explain their decision on the basis of patriotic feelings or a sense of civic obligation. They may ostensibly appear to be "willing to risk everything in service to their country," but in the midst of conflict they think "more of food than fame, [long] more for home than heroism" (Bellesiles 2012: 3).

Gerena Valentín belongs in this latter category of participants. He did not join to prove that he deserved to be a U.S. citizen. He was not expecting to receive governmental benefits after the service, and he did not need to be told that he had an obligation to serve his nation; that would have been futile since he did not think of himself as a national of the United States. By his own admission, family was more important than nation, if nation meant the United States. The price to pay for refusal to comply with the draft was the loss of freedom. The risk of military service was death. Yet, Gerena Valentín was persuaded that, for the sake of his family, the army was a better alternative than prison. Under the terms of the Selective Training and Service Act of 1940, Gerena Valentín had the option of refusing to serve as a conscientious objector, that is, as someone who opposed war in any form by reason of religious training and belief (Axelrod 2007: 392). This choice was available to all men qualified for the draft. For reasons that we can only guess, Gerena Valentín did not follow that path.

Even though the U.S. appeared to see no reason to intervene in the war before 1941, in 1940 the U.S. Congress was prodded by President Roosevelt to appropriate substantial amounts of money for national defense on three separate occasions—$1.8 billion in January, $2.5 billion on May 16, and $1.3 billion on May 31st. In order to make provision for war, the National Defense Act of 1940 raised the national debt limit by 9 percent from $45 to $49 billion. Another obviously war-related measure was the Two-Ocean Navy Act, approved on July 20th, which allocated funds to make the U.S. Navy capable of fighting Germany in the Atlantic Ocean and Japan in the Pacific (Axelrod 2007: 391). In August 1941, Roosevelt and Winston Churchill signed the Atlantic Charter, which cemented the alliance between England and the United States for the explicit purposes of restoring sovereign rights and self-government to those who had been deprived of them by force and to establish a lasting and just peace among nations. The Charter made explicit reference to the timing of peace: it would follow "the final destruction of the Nazi tyranny." Yet, by November 1941, the U.S. continued to follow a policy of neutrality even as it waged an undeclared naval war with Germany and authorized the arming of merchant vessels in response to German attacks (Axelrod 2007: 394–5).

By the time Gerena Valentín made it to a theater of war in 1943, the United States had taken over the islands of Guadalcanal and Bougainville, as well as the Gilbert Islands in the Pacific Ocean. Early in 1943, the Allies scored a significant victory in North Africa, and before Gerena Valentín departed to New Guinea in December, Sicily fell to the Allies, Italy surrendered, and U.S. forces landed in Salerno, the capital of the province of Salerno, in the Italian region of Campania (Axelrod 2007: 378).

Gerena Valentín participated in air missions, was forced to parachute in enemy territory, and nearly lost his life. He was in the Philippines but did not experience the horror of the Bataan Death March, which took the lives of 10,000 men. Black Puerto Ricans, whether from the island or from New York, experienced segregation in the military during and after World War II (Bonilla 2000), but Puerto Ricans in the United States did not go through the ordeal of arrest and detention that residents of German and Italian descent experienced, nor the degradation of internment in concentration camps suffered by more than 100,000 Nisei (citizens) and Issei (noncitizens) Japanese residents (Axelrod 2007: 379, 398–9).

Based on a 1945 article in the soldier magazine YANK, Linda Delgado claims that "more than eighty Puerto Ricans were wounded or killed in action during World War II, at a time when no Puerto Rican units were officially reported as being on the front" (2005: 79). It makes sense that no report of a Puerto Rican unit being on the front existed because the only Puerto Rican unit in the U.S. Army at the time was the 65th Regiment, which was not allowed to participate in combat until the Korean War. Thus, whatever the number of Puerto Rican dead and wounded, they must have been Puerto Ricans who, like Gerena Valentín, were drafted in the United States.[8]

Gerena Valentín's military experience is not the experience that is typically portrayed in the literature on Puerto Rican participation in the military. Aside from the fact that secondary sources do not distinguish between the experience of Puerto Ricans from the island and Puerto Ricans born or residing in the United States, their emphasis is on the patriotic eagerness, loyalty, and bravery of Puerto Rican soldiers (see Curbelo 1992; Cruz 2000a; Delgado 2005). Gerena Valentín's experience may be the tip of the iceberg of stateside Puerto Rican participation in the U.S. military. Whether his tour of duty is representative or exceptional remains an important question. Yet his record of participation is perfectly in tune with a strand in the larger narrative of American participation in the service. Ever since the Civil War, Americans have shown their reluctance to join the U.S. military when they either did not understand what the conflict was about or did not agree with U.S. policy. Many are known to have gone beyond a grudging participation to outright avoidance, by fleeing their states, going to Canada, or through subterfuges that gained them a medical exemption (Bellesiles 2012: 110). Also, like Gerena Valentín, many American soldiers eventually became sympathetic towards the "enemy," once they understood that the war—against Mexicans, Native Americans, or the Vietnamese—was unjust or a mistake (Bellesiles 2012: 75, 138, 275, 279–80).

After the war, black and Hispanic veterans returned to the status quo ante: prejudice, segregation, and discrimination. Black veterans demanding their citizen rights could count on the National Association for the Advancement of Colored People (NAACP) and Progressive Democrats, a group organized by the end of the war, for assistance (Nieman 1991: 140). In 1949, in Corpus Christi, Texas, Mexican American veterans organized the American G.I. Forum to defend their rights. The Forum quickly became an effective advocate for the civil rights of all Mexican Americans. (Gutiérrez 1995: 154). In 1958, Puerto Ricans in New York organized the National Congress of Puerto Rican Veterans. "We have served with honor," said retired army colonel Rafael Pagán, "we are not asking [for] favors. We are asking this nation to give our veterans their fair share" (Narváez 1973: 76).

Even though these words were said in 1973, it is striking that, as far as the claims of Puerto Rican World War II veterans is concerned, they go to the crux of the matter.[9] Yet, in 1947, the problems of Puerto Rican veterans in New York were overshadowed by the "Puerto Rican problem"—a concept created by the media to blame Puerto Ricans for overcrowded housing, increases in unemployment and crime, and a deterioration of public health in the city. The alleged unwillingness of Puerto Rican migrants to assimilate only made matters worse (Meléndez 2010: 201).

In 1946, Gerena Valentín donned his civilian clothing, returned to New York, and went back to work—he did so literally, in the ordinary, making-a-living sense. His old job at the Commodore Hotel was there, waiting for him. He also went back to work in a more expansive sense: by devoting himself to the issues and projects that made him a fabled member of the Puerto Rican political elite in New York City.

THE POLITICAL SCENE

In the Puerto Rican narrative of politics in New York City, where does a figure like Gerena Valentín fit? The story of Puerto Rican politics in the city twists and turns differently over time. Generally, we can say that during the twentieth century Puerto Ricans in New York confronted exclusionary rules, partisan neglect, and discrimination. Some within the community suffered persecution, repression, and imprisonment for defending what they believed to be the island's inalienable right to independence. Most were considered politically apathetic.

Nothing ever sits permanently still, and the Puerto Rican political experience in New York conforms to that axiom. But change also coexists with continuity, and one element that illustrates that feature in the case of Puerto Ricans is the persistent affirmation of a national identity framed by, but not entirely and not always defined in terms of, American citizenship. This process of cultural affirmation has had distinctive features. For more than a century, Puerto Ricans in the United States have lived immigrant lives without being immigrants in a formal sense. They have been defined as political exiles, as an ethnic group, as an oppressed nationality, and as a racial minority. Other concepts that academics have used to designate Puerto Rican identity include "commuter nation," "transnational," and "translocal." As a group, Puerto Ricans are diverse in terms of class and race. Whether born in Puerto Rico or in the United States, they see themselves as Puerto Rican; no

Puerto Rican born in the United States uses the term Puerto Rican-American as an identity label, but when push comes to shove, all claim a dual identity as Puerto Rican and American; or as poet Tato Laviera put it: AmeRican.

In the New York community, the period from 1920 to 1950 was marked by efforts related to settlement. This is the stage that James Jennings describes as the time of "relative nonparticipation" (1984b: 141). Electoral politics was part of the mix but the most prominent activities were community organizing and institution building. Mobilization centered on social and cultural projects, including the establishment of civic, mutual aid, and charitable groups. While some of these groups were also expected to perform political functions, others were established to be explicitly political but in effect were social (Sánchez Korrol 1994: 173). The period from 1950 until the mid-1960s was also characterized by socio-cultural organization, but politics becomes more important as well. From the mid-'60s up to 1975, Puerto Rican politics takes a new turn, simultaneously becoming more focused on the electoral process while shifting decisively to a bureaucratic style. Puerto Rican radicalism also grew during this period. With the end of the War on Poverty, politics at the community level moved away from transformative goals to focus on service provision, cultural affirmation, and the promotion of social integration and upward mobility. Since 1975, the main arena of participation has been the electoral and policy process, and the goals of representation, agenda-setting, and policymaking favorable to Puerto Ricans have been its target.

Despite the many political changes fostered by Puerto Ricans in New York—the elimination of literacy tests as a requirement for registration and voting, the use of bilingual ballots, and the creation of a police review board, among others (Cruz 2011: 82)—their politics has the quality of caretaking as well as transformation. This is so in the sense that the assumptions and principles associated with liberal democracy were sustained as much as they were challenged by them, rhetorically and in practice. Puerto Ricans added discursive references to individual and group rights, inclusive political participation, economic justice, the right to descriptive representation, communitarianism, internationalism, working-class hegemony, and socialism to the political vernacular. They also made claims and achieved practical results, mostly within the parameters of liberal democratic politics, i.e., a politics of social mobilization and electoral participation seeking inclusion, descriptive representation, and socioeconomic equality through public policy as well as through self-help.[10]

Gerena Valentín himself helped bring about some of the changes noted above. The work by Aspira and the Puerto Rican Forum to promote bilingual education and to set up the Puerto Rican Family Institute, respectively, further illustrates the pattern. The work of radicals at the United Nations (UN) to make the international organization proclaim the colonial nature of the status of Puerto Rico illustrates the mixed nature of Puerto Rican politics and their success confirms the prevalence of the liberal democratic paradigm: UN resolutions represented rhetorical victories that had no transformative impact; Puerto Rico's colonial status persists to this day.

Despite low levels of electoral participation, Puerto Ricans were not marginal in New York City—they created political clubs, organized voter registration drives, ran for office, elected representatives to the State Assembly, the State Senate, and the New York City Council, received numerous appointments to administrative agencies, pursued and achieved judgeships, built lasting social service, cultural, and academic institutions, liberalized access to higher education, and helped broaden the scope of the franchise. One could say that, contrary to the notion that reality is constituted by visibility and perception, Puerto Ricans in New York were real players in the political process even though the perception of their initiatives and their impact was low. To policymakers and fellow citizens they may have been selectively out of mind, but, for better or for worse, they were never completely out of sight.

In the democratic process, elections alone are an inadequate gauge of participation; this has been evident to a good number of political scientists for a while and much more so to historians, anthropologists, and sociologists. The Puerto Rican story in New York City illustrates that insight with particular clarity. For example, The Puerto Rican Forum and ASPIRA were seen by some of their creators as building blocks in a strategy for political empowerment. Some did not agree with a scheme in which the Forum would serve as institutional incubator of related projects. ASPIRA never went beyond the boundaries of its educational agenda, but the Forum did try to perform this brokerage function. As community leader Josephine Nieves put it:

> The Forum was about brokering power and pushing for influence and becoming a watchdog for our community at the level of the NAACP and the Jewish organizations. We had a project in which we, and this was in East Harlem, we

> did an intensified campaign to put someone in office; that
> was a training ground for so many of us that we learned
> what running a campaign was all about. De esa [That is how]
> Johnny Carro salió siendo [became] the first Puerto Rican
> assistant to the mayor, Mayor Wagner. (Nieves 1988)

Groups such as the Association of Puerto Rican Social Workers and the Gurabo Social Club promoted interest in the political process through their participation in the mock election of the "Mayor of Puerto Rican New York," an event initiated by the newspaper *La Prensa* in 1961 (Nuevos Candidatos 1961: 6). In 1962, the Puerto Rican Association for Community Affairs brought together civic and political leaders to discuss Puerto Rican culture and the problem of urban education (No Basta 1962: 1). In 1966, a group of Puerto Ricans established the Comité Boricua Contra la Brutalidad Policíaca to fight against the use of excessive force by the police (González 1966: 4). During the 1970s, United Bronx Parents, led by Evelina Antonetty, was instrumental in the promotion of political participation of Puerto Ricans at the school board level (United Bronx Parents 1977). All of this, and much more, would be missed by focusing solely on electoral politics.

It is usually a mistake to see the politics of a particular community as an integrated whole, dominated by one type of discourse and agenda. Nevertheless, it is safe to say that Puerto Rican politics before, during, and after Gerena Valentín, were fundamentally liberal democratic in the sense I have specified above. Puerto Rican *tabaqueros* may have dreamt of socialism during the late 1910s and early 1920s (Vega 1984: 23–4), but Puerto Rican voters were more inclined to participate in the regular electoral process. Early on, they voted for out-group candidates if they had to—the support given to James Lanzetta, Fiorello LaGuardia's opponent in 1932, is an example.[11] But when they had the opportunity to vote for one of their own they took it— something they did successfully as early as 1937, in the election of Oscar García Rivera to the New York State Assembly. Even a radical like Bernardo Vega was taken up by the liberal net during the 1948 presidential race in support of Progressive Party candidate Henry Wallace (Vega 1984: 233). During the late 1950s and early 1960s, the Puerto Rican elites who believed that Puerto Ricans had no future within the framework of Democratic machine politics, decided to work with whomever was willing to work with them, within or without the political parties (Carro 1988), but always within the parameters of liberal democratic principles and goals. In Gerena Valentín we find corroboration of this attitude in his involvement with the Communist Party: he worked with Communists, but he was not a member of the party. His nationalism was intense, but it did not question the legitimacy of liberal democracy.

At this point the reader may ask: What about the Young Lords? How do *they* fit in the liberal democratic framework? The Young Lords did not pioneer a radical style and orientation within the Puerto Rican community, but theirs was the first truly homegrown expression of Puerto Rican radicalism in New York. Their significance in the overall narrative of Puerto Rican politics has been exaggerated, but the group did make a unique contribution (see Whalen 1998; Fernández 2004; Ogbar 2006). The verse in Mariposa's[12] poem, "Ode to the Diasporican," *No nací en Puerto Rico/Puerto Rico nació en mí* [*I was not born in Puerto Rico/Puerto Rico was born in me*], encapsulates the basic distinction between the politics of the Young Lords and the politics of their radical predecessors, the Nationalist Party and the Movimiento Pro Independencia. Members of the latter were born in Puerto Rico, and in their politics the island was always first. The Young Lords were born and raised in the U.S.A., and their politics were initially focused on their oppression in the United States; only later did they come to believe that their plight was connected to the plight of Puerto Rican islanders. In essence, however, the Young Lords were nationalists dressed in army fatigue jackets. In context, it is understandable that their *outré* style of politics passed as radicalism. In effect, they were more loyal critics than revolutionaries, ostensibly interested in systemic transformation but practically invested in the reproduction of liberal democracy.

The Puerto Rican Nationalist Party was never interested in the social transformation of the United States. The Movimiento Pro Independencia (MPI) was in the same political boat as the Nationalists until the island organization decided to follow in the footsteps of Fidel Castro and Ché Guevara, and the Misión Vito Marcantonio changed its name to Puerto Rican Socialist Party-USA Branch (PSP). In this, the Young Lords beat the MPI to the punch. But as the Lords began to disintegrate and the MPI changed its label, the latter picked up where the former left off. Beginning in 1973, and for about ten years, the PSP articulated a political vision that hinged on the national liberation of Puerto Rico and the socialist transformation of the United States. Did this mean that from 1969 to about 1982, the Young Lords and the PSP, along with a small assortment of additional groups and organizations,[13] managed to impose a shift in Puerto Rican politics from its dominant liberal political orientation toward a radical agenda? (see Rodríguez-Morazzani 1992; Thomas 2010).

Not quite. At best, so-called radicals offered a critique and rejection of liberal politics and liberal democracy but without moving away from this established tradition and practice. There was no shift for three reasons. First, homegrown radicals emerged, almost out of the blue, as adversaries of liberalism and capitalist democracy without any kind of connection or even clear notion of what liberal mainstream politics was. Theirs was rather a gut reaction against existing conditions, a reflex almost, prompted by individual experiences. In some cases, these individual experiences were vicarious, and the virtual stimulus was collective in nature. For example, some individuals became radicals based on the example provided by the participation of their parents in New York's public schools decentralization struggle of 1968 or, at the macro level, as a result of their particular way of processing the struggles of blacks in the South or the struggle of the Vietnamese for national liberation.

Second, radical politics was steeped in the politics of the moment, and, despite its programs and platforms, it had no real strategic orientation—in other words, it did not fully know what it was against or where it was going. Esoteric theoretical debates and internecine conflicts were both symptoms and proof of this lack of strategic orientation. With its systematic program of political education, its newspaper, and its programmatic platform, the PSP had all the trappings of an organization firmly grounded in hard-headed scientific analysis of Puerto Rican life *en las entrañas del monstruo* [in the belly of the beast]. This turned out to be an illusion, more sound than fury, a veritable Wizard of Oz scenario. For all of its seemingly deep theory and scientific strategy, the PSP could lay claim to very little by way of understanding or practical results. And despite all appearances of planning and democratic control, decisions were made almost in a moment-to-moment fashion and according to the whim of the Secretary General of the party, Juan Mari Brás, and his minions in the *comisión política*—the PSP equivalent of the Soviet *politburo*. Latter-day reviews have tried hard to make silk gloves out of the sow's ears of the PSP experience, but that is a difficult story to spin.

Third, the Young Lords and the MPI-PSP had more sympathizers than followers. For every Puerto Rican who described the Lords as folk heroes, there was another who considered them *títeres*, i.e., hoodlums or troublemakers. The PSP (both the island and USA branches) managed to rally 20,000 people at Madison Square Garden in 1974. In Puerto Rico, the main branch printed 100,000 copies of the newspaper *Claridad* before the 1976 general election. Yet in that electoral contest the party received the support of only 0.6 percent of the voters; in 1981 appeals by the PSP-USA to Puerto Ricans in New York to support Frank Barbaro for mayor were roundly ignored in favor of the re-election of Edward Koch.[14]

Instead of shifting, Puerto Rican politics fluctuated between liberalism and its alternatives. The trajectory of the community was fundamentally recursive rather than progressive. "Radicalism" represented a parallel emergence—in some cases it was an outlier—rather than a shift. Instead of displacement there was co-existence within the prevailing orientation and context. All in all, Puerto Rican politics in New York was a highway system of sorts, with scores of people moving both in the same and opposite direction, sometimes colliding, sometimes yielding, sometimes sharing the lane, sometimes driving together, going through different exits or points of entry alone or together, sometimes moving in sequence and sometimes in parallel. In that system, Gerena Valentín drove, along with others, propelled by the twin engines of trade unionism and nationalism.

Puerto Rican linkages to the civil rights, anti-war, and feminist movements of the 1960s and '70s provide further evidence of the mainstream-oriented, liberal character of Puerto Rican politics during the time that Gerena Valentín was active in New York; he embodied some of those connections. In 1965, for example, he was head of the National Association of Puerto Rican Civil Rights. A year later he was ranked number one among fifteen Puerto Rican community leaders identified as the most "influential decision-makers...in anti-poverty, civil rights, and voting amendment programs" (Kihss 1966: 118).   He is credited with organizing a large Puerto Rican mobilization as part of Martin Luther King's 1968 Poor People's Campaign (Torres 1998: 5). Of course, during the 1960s these movements felt radical in nature. It is only in retrospect that we understand how they fit within a liberal democratic framework. The Black Panthers and the Nation of Islam may not have wanted integration à la Southern Christian Leadership Conference, and they may have been to the left of the Student Non-Violent Coordinating Committee, but all of them wanted recognition and equal treatment under the law.

One could argue that the visibility, strength, and moral appeal of the civil rights, anti-war, and feminist movements made the involvement of Puerto

Ricans in New York in those types of struggles natural. Puerto Ricans and blacks in particular were both second-class citizens, subject to the same kind of racially discriminatory treatment, and in the case of Puerto Ricans, regardless of color. Gerena Valentín, for example, could pass as white only if he did not speak. Otherwise he was vulnerable to discrimination as his accented English made it apparent that he was the Other. Alliances with blacks, however, were crafted rather than natural, and the relationship included a good dose of caution, competition, and conflict (Lee and Diaz 2007; Rodríguez-Morazzani 1998: 36–7).

Aponte-Parés and Merced suggest that because of class, racial, and ethnic differences, the gay liberation movement did not appeal to many Puerto Rican gays. On the other hand, those Puerto Rican gays who were interested were rejected by the movement out of fear or prejudice (1998: 297–300). Looking at African Americans and Puerto Ricans in Hartford, Connecticut, I found that their relationship was driven by three sets of paired variables: compartmentalization and ambivalence, resentment and paternalism, and cooperation and conflict. Compartmentalization entailed dissimilar histories, while ambivalence referred to the duality of Puerto Rican racial identity. Resentment and paternalism were African Americans attitudes toward Puerto Ricans; cooperation and conflict are self-evident: Puerto Ricans and blacks were friends as well as adversaries (Cruz 2000b). These features were also part of the New York scene during the time in which Gerena Valentín did his work as politician and activist (Cruz Forthcoming).

Civil rights organizations, voter registration and education campaigns, and grassroots efforts to improve socioeconomic conditions of Puerto Ricans were expressions of an approach that entailed political challenges that did not question the legitimacy of the political order—this was an insider type of politics. In this approach the goal was not to transform the political system but rather to align the system's performance with its promise. Even the activism that sought to develop the political capacity to transform American politics and society relied on strategies and tools for action that were acceptable to the political establishment and promoted liberal integration—this was an outsider type of politics whose unintended integrationist effects I have called "pushing left to get to the center" (Cruz 1998);[15] within this type of politics there were expressions of terrorism, but these were few and politically ineffective. Within the Puerto Rican community the most significant representatives of outsider politics were the Puerto Rican Socialist Party and the Young Lords

Party; the most notorious were Los Macheteros and the Fuerzas Armadas de Liberación Nacional (FALN).

In a practical sense, Puerto Rican politics in New York developed as a set of expressions of these two tendencies; once the terrorist factor is removed from the equation, both insider and outsider politics generally fit within the framework of liberal democratic aspirations that have also served as the mainspring of Puerto Rican politics.

In this context, as a political actor, Gerena Valentín understood that it was important to work with oppositional groups and other minorities but always with eyes fixed on the prize of Puerto Rican advancement. He operated as an outsider in rhetoric and style, while remaining within the parameters of insider politics in terms of methods, substance, and goals. Thus, marching, rallying, and participating in boycotts did not exclude membership in governmental commissions or being an elected official. For him, being a part of movements promoting social, economic, or political transformation in the United States was worthwhile only if there was something in it for Puerto Ricans in the here and now, whether in terms of socioeconomic advancement or nationalist vindication or both. The Popular Front model was acceptable for trade union or nationalist politics, but travels with the Communist Party USA stopped at the systemic transformation shore.

It is hard to say whether Gerena Valentín acted in full awareness of the sources of his approach to political action or not, but it is nevertheless clear that his reliance over time on a combination of bargaining and compromise tactics with demand-protest actions, using open challenges to established organizations and political institutions as a point of entry into the structure of political representation, gibes almost perfectly with the features of the larger context of politics in which he participated. The reliance of social movements on pressuring mainstream parties into adopting a more responsive stance, challenging objectionable incumbents, or electing sympathetic or descriptively representative candidates committed to a progressive agenda are features that also defined Gerena Valentín's political trajectory over time.

In 1996, an alliance of Puerto Rican organizations marched on Washington, D.C., to bring attention to the public policy needs of Puerto Ricans in the United States and Puerto Rico. Dubbed Boricua First!, this coalition was organized by agency executives, former and unreconstructed radicals, veterans, and cultural nationalists. These activists believed that, while other minority groups were making significant socioeconomic and political gains, Puerto Ricans remained marginalized, underrepresented, and underserved (Torres, et al. 1996). Although turnout was expected to be 25,000, only 2,500 traveled to Washington. The activities were poorly organized, publicity was deficient, and many were turned off by the focus on political prisoners. A policy agenda that the coalition outlined was presented to leaders of Congress. Participants who lobbied legislators could not believe how easily they were dismissed by staffers who felt no obligation to a constituency that either barely turned out or voted against their party.

To some, the whole effort reflected political immaturity and poor strategizing. On the other hand, there were those who praised the march as a sincere attempt at promoting unity among Puerto Ricans; to them any expression of ethnic pride and any demands for justice and respect for Puerto Ricans had to be commended, regardless of the outcome. Critics dismissed the claim that the march had been a success, since it highlighted the fact that Puerto Ricans were divided over many issues, that community resources were limited, and that Puerto Rican elites did not know how to use existing resources very well.

In a post-march incident that was highly symbolic, a security guard kept Congressman Luis Gutiérrez from entering the Capitol building. After refusing to accept his congressional identification, the guard told Gutiérrez to "go back to the country you came from" (Bowles 1996). Meanwhile, the Boricua First! National Steering Committee went into a coma. Critics of the group went public with their concerns, and the financial practices of the treasurer were questioned. By the end of June many were wondering whether the organization was dead (*Crítica* 1996: 2). When 35,000 Latinos from across the country marched on Washington in October, the Puerto Rican members of Congress attended and spoke at the main rally (Torres 1996). Boricua First!, however, was nowhere to be found. In 1997, the demise of the group was confirmed publicly (*Crítica* 1996-1997: 9–10). By then, Gerena Valentín had returned to the country he came from.

Gilberto Gerena Valentín lived through the various phases of Puerto Rican political development in New York as an active protagonist until his return to Puerto Rico in 1985. After the war he went back to labor organizing, but in a context that was not as friendly to labor as before. He lived and worked through a time in which Puerto Ricans were neither able to benefit fully from public services nor "to shape the policies of public agencies" (Sexton 1965: 105). During the 1960s, initiatives aimed at improving the socioeconomic condition of the community were profitable in the short-term, but not all achieved lasting results. During the War on Poverty, Puerto Rican elites were more successful in the local antipoverty establishment than in other arenas of representation. According to James Jennings, this resulted in a "dependent politics, one in which independent political power is not developed" (Jennings 1984a: 92).

Gerena Valentín would disagree. In fact, it could be argued that Gerena Valentín's work is an example of a Puerto Rican politics that was not just independent but, also, systematic and persistent against all odds. It was an independence forced on Puerto Ricans by the negligence of the Democratic and Republican parties, racial discrimination, and socioeconomic disadvantage; and it was practiced to perfection by activists like Gerena Valentín, who didn't care to go along to get along. Gerena Valentín's principled style of activism was incompatible with the idea articulated by Woodrow Wilson in *Congressional Government*, which states that "nothing can be accomplished in politics by mere disagreement" (1956: 213). It is, perhaps, for this reason that his accomplishments were greater in the civil than in the political society.[16]

While at face value Gerena Valentín's political style and trajectory seems to point toward the idea of "going against the grain," this idea does not fully define his record of participation.[17] As a New York City councilman he introduced resolutions against the presence of the U.S. Navy in Vieques, Puerto Rico; against the movie *Fort Apache, The Bronx*, and against the dictatorship of Anastasio Somoza in Nicaragua. Gerena Valentín saw the council more as a bully pulpit than as a policymaking tool, and in office he acted more as an ideologue than a policymaker. Nevertheless, his actions almost always had a constituency, and he was recognized as someone who could put "boots on the ground" when necessary. Ironically, when he lost his city council seat in 1982, columnist Luisa Quintero noted that his problem was that he was not Machiavellian enough (Quintero 1982: 20).

Gilberto Gerena Valentín was not a prince, but he was as Machiavellian as they come. To those who don't know Machiavelli, this may be insulting. I leave it to the *cognoscenti* among us to recognize the compliment or to agree to disagree. The context in which Gerena Valentín lived and worked structured his activism, sometimes facilitating and sometimes hampering political action. Yet, his life in New York is stamped with the seal of his originality. It should be easy for the reader to appreciate that in the pages that follow.

NOTES

1 See U.S. Census Bureau (1940); Gibson (1998); Department of City Planning (1993).

2 García Rivera ran on the Republican and American Labor Party lines. At the time, Assemblymen served for one-year terms and García Rivera served in 1938 and 1939. In 1940 he was defeated by the Democratic candidate, Hulan Jack, 12,171 to 9,026 (see *The New York Red Book* 1938, 1941).

3 By 1941, the work week was reduced to forty-hours. The prohibition on child labor applied only to children under sixteen in industries whose scope of commerce was inter-state.

4 According to the Gotham Center's Garment Industry History Initiative, "increasingly in the decades after WWII, production moved South, West and then overseas to lower-cost areas" (Gotham Center for New York City History n.d.).

5 A good example is the Women's Trade Union League of New York (WTUL). By 1955, the organization was little more than a social welfare group, convinced that unions could exert pressure but only government could effect change. After World War II, instead of organizing, WTUL activists spent their time in Albany lobbying, and many moved into bureaucratic positions in the wartime agencies that morphed into permanent administrative units or in state boards and agencies (Schrom Dye 1980: 162–3). In New York, the best example of union alignment with Cold War policies is that of the Building and Construction Trades Council of Greater New York under Peter J. Brennan. Though an activist Democrat during the 1950s and '60s, during the 1970s Brennan supported Republican candidates and was ardently in favor of the war in Vietnam. During his vice presidency of the New York State AFL-CIO, two hundred workers were mobilized by the organization to attack an anti-war demonstration on Wall Street. Dubbed the "Hard Hat Riot," the disturbance resulted in more than 70 people injured and six arrested (McFadden 1996; Bigart 1970). The United Auto Workers, which had been the epitome of militancy during the late 1930s and '40s, by the end of the 1950s was policing its members to maintain contractual agreements that were more focused on money than working class power and economic democracy. Labor also actively supported Truman's anti-communist policies, the Marshall Plan, American participation in NATO, and the Korean War. When the CIA decided to actively undermine leftist labor movements in Europe and Latin America, the AFL and the CIO were more than happy to help (Dubofsky and Rhea Dulles 2004: 344–6).

6 The Sudetenland comprised areas of Czechoslovakia that were inhabited mostly by Germans.

7 The second Neutrality Act was passed in reaction to the Spanish Civil War in 1936.

8 Unlike African-Americans, who were granted citizenship *after* performing with bravery and distinction during the Civil War, Puerto Ricans served in World War I at the same time that citizenship was conferred to them in 1917. A year after the U.S. invasion of Puerto Rico, Congress created the Puerto Rican Volunteer Regiment. Renamed the Puerto Rican Infantry Regiment of the United States in 1917, its members discharged their military duties in the Panama Canal Zone. In 1920, the regiment was baptized the 65th U.S. Infantry, and under that name Puerto Rican soldiers from the island served in the African, Italian, French, and German theaters during World War II (Curbelo 1992: 55). Puerto Ricans from the island were used initially as support troops. As a unit they did

not participate in active combat during World War II. Only after they demonstrated their ability during maneuvers held in Vieques in 1950, were they allowed to fight in Korea (Harris 1980: 43, 158).

9   In 1972, the Congress received a $1.3 million grant to help returning G.I.'s adapt to their peacetime environment and to assist them in their dealings with the military bureaucracy. In 1973, it lamented the fact that more than 60 percent of Vietnam veterans of Puerto Rican origin in the New York metropolitan area were unemployed. The group claimed that the provisions of the G.I. Bill were such that Puerto Rican veterans were all but excluded from access to benefits. Further, the Congress noted that veterans experienced discrimination from businessmen and employers (Narváez 1973: 76).

10   This is not the typical definition of liberal politics. I offer this definition because the exclusion of the social or group dimensions of politics from traditional definitions of liberal politics is useful as an analytical strategy but limited as an epistemic criterion. I am also reacting to the tendency to reduce liberalism to its market-centered dimension. The liberalism of Puerto Ricans did not challenge the idea of the market but focused on the state as the primary arbiter of the contest for rights and benefits.

11   Ronald H. Bayor notes that La Guardia's loss to Lanzetta was due in part to overconfidence. He writes: "Lanzetta and Tammany [Hall]...were ahead of La Guardia in establishing contacts with Puerto Ricans...Tammany was aggressive in organizing and controlling the vote of this new group, whereas La Guardia and his people were lax in responding to the ethnic succession going on in the district as the Jews began to move out" (See Bayor 1993: 79). Interestingly, in 1934 Puerto Rican voters turned against Lanzetta and helped elect his opponent, Vito Marcantonio, to Congress (Sánchez Korrol 1994: 187–90); as a result, a long-term and close political relationship between Marcantonio and Puerto Ricans followed, focused on issues pertaining to the island as well as New York (see Meléndez 2010: 203–12; Meyer 2011: 91).

12   a.k.a. María Teresa Fernández.

13   A prominent group within this lesser-known assortment of organizations was El Comité-MINP. In contrast to the Nationalist Party, the PSP-USA, and the latter Young Lords, El Comité-MINP put the struggle for Puerto Rican democratic rights in the United States front and center (see Muzio 2008).

14   Frank Barbaro ran against Ed Koch in the September 22, 1981, primary for the Democratic nomination. Barbaro won in mostly black districts but Koch beat him by a 3-2 margin. Koch was endorsed by the *New York Times* and also won the Republican nomination. Barbaro stayed in the race as the candidate of the Unity Party, formed in that year, and went on to lose the election by almost 800,000 votes despite being favored by minority and progressive elites. The Puerto Rican Socialist Party-USA endorsed Barbaro. Puerto Rican voters supported Koch. They also rejected their compatriot Jerónimo Domínguez, who ran for mayor in the heels of his 1980 defeat in the race for Bronx Borough President. According to *El Diario-La Prensa*, Domínguez was not a credible candidate. His campaign was seen as an embarrassment to the community and his leadership more fit for a cult than political office (see Meislin 1981: 1; Once Again, the Primary 1981: E20; Lynn 1981a: A1; Lynn 1981b: A1; de Dios Unanue 1981: 2).

15   While this may seem to be a different name for what Herbert Haines calls "positive radical

flank effects" (1988: 4), there is an important difference: Haines made a clear distinction between mainstream and radical black politics. I suggest that Puerto Rican politics was fundamentally liberal democratic.

16 The contribution of Gerena Valentín to the formation of the Congress of Puerto Rican Hometowns and the Puerto Rican Day Parade was substantive as well as controversial (see Puerto Rican Leader, Gilberto Gerena Valentín 1964). By his own admission, political office was just a platform to push for certain issues (see Gerena Valentín 1980).

17 For a different categorization, see Baver (1984).

REFERENCES

Acosta-Belén, Edna and Carlos E. Santiago. 2006. *Puerto Ricans in the United States, A Contemporary Portrait*. Boulder, CO: Lynne Rienner Publishers.

Aponte-Parés, Luis and Jorge B. Merced. 1998. Páginas Omitidas: The Gay and Lesbian Presence. In *The Puerto Rican Movement: Voices from the Diaspora*, eds. Andrés Torres and José E. Velázquez. 296–315. Philadelphia: Temple University Press.

Axelrod, Alan. 2007. *Political History of America's Wars*. Washington, D.C.: CQ Press.

Ayala, César J. and Rafael Bernabe. 2007. *Puerto Rico in the American Century, A History Since 1898*. Chapel Hill: University of North Carolina Press.

Baver, Sherrie. 1984. Puerto Rican Politics in New York City: The Post-World War II Period. In *Puerto Rican Politics in Urban America*, eds. James Jennings and Monte Rivera. 43–59. Westport, CT: Greenwood Press.

Bayor, Ronald H. 1993. *Fiorello La Guardia, Ethnicity and Reform*. Arlington Heights, IL: Harlan Davidson.

Bellesiles, Michael A. 2012. *A People's History of the U.S. Military*. New York: The New Press.

Bigart, Homer. 1970. War Foes Here Attacked By Construction Workers. *New York Times* 9 May. Accessed 8 September 2013. http://select.nytimes.com/gst/abstract.html?res=F60C10FE3F 5D137B93CBA9178ED85F448785F9/.

Bonilla, Frank. 2000. Telephone conversation with José E. Cruz, 26 May.

Bowles, Scott. 1996. Lawmaker Says Capitol Security Aide Used Ethnic Insult. *The Washington Post* 18 April: B3.

Carro, John. 1988. Interview with Carlos Sanabria, 25 May. Center for Puerto Rican Studies Archives, Hunter College, CUNY, New York.

Cayo Sexton, Patricia. 1965. *Spanish Harlem, An Anatomy of Poverty*. New York: Harper & Row.

Crítica. 1996. Contradicciones. June: 2.

_____. 1996-1997. Contradicciones. December-January 2: 9–11.

Cruz, José E. 1998. Pushing Left to Get to the Center: Puerto Rican Radicalism in Hartford, Connecticut. In *The Puerto Rican Movement: Voices from the Diaspora*, eds. Andrés Torres and José E. Velázquez. 69–87. Philadelphia: Temple University Press.

_____. 2000a. Nosotros Puertorriqueños: Contributions to Politics, Social Movements, and the Armed Forces. In *Adiós Borinquen Querida: The Puerto Rican Diaspora, Its History and Contributions*, eds. Edna Acosta-Belén, et al. 37–57. Albany, NY: CELAC.

_____. 2000b. Inter-minority Relations in Urban Settings: Lessons from the Black-Puerto Rican

Experience. In *Black and Multiracial Politics in America*, eds. Yvette M. Alex-Assensoh and Lawrence J. Hanks. 84–112. New York: New York University Press.

_____. 2011. Puerto Rican Politics in New York City during the 1960s, Structural Ideation, Contingency, and Power. In *The Politics of Inclusion and Exclusion, Identity Politics in Twenty-First Century America*, ed. David F. Ericson. 67–90. New York: Routledge.

_____. Forthcoming. *Out of the Margins: Puerto Rican Politics in New York City, 1960-1990.* Gainesville: University Press of Florida.

Curbelo, Silvia Alvarez. 1992. A Meditation on the 65th Infantry. *CENTRO: Journal of the Center for Puerto Rican Studies* 4(1): 54–8.

Davis, Colin J. 2003. *Waterfront Revolts: New York and London Dockworkers, 1946-61.* Urbana: University of Illinois Press.

de Dios Unanue, Manuel. 1981. Betancourt: única esperanza de tener representación hispana en N.Y. *El Diario-La Prensa* 3 November: 2.

Delgado, Linda C. 2005. Jesús Colón and the Making of a New York City Community, 1917 to 1974. In *The Puerto Rican Diaspora, Historical Perspectives*, eds. Carmen Teresa Whalen and Víctor Vázquez-Hernández. 68–87. Philadelphia: Temple University Press.

Department of City Planning, City of New York. 1993. Puerto Rican New Yorkers in 1990. December.

Dubofsky, Melvyn and Foster Rhea Dulles. 2004. *Labor in America, A History.* Wheeling, IL: Harland Davidson, Inc.

Fernández, Johanna L. del C. 2004. Radicals in the late 1960s, A History of the Young Lords Party in New York City, 1969-1974. Ph.D. dissertation, Columbia University.

Gerena Valentín, Gilberto. 1980. Interview with Esperanza Martell, 18 September. Center for Puerto Rican Studies Archives, Hunter College, CUNY, New York.

Gibson, Campbel. 1998. *Population of the 100 Largest Cities and Other Urban Places in the United States: 1790 to 1990.* United States Census Bureau, June.

González, Mario. 1966. Constituyen Comité Boricua contra brutalidad policíaca. *El Diario-La Prensa* 15 November.

Gotham Center for New York City History. nd. Garment Industry History Initiative, Historical Overview. Accessed 23 August 2013. http://www.gothamcenter.org/garment/.

Gutiérrez, David G. 1995. *Walls and Mirrors, Mexican Americans and Mexican Immigrants and the Politics of Ethnicity.* Berkeley: University of California Press.

Haines, Herbert H. 1988. *Black Radicals and the Civil Rights Mainstream, 1954-1970.* Knoxville: University of Tennessee Press.

Harris, William Warner. 1980. *Puerto Rico's Fighting 65th U.S. Infantry.* San Rafael, CA: Presidio Press.

Isaac, Larry. 2002. In Search of American Labor's Syndicalist Heritage. *Labor Studies Journal.* 27(2): 21–37.

Jacobs, James B. 2006. *Mobsters, Unions, and Feds: The Mafia and the American Labor Movement.* New York: New York University Press.

Jennings, James. 1984a. Puerto Rican Politics in Two Cities: New York and Boston. In *Puerto Rican Politics in Urban America*, eds. James Jennings and Monte Rivera. 75–98. Westport, CT: Greenwood Press.

_____. 1984b. Conclusion: Puerto Rican Politics in Urban America—Toward Progressive Electoral Activism. In *Puerto Rican Politics in Urban America*, eds. James Jennings and Monte Rivera. 139–43. Westport, CT: Greenwood Press.

Kihss, Peter. 1966. 15 Puerto Rican Leaders are Rated in Study Here. *New York Times* 5 June.

Krebs, Ronald R. 2006. *Fighting for Rights, Military Service and the Politics of Citizenship*. Ithaca, NY: Cornell University Press.

Lee, Sonia S. and Ande Diaz. 2007. I was the One Percenter: Manny Diaz and the Beginnings of a Black-Puerto Rican Coalition. *Journal of American Ethnic History* 23(3): 52–80.

Lynn, Frank. 1981a. Koch Plans Extensive Campaign Despite 2-Party Primary Triumph. *New York Times* 24 September: A1.

_____. 1981b. Mayor Takes 75%. *New York Times* 4 November: A1.

McFadden, Robert D. 1996. Peter Brennan, 78, Union Head and Nixon's Labor Chief. *New York Times* 4 October. Accessed 8 September 2013. http://www.nytimes.com/1996/10/04/nyregion/peter-brennan-78-union-head-and-nixon-s-labor-chief.html/.

Meislin, Richard J. 1981. Primary Date Set, Candidates Begin 'Second Campaign.' *New York Times* 13 September: 1.

Meléndez, Edgardo. 2010. Vito Marcantonio, Puerto Rican migration, and the 1949 mayoral election in New York City. *CENTRO Journal of the Center for Puerto Rican Studies* 22(2): 198–233.

Meyer, Gerald J. 2011. Pedro Albizu Campos, Gilberto Concepción de Gracia, and Vito Marcantonio's Collaboration in the Cause of Puerto Rico's Independence. *CENTRO: Journal of the Center for Puerto Rican Studies* 23(1): 86–123.

Michels, Tony. 2005. *A Fire in their Hearts: Yiddish Socialists in New York*. Cambridge, MA: Harvard University Press.

Muzio, Rose. 2008. Puerto Rican radicalism in the 1970s: El Comite-MINP. Ph.D. dissertation, City University of New York.

Narváez, Alfonso A. 1973. Puerto Rican Veterans Here Seek Aid. *New York Times* 25 November.

Nieman, Donald G. 1991. *Promises to Keep, African-Americans and the Constitutional Order, 1776 to the Present*. New York: Oxford University Press.

Nieves, Josephine. 1988. Interview with Amílcar Tirado and Carlos Sanabria, 24 May. Center for Puerto Rican Studies Archives, Hunter College, CUNY, New York.

No Basta con Querer ser Líder; Hay que Capacitarse Para Serlo: Pantoja. 1962. *La Prensa* 15 April.

Nuevos Candidatos a Alcalde del Nueva York Puertorriqueno. 1961. *La Prensa* 31 January.

Ogbar, Jeffrey O. G. 2006. Puerto Rico en mi corazón: The Young Lords, Black Power and Puerto Rican nationalism in the U.S., 1966–1972. *CENTRO Journal of the Center for Puerto Rican Studies* 18(1): 149–69.

Once Again, the Primary. 1981. *New York Times* 20 September: E20.

Puerto Rican Leader, Gilberto Gerena Valentín. 1964. *New York Times* 2 March 2: 18.

Quintero, Luisa A. 1982. ¿Quienes le Temen a Gerena Valentín? *El Diario-La Prensa* 7 November: 20.

Rivera Batiz, Francisco L. and Carlos Santiago. 1994. *Puerto Ricans in the United States: A Changing Reality*. Washington, D.C.: National Puerto Rican Coalition.

Rodríguez, Clara E. 1989. *Puerto Ricans, Born in the U.S.A.* Boston: Unwin Hyman.

Rodríguez-Morazanni, Roberto. 1992. Puerto Rican Political Generations in New York: Pioneros, Young Turks and Radicals. *CENTRO: Journal of the Center for Puerto Rican Studies* 4(1): 91–116.

_____. 1998. Political Cultures of the Puerto Rican Left in the United States. In *The Puerto Rican Movement: Voices from the Diaspora*, eds. Andrés Torres and José E. Velázquez. 25–47. Philadelphia: Temple University Press.

Sánchez Korrol, Virginia. 1994. *From Colonia to Community, The History of Puerto Ricans in New York City*. Berkeley: University of California Press.

Schrom Dye, Nancy. 1980. *As Equals and as Sisters, Feminism, the Labor Movement, and the Women's Trade Union League of New York*. Columbia: University of Missouri Press.

The New York Red Book. 1938. Albany, NY: J.B. Lyon Company.

_____. 1941. Albany, NY: J.B. Lyon Company.

Thomas, Lorrin. 2010. *Puerto Rican Citizen, History and Political Identity in Twentieth Century New York City*. Chicago: University of Chicago Press.

Torres, Andrés. 1998. Introduction: Political Radicalism in the Diaspora—The Puerto Rican Experience. In *The Puerto Rican Movement: Voices from the Diaspora*, eds. Andrés Torres and José E. Velázquez. 1–22. Philadelphia: Temple University Press.

Torres, Jennie, et al. 1996. *National Puerto Rican Leadership Agenda*. Washington, D.C.: Boricua First/National Puerto Rican Coalition.

Torres, Joseph. 1996. Latinos Speak Out. *Hispanic* December: 18–24.

United Bronx Parents, Minutes, Board of Directors Meeting, 19 April 1977. Records of United Bronx Parents, Series I, Box 1, Folder 4. Center for Puerto Rican Studies Archives, Hunter College, CUNY, New York.

U.S. Census Bureau, Census of Population and Housing, 1940 census, Vol. 1. Number of Inhabitants, Table 21. Accessed 9 September 2010. http://www.census.gov/prod/www/abs/decennial/1940.html/.

Vega, Bernardo. 1984. *Memoirs of Bernardo Vega: A Contribution to the History of the Puerto Rican Community in New York*. Ed. Cesar Andreu Iglesias. Trans. Juan Flores. New York: Monthly Review Press.

Whalen, Carmen Teresa. 1998. Bridging Homeland and Barrio Politics: The Young Lords in Philadelphia. In *The Puerto Rican Movement: Voices from the Diaspora*, eds. Andrés Torres and José E. Velázquez. 107–23. Philadelphia: Temple University Press.

Wilson, Woodrow. 1956. *Congressional Government, A Study in American Politics*. Cleveland and New York: The World Publishing Company.

Yellowitz, Irwin. 1965. *Labor and the Progressive Movement in New York State, 1897-1916*. Ithaca, NY: Cornell University Press.

1.
THE BEGINNING

I came into the world on August 10, 1918, in Lares, Puerto Rico, a town deep in the island's mountainous interior. Following the Hispanic tradition of naming children according to the saints' calendar of the Church, my mother gave me the name Lorenzo. Eleven days later, I was baptized in the Iglesia San José. Just over two months after I was born, on October 11, an earthquake estimated today at 7.5 on the Richter scale, followed by a tsunami, hit the island, leaving more than 150 dead. It was a foreshadowing of the adversities I would face throughout my childhood.

On January 25, 1919, shortly after my family moved to the "big city"—Santurce, right outside San Juan—my mother registered me with the Civil Registry. For many years I thought January 25 was my real date of birth, and even today I celebrate my birthday on that date. And that was not all. She registered me as "Gilberto Valentín." Despite the fact that all my official documents—diplomas, Army ID, driver's license, Social Security card—bear my two last names, both father's and mother's, as I write these lines the bureaucrats in the Commonwealth of Puerto Rico's Demographic Registry are still asking for evidence that I am in fact named, as everyone knows me, Gilberto *Gerena* Valentín.

I am the son of Cándido Gerena and María Valentín. My father's family, the Gerenas, came to Puerto Rico in the sixteenth century and settled in the center of the island, near Lares. Many members of the family owned sugar-cane or coffee haciendas or were merchants in town. Cándido was illegitimate. Although his father gave him his surname, the father's side of the family refused to recognize him. He lived as best he could, hand to mouth, until a kind lady named Juana Quiñones, God bless her, took pity on him and brought him up as though he were her own son. They lived in a humble little house, almost a shack, in the Anón barrio of Lares.

My father was earning his living as an agricultural worker, a peón, when he met my mother. Her forebears, the Valentíns, were Basques; her parents had arrived in the late nineteenth century to work a piece of land that had been granted to them by the Spanish crown. When she met my father, my mother was working as a domestic. Her first husband, whose surname was Luiggi, had abandoned her, leaving her to take care of her three children, Monserrate,

Alfonso, and Sara. Cándido and María took a liking to each other, as they say in the country, and, following the common practice among poor people of the time, decided to live together. I don't know whether they ever actually got married in a civil ceremony; I just know that they lived together "till death did them part."

When my mother became pregnant, my father moved with her to Bajaderos, another poor barrio near the center of town. It was perched precariously on the side of a steep hillside divided from top to bottom by an old, rickety staircase. My parents lived at the very foot of the staircase in a little wooden house, and there I was born, the only child of that union.

At the time of my birth, the socioeconomic situation of Lares and other towns in the interior of the island was deteriorating. Upon the transfer of Puerto Rico to the United States in 1898, after the Spanish-American War, the new administration imposed its own economic priorities. Several radical changes in the island's industrial landscape—the rapid expansion of the sugar industry, which in its advance mercilessly wiped out all other crops; the ruin of the coffee industry; and the creation of workshops and factories in urban areas, especially around San Juan—led thousands of campesinos to move to the capital in search of work. Many settled in Puerta de Tierra, the narrow strip of land that connects Old San Juan to the "big island" of Puerto Rico, creating several large slum areas along that "land bridge."

Like many residents of Lares before them, my parents saw San Juan as a place to try their luck, as a place where they might improve their lot. The earthquake and tsunami that struck the western part of the island was a spur to their decision. With the help of my Tía Monchita, my mother's "almost-sister" (she had been taken in by my mother's family and raised like one of their own children), who had been living in Santurce for some time, my parents found a little wooden house in a modest neighborhood called Sunoco. The area had neither running water nor electricity, and not long after we moved there it was included in an urban-renewal project that was never fully implemented but was intended, in part, to relocate the residents of several of the slums in Puerta de Tierra that were seen as obstacles to developers' plans. The "new" neighborhood was ever afterward known as Barrio Obrero—"the workingman's barrio."

Between November 1918 and January 1919, when I was just a little flea, as my mother used to say when she told me about my early years, my parents packed up the few belongings they had and moved with their three youngest children—Alfonso, Sara, and I—to number 19, Calle Gautier Benítez. Monserrate, whom everybody called Catate, stayed in Lares with her godparents, who looked after her until 1925, when she graduated from high school and went to New York City in search of a better life.

The fact is, I have very few memories of my father. I know that he was a calm, very hard-working man. One recollection, though, is engraved in my memory: a night when my father and I were walking down Barrio Obrero's main street in a crowd of hundreds of people carrying lighted torches. As I walked along holding my father's hand, I was carrying a little torch of my own. Years later, I discovered that that march was a demonstration by the Puerto Rico Socialist Party, which at the time was the principal defender of Puerto Rican working men and women.

I also remember visiting my father at the stand he set up just outside the wrought-iron fence that encircled the monastery at the neighborhood church, where he earned a living selling fruit, soft drinks, and coffee. My mother was always next to him, helping with the business. I would be at home, in the care of Tía Monchita. So there are only a very few memories, as there was only a short time that I was able to be with him.

The poorer barrios of the cities, with their overcrowded, unhealthy conditions, were incubators of disease, especially the terrible scourge of tuberculosis, which for many years was the main killer of poor Puerto Ricans. In the early twenties, consumption, as it was also called, attacked the island like a plague. My father was infected shortly after we settled in Barrio Obrero and he, in turn, passed it on to Sarita. My poor sister, who had always been somewhat sickly, was the first of the two to leave us. She died in the very spring of her life; she was barely 18 years old.

Within a few months, in 1922, my father followed her. Tía Monchita, whom I loved so much, died soon after. Unlike my father and sister, my aunt died not from tuberculosis but rather from a terrible illness that affected her mind: what we called *mal de amores*, or lovesickness. She took her own life by swallowing some pills, I think arsenic, when, my mother told me, she found out that the man she loved was married. And then, to make matters worse, my mother got sick. Her body consumed by illness, she was eventually forced to close the fruit stand that had been our only source of income.

Although our financial situation had become dire, we were not totally destitute. Alfonso, my older brother, found work as a fisherman. Like the good son he was, he sent my mother part of the money he made from selling his catch. Not long after, Fonso, as we called him, started going out with a girl named Juana O'Farrill, much against my mother's wishes. It seems that Juana was black. My mother, like many Puerto Ricans in those days, and still perhaps today, was against "the mixing of the races," and especially interracial marriage.

In 1925, Fonso, who had been sent for by Catate, set sail for New York City. There he quickly found work at the General Tire Company factory. Always concerned about my mother, Fonso continued to help her financially, religiously sending her a money order for $3.50 every week. Ironically, Juana, whom my mother had rejected for the color of her skin, was the one who made sure that Fonso fulfilled his filial duties. With that little bit of money, my mother managed to pay the rent and buy food for us.

2.
MY MOTHER AND I

Although I have very few memories of my father, not a day passes that some recollection of my mother doesn't come to me. Maria Valentín was an extraordinary woman. She was tall—5 feet, 8 inches—and slender, though very strong. Hardened by work and poverty, she had learned to fend for herself in a world of men, and she was known to "duke it out" with the best of them. She was profoundly religious and extremely affectionate, but when she thought stronger medicine was in order she didn't hesitate to use a switch to discipline us. She was my first teacher in life. From her, I learned to persevere, to be firm in my convictions, to accept responsibility for my actions, to respect those who merited respect, to fear only God, and to mistrust anyone in a position of power. One of her favorite expressions was "the man that makes the law, sets the trap."

By the time I was born my brothers and sisters were practically grown. After the death of my sister, father, and aunt and Fonso's decision to go off to New York, my mother, as sick as she was, dedicated herself body and soul to me. We had an excellent relationship, although I must confess that I was not the easiest boy in the world to raise. I was impertinent, spoiled, and a bit of a troublemaker. Since I was blond and had blue eyes, the boys in the neighborhood would often tease me, saying I looked like an "Americanito," which made my blood boil, and as often as not I'd take out my anger with my fists. In fact, it was my mother who taught me to fight, to defend myself. The only problem was that I discovered that I *liked* to fight.

As was the custom among the poor Puerto Ricans of those years, one Easter Sunday my mother made an *arroz con bacalao*. Steam was still rising from the pot, but I was hungry, so without a second thought I took a bite, and the pain was followed by a curse word. My mother whirled around—"What did you say?" And since I was a tough guy, I repeated it. The next thing I knew, my mother had smacked me in the face and I was on the floor. She told me to strip, and she held out a cassock and told me to put it on. She gave me four licks with a switch she always kept handy and made me kneel on a grater before an image of the Virgen de Perpetuo Socorro, the image of the Virgin that she prayed to. The punishment wouldn't have been so bad if she hadn't put an iron bar weighing close to six pounds in each hand. Thinking she'd left me alone in my "penitence," I angrily said to the Virgin, "Help me, you bitch! Why are you leaving me like this, and not helping me? Help me!" Words I would learn to rue, I'll tell you! My mother, who was standing near the door, heard me and said, "What are you saying to the Virgin?" And with that, she tore off my cassock and gave me another good lashing with the switch. I could hear the neighbors out in the street yelling, "That's it, María! Give it to him! Harder, harder! Teach him to talk to the Virgin that way!" That was the way parents punished their kids back then. . .

Even as a young man, Fonso liked his liquor. When my mother found out, she warned him: "I catch you drinking, you'll answer to me." One day somebody told her that Fonso was down in the café on the corner drinking. My mother said, "Come with me," and grabbing me by the hand she stalked down to the café. She walked in like she owned the place and without a word to anyone she balled her fist and hit Fonso in the mouth. Her only words were, "I warned you!" My dear brother Fonso never learned his lesson, although it was years before I took my first drink of alcohol.

After we were left alone, my mother would take me with her when she ran errands. On one occasion, we went to visit my father in the hospital. I had a stomach ache, so she gave me a laxative before we left the house. When we were coming back on the bus, my insides started gurgling and churning. The pain was so bad that I couldn't control myself, and I dirtied my pants. Some of the other passengers started yelling, "Ugh! Get him out of here, he stinks!," but my mother refused. Finally there was so much yelling that the driver stopped the bus and made us get off, halfway home. It was one of the few times I ever saw my mother cry, but the tears were not from embarrassment or sorrow; they were from anger and humiliation at the injustice done us.

I also remember the first time she carried me to an *espiritista* gathering. We sat down in front of a big table covered with a white tablecloth, with lots of candles and goblets of water. The second the ceremony began, the medium went into a trance and my mother, who was a faithful believer in *espiritismo*, started to act strange. I thought all this rigamarole was so funny that I couldn't help laughing out loud. My mother got up and gave me a slap on the back of the neck, saying, "You don't laugh at religion, young man."

I never hit my children, but when I relive that historic moment and the other circumstances of my childhood, I find nothing to reproach my mother for. She lived for me. If there is anything I'm thankful for, it's that her method of disciplining me and showing me the right path was always guided by a profound sense of love, respect, and justice.

Although my mother was illiterate, she always insisted on the importance of an education. I learned to read in a neighbor's house. To practice my reading, my mother had me read to her at night—a newspaper she borrowed, since she couldn't afford to buy it. I had mastered the rudiments of reading when, in 1923, my mother enrolled me in the Manuel Boada Elementary School, located on Avenida Borinquen in Barrio Obrero. In the most representative tradition of urban planning by our colonial government, the school had been built on the grounds of an abandoned cemetery. However, this turned out to be an advantage. The school had no materials or equipment for physical education, so during recess we students would entertain ourselves by digging around on the school grounds to find bones—a tibia here, a femur there—and we used our imaginations to invent games with them.

The principal of the school was Julia M. de Velázquez. I learned much later that she and her husband were leaders of the Puerto Rican Nationalist Party. The first day of class, my mother took me to my homeroom and said to the teacher, with that self-assurance so natural to her, that I was more advanced than the rest of the children, so I ought to be enrolled in a higher grade. And to me she said, looking at me sternly, "You stay here." I didn't dare disobey. Three weeks later, the principal contacted her to tell her that she was right, and they were moving me up to the second grade.

In September of 1928, when I was in the fifth grade, a category 5 hurricane, San Felipe,[1] struck the island, killing more than three hundred people and destroying thousands of homes. I can still see my mother's anguish as she pulled me out of our little wooden house and hurried down Calle Gautier Benítez, sheets of galvanized metal from the barrio's roofs flying over our heads. We finally reached a store built of concrete, where we took refuge. When we emerged, hours later, we saw that San Felipe had destroyed practically every house in the neighborhood. Miraculously, ours was the only house left standing. This is one of the clearest memories I have of my mother. A few weeks after this terrible event, in early November of that year, she died of cancer, at barely forty years of age.

My mother had been diagnosed with cancer in Presbyterian Hospital. At that time "Presby," as it is known today, was administered by American missionaries, and part of its philanthropic mission was to provide free medical services to the poor. Ironically, in that same hospital, in 1931, the American doctor Cornelius Rhoads, as he acknowledged in a letter written in his own hand, did everything he could to hasten the extermination of the Puerto Rican people, killing eight by injecting them, along with many others, with cancer cells.[2]

I often accompanied my mother when she went to Presbyterian—first to visit my father and then for her doctor's appointments. These were my first trips out of Barrio Obrero; on them, I discovered the other face of Puerto Rico: lighted streets, paved roads, large stores and businesses, middle-class houses and the mansions of the wealthy. They were also the first time I saw the ocean and the beach.

I remember hearing that you had to be careful on the beach because there were sharks, and they attacked people. On one occasion I saw some kids, paler than I was, playing on the beach. I went over to them, and one of them threw sand in my face. Crying, I ran to my mother, who asked me what had happened. I told her I'd been attacked by a shark. "A shark?" she repeated, incredulous. "Yes," I said, pointing down the beach at the kids. When they saw my mother headed their way, the kids started running. My mother laughed and said, "Look at that shark of yours running on two legs! It's a gringo shark!" Now that I think about it, that was my first encounter with an American.

The moment came when my mother could no longer take care of herself, and she had to be hospitalized. Some neighbors took charge of me. When she sensed that she was about to die, my mother sent to school for me. By the time I reached her bedside, she was dying.

I clung to her hand long after she had breathed her last breath; I still remember it slowly turning cold. I cried inconsolably at her passing. She was buried, like my father, in the San José Cemetery in Villa Palmeras.

3.
BACK TO LARES

The worry that tormented my mother on her deathbed was what would happen to me when she died. When we left Lares, she had lost contact with her brother. Three of the four family members I had known—my father, my aunt, and my sister Sarita—had died. The other, my brother Fonso, lived in the United States, and at that moment it was simply impossible for him to come to Puerto Rico to take care of me, or for him to bring me to New York. To my mother's relief, and mine, doña Gloria, a neighbor who went often to the hospital and who had become attached to me, promised that she'd take care of me.

I lived in doña Gloria's house for about a month and a half. During that short time, she treated me like a son. She told me not to worry, she was going to adopt me. I was getting used to the idea that that was going to be my new home when without warning a stranger came to the house and asked for me. It was my mother's brother, Tío Juan. He explained to doña Gloria that Fonso had written and told him about the death of my mother, about my situation in general, and asked him to take me in. I later learned that Fonso had also sent him the money for the car he rented to come to San Juan to find me, and that he sent money from time to time to help pay my expenses. And so I left the world I had known up to then and went back to the town where I was born but knew only by name.

I returned to Lares in 1928. My uncle was a small landowner, and very poor. He had 24 *cuerdas*[3] of land in Barrio Espino, on which he grew coffee, bananas, and plantains. He and his wife had five children—two boys and three girls. Since there was no market for his produce, and even less money to hire workers, the sons worked the land while the girls took in sewing for small factories in the area. They made handkerchiefs and gloves, for which they were paid a penny a piece. Their work was a tremendous help, as the money they earned was used to buy the food that couldn't be grown or raised on the farm, and for other necessities.

Now, with my arrival, there was another mouth to feed. Since I was "the orphan," I was last in line for everything. They gave me a cot to sleep on and a tattered sheet to cover myself with. I wasn't used to the lower temperatures in the mountains, so I suffered at first in those (to me) frigid nights. There were not a few times that I wet my bed, from shivering in the cold.

As Fonso had asked him to do, Tío Juan enrolled me in the town's school, Henry Clay Elementary. Later I learned that the school had been named for an American legislator from the South. Owner of slave plantations and promoter of territorial expansion, Clay in a most Christian way opposed the mixing of races, and he had the brilliant idea of deporting freed slaves and free blacks to Africa to prevent them from destabilizing the American slave society. Still today, the school bears that name. Ironically, it is located on a street named for Pedro Albizu Campos, the revered leader of the Puerto Rican independence movement and a black man, the grandson of a freed slave woman. The things that happen in a colony. . .

Clay was in the center of town. To get there from Barrio Espino I had to walk about four and a half kilometers, almost three miles, along a steep unpaved road through the mountains, one curve after another. I would leave at seven in the morning with a sip of bitter coffee for breakfast—there was no money to buy sugar with—and come back after three in the afternoon.

As might be expected, my uncle integrated me into the family economy. When I got back from school, I had to do my chores, which included cutting grass for the horse and cow we had on the farm, finding firewood for the stove, and fetching water for drinking and cooking. To get the water, I had to walk to a well that had been dug in a hollow, then climb down the side of a hill, holding on to branches and shrubs so as not to fall. I carried the water in a five-gallon lard can. I remember how hard it was when it rained, because the side of that hill was like somebody had poured soap on the ground.

Once I had finished my chores, I could start studying for the next day. There was no electricity, so when it got dark I had to use a kerosene lantern to do my homework. The smoke and smell from it, especially when it was windy outside, was so bad that when I blew my nose the handkerchief would have black soot on it.

Saturdays, I would work on the farm, doing whatever needed doing. That meant, among other things, weeding, cleaning the paths and roads, cleaning up after the animals and carrying the manure in buckets to use as fertilizer on the crops, and picking coffee during harvest time. We would drop the beans into cans, and from the cans pour them into sacks we hung around our necks and over our shoulders. At the end of the day the coffee would be weighed, so you'd know just how much weight you'd been dragging around by your neck all day. (The coffee industry used an old Spanish unit of measure, the *almud*, equivalent to 28 pounds.) Fortunately, after Saturday came Sunday, and since

Tío Juan was a religious man, Sundays were sacred; you didn't have to work at all that day.

Despite the sadness I felt at the loss of my mother, and the shock of the radical change in my way of life when I moved back to Lares, I ended the school year with good grades. Hunger, however, went with me to school almost every day. Back then, you had to pay a penny to eat in the lunchroom. Tío Juan didn't have a penny to give me, so many were the times I went back home dead tired and starving.

Luckily, doña Juana, the lady who had taken pity on my father, and who turned out to be my godmother from when I was baptized, found out that her godson had come back to town. As she'd done with my father, that wonderful woman found a way to help me.

Juana—or *abuelita*, "granma," as I affectionately called her—still lived in the little place known as Anón. She had two sons. One of them, Delfín Nieves, whom I came to consider my uncle, was married and had a stall in the tallest building in Lares—later it housed the U.S. post office—out of which he sold milk and meat. Abuelita convinced Delfín to give me a penny a day for lunch. To get the penny, I had to leave school after the last class in the morning and walk about three hundred yards to Delfín's shop. You can't imagine how sad I would be on those days when I got to Delfín's shop and found that he was out running some errand or other. In addition to going back to school on an empty stomach and without the penny, I would be tired from the hot walk, and then after school I'd have to make the long trek home to Tío Juan's house.

Near the end of the fifth grade, things got a little better. Abuelita got a little job as a cook in the lunchroom. So I didn't have to worry about the penny anymore, because abuelita made arrangements for me to go into the lunchroom without paying, and she would serve me my lunch. Sometimes I'd have seconds, because I was always hungry.

As I explained in an earlier chapter, in Barrio Obrero I was always getting into fistfights with the kids in the neighborhood. In fact, I would fight so often and so well that my mother was always saying that when I grew up I was going to be a boxer. But I became a boxer long before my mother thought. With a friend who acted as my promoter and manager, I started boxing at school, a penny a match. A little dirt hill near the school was the ring. My friend would put a piece of dry grass on my shoulder and bet a penny on me, then dare somebody to knock the straw off. Whoever did would have the fight. Soon the "White Horse," as I was known, became famous. All the tough guys in school wanted to have a go at me, and they'd come one by one to knock the straw off my shoulder. One day, though, things blew out of proportion. I fought a boy who turned out to be a real hothead. Unhappy at losing, he came back with a knife and cut me on the arm—I was lucky it wasn't worse. What a scandal that caused! I was given first aid and the boy was accused of assault with a deadly weapon. And that ended my career as a boxer.

Fonso, who had transferred that deep love he felt for my mother to me, was still looking out for my well-being from New York. Once, concerned that I was having to walk barefoot to and from school, he sent my uncle money to buy me a pair of shoes. My uncle, being a practical man, had the shoemaker make me a pair of leather shoes three sizes larger than I needed, so I'd "grow into them." From time to time, Fonso would also send me clothes. I remember the time he sent me some pants that reached about halfway down my shins and a pair of checked sneakers. My uncle made me wear the clothes to school, and as you might expect, the other students had a lot of fun at my expense. But the fun stopped when I dealt with about three of the jokers.

In the sixth grade, I had a teacher named Elisa López. She was very intelligent and was always trying to help her students. One day she said to me, very seriously, "Stay after when the bell rings, I want to talk to you." I thought she was going to reprimand me for something I'd done. When the class was over, I stayed at my desk, ready for my punishment. Instead, to my surprise, Miss López said I was in the wrong grade and she suggested that I take a competency test to see if I could be promoted to the eighth grade. She also said she'd be glad to tutor me in anything I needed so I could pass the exam. I thanked her effusively; I was excited by her suggestion, and wanted to see what might happen.

As she had promised, my teacher bent over backward to prepare me for the exam. The day of the test I was very nervous. When I entered the room where I was to take it, I found that there were other students there, too, among them Luis Estades, a teacher's son; a student whose last name was Planell, and Alicia Labiosa and Enrique Segarra. All five of us passed the exam, and we were moved ahead a grade. Because of those coincidences of fate, almost fifty years later I took an active part in the committee to support Juan Enrique Segarra Palmer, Enrique's son, when he was accused of sedition in the eighties for his struggle on behalf of Puerto Rican independence.

I graduated from the eighth grade with excellent marks. When the long-awaited graduation day came, I was the only student who didn't attend the ceremony, since I didn't have the appropriate clothes and shoes for the occasion. I stayed at home, back on the farm. After a few weeks, I went by the school to pick up my award and the diploma that represented, if nothing else, my perseverance in getting an education.

4.
PERSEVERANCE PAYS

When I found out that I was being moved ahead a grade, I went to tell my uncle the news. He blessed me by making the sign of the cross over me—which parents and guardians always did to show their pride and love—and told me he was happy, because when I finished the eighth grade I could stay and work on the farm. His words completely knocked the wind out of my sails—I couldn't believe what I'd just heard. I told him I wanted to stay in school, to go on, to graduate from high school. This was his answer: "You have a home and food here, but I can't give you money for high school. You've got to work on the farm and help out." I told him, in all honesty, that I didn't know what I was going to do—what I did know was that the decision I made at that point would determine the whole rest of my life.

After meditating on my situation, I hit on a solution. I'd speak with my godmother Juana. At that time, her older son Peyo and a granddaughter named Encarnación were living in her house. When I explained my situation to her she told me that if I wanted to stay in school I could come and live with them. Everything was set for my move.

At my uncle's a hen was sacrificed every Sunday for lunch. It was the only day of the week we ate meat. On Sunday, while the family was gathered for lunch, I sneaked off out behind the house with a little box that contained everything I owned: a cheap fountain pen, the kind that leak ink and ruin everything they come in contact with, and a few pieces of clothing. As I was crossing Juan Vivó's place, his bulldog, which weighed about a hundred pounds, appeared. But I knew there was a guard dog, so I'd taken precautions. I was carrying a switch from a guava tree. When the dog approached, growling and showing his teeth, I brought the switch down across his nose and he tucked his tail between his legs and ran off squealing. I continued my walk, but as I jumped the barbed-wire fence at the road I scratched my leg. I crossed the road and cut across the Hacienda de los Canales and finally came to my godmother's house. She was waiting for me with open arms. To celebrate the occasion, she'd killed and cooked a hen for lunch.

Moving to my abuelita Juana's house made things a little easier for me. Although we lived in a small house without running water or electricity, and I had to sleep in the same bed with Peyo, at least I didn't have to walk three miles to school, or do chores around the farm every afternoon. My life also took a new turn when, in the eighth grade, I met the brothers Ángel and Luis Garrastegui and with them, their parents, doña Juanita Pellicier and don Juan Garrastegui, who were both teachers. Doña Juanita was a very pleasant, warm, wise woman; she gave me many, many little pieces of advice, words of wisdom I've treasured all my life. Don Juan was a very upright man, deliberate in his words and actions, and very well educated.

Ángel, Luis, and I became good friends. Ángel, the older of the two brothers, was a classmate of mine. We spent a lot of time with each other, and played baseball together. As a result of that friendship, I became like a son to doña Juanita and don Juan. When they found out about my tribulations, they invited me to live with them. After discussing it with my godmother, who realized that that was the best solution, I moved in with them.

The Garrastegui family lived in a house they rented across the street from the high school, which today is the Mariano Reyes Elementary School, and they later moved to the big Torres' house, on the highway that led to the La Sierra sector of Lares, at the entrance to town, near the road to Arecibo. It was a beautiful house, built of native wood, and it had a history. The Puerto Rican separatists who lived in Lares met in it to organize the struggle against Spain that culminated in the ill-fated "Grito de Lares" in 1868.[4]

Don Juan had leased a little plot of land near the house. At the time, La Sierra was just forest. There was a creek that provided water to all the surrounding land. Don Juan prepared the land and planted tomatoes, lettuce, corn, and peppers. In the afternoon after school, his sons and I would go with him to work in the garden, which helped round out the family's diet.

At this time, high school was not free. Each credit cost $2.50, and 17 credits were needed to graduate. In addition, you had to buy your own books. The Garrasteguis gave me the push I needed to enroll in high school. It was they who gave me the money to pay the tuition. Ángel, in turn, made a deal with me to solve the problem of the texts I needed: we agreed that he'd lend me his books after he'd done his studies for the night, in exchange for my help with his homework when he needed it.

Around then I had found other, less risky ways to make money than letting somebody knock the straw off my shoulder. While I was living with Tío Juan, he offered to pay me five cents a month if I would deliver a pitcher of milk to the Lópezes. I agreed. Dr. López was the town's dentist. A beginner at this, I didn't know that delivery boys and service people were supposed to enter through the kitchen. The minute I entered the house through the front door, the lady of the house, who for the obvious reason was called "Cross-Eyes" by all the boys in town, stopped me, sternly saying, "You, young man, are a peon! You do not enter through that door, you enter through the kitchen!" A mixed feeling of humiliation, anger, and sadness came over me. I bit my tongue to keep myself from shouting at her that I was no peon, I was working so I could go to high school and get ahead in life. I left through the front door and made my delivery "the right way," but I've never forgotten that moment.

A short time later, Delfín suggested another way for me to make money: buy candy by the box and sell it in front of the San José Theater, the only movie theater in Lares. He was well aware of my entrepreneurial inclinations, and he bought my first assortment of candy. So I started selling chewing gum, chocolate bars, roasted peanuts, and a delicacy called *gofio* at night in front of the movie theater.[5] The first night was a complete success. I sold my entire stock and, the icing on the cake, the manager invited me inside to see the movie. It was the first time in my life I'd seen a movie. It was called *The Perils of Pauline*, dubbed, of course, into Spanish. The first thing I did with the money I'd made was pay back the Garrasteguis' loan to me.

But selling candy didn't bring in enough to cover all my needs, so I decided, following doña Juanita Pellicier's recommendation, to try my luck at another business: selling high-school textbooks. Since I didn't have enough money to buy the books, I sold used books on consignment. I made very little, because the sale depended on the buyer, who was a poor kid like me, being able to pay for the old beat-up book that had passed through who knew how many hands. With the little money this business generated, I paid my tuition.

Although it's true that financially things were not easy, my desire to get ahead was invincible. I decided to speed up my studies so I could be independent sooner and eventually study at the University of Puerto Rico. When I finished my junior year of high school, I lacked only two credits for graduation. Back then, there was a summer program that allowed a youngster to study on his own and then take the examinations in a school designated for that. I decided to take advantage of that opportunity. I studied hard, and when the time came, a friend of mine let me ride behind him on his horse from Lares to the high school in Arecibo to take the examinations. We had to leave at six in the morning in order to be there by 8:00 am, when the exams were to begin. We arrived late. At first, they wouldn't let me in the room, but after I argued my case, they let me in. I passed with high honors. Now I was ready for a new stage in my life.

5.
MY FIRST *GRITO*

From the moment of my birth, I lived in poverty. And although even as a youngster I fought instinctively to rise above it, I saw poverty as a natural condition, a fact of life. It wasn't until I heard the redemptive arguments of nationalism as preached by Pedro Albizu Campos that I began to make the connection between the poverty that we Puerto Ricans were living in at that moment and the political system that governed the island—and that continues still today, to the misfortune of us all.

It happened in 1932. I was in my first year of high school, which back then was the ninth grade. In mid-September there was an announcement in school that on the 23rd of that month Pedro Albizu Campos, the young leader of the Puerto Rican Nationalist Party, would be coming to Lares to plant a tamarind tree in the town square.

Even though since 1930 Albizu had been making an annual pilgrimage to Lares, his name was unknown to me until that announcement. When I came home with the news about the tree-planting, Don Juan Garrastegui, who was an *independentista* and had gone to high school with Albizu in Ponce, told me about Albizu's life, how the poor boy of color had risen above his conditions of birth and gone on to study at prestigious Harvard University, travel throughout Latin America to generate support in our sister republics for the independence of Puerto Rico, and, on his return, become the undisputed leader of the nationalist cause. I also learned the story behind the tamarind tree that "El Maestro," as don Pedro was already known among the young people in the Nationalist Party, would bring with him on the 23rd of September.

The little tree, the story goes, was an offshoot of the tamarind under which Simón Bolívar, the Liberator of the Americas, had rested from war. That original tree was on the San Pedro Alejandrino estate, where Bolívar also died. On her first visit to the island in 1931, the distinguished Chilean poet Gabriela Mistral had brought it as a gift for Albizu as a demonstration of Mistral's solidarity with the struggle for Puerto Rican independence. Don Pedro, for his part, decided to replant it in Lares, the place he called the "Altar of the Homeland." Planting it in the town where the first grand blow was struck for Puerto Rican independence symbolized the brotherhood of Puerto Rico with the rest of Latin America and, like the fruit's taste, the bittersweet nature of the sacrifices made for freedom.

The activity had been organized by the Nationalist Party. At that time, many of us students in the high school sympathized viscerally with independence. One of our teachers—I don't remember her name—asked us why we didn't try to find some way to integrate ourselves into the ceremony. That was the moment when I fully understood the significance of what my father tried to show me when he led me by the hand in the demonstration with the torches: freedom is the fruit of a collective effort.

I was recognized as a leader among the students. In response to our teacher's encouragement, I helped organize the students so we could take an active part in the planting of the tree in the town square. The assignment was to collect a handful of dirt from each of Lares' eleven barrios, which we would then contribute to the ceremony.

That September 23, we stopped classes and marched to the plaza. We were joined by students from the elementary school. Already in the square, farmers, day-laborers, students, teachers, and people from all around the center of Lares had gathered, along with visitors from other towns around the island. The mayor, don Aurelio Bernal, welcomed Albizu Campos, the leaders of the Nationalist Party, and those who had come from other towns, and the tamarind tree was planted alongside the obelisk that had been erected in 1927 in the town square, the Plaza de la Revolución, in honor of the heroes from Lares and the surrounding countryside who had risen against Spanish domination in 1868.

Before Albizu spoke, a student was asked to say a few words. My classmates urged me to say something, but for the first time in my life I didn't know what to say, so I declined the offer. The solemnity of the ceremony and the imposing presence of Albizu had rendered me speechless. Albizu, it was clear, was profoundly moved by our initiative.

Although I didn't become a member of the Puerto Rican Nationalist Party until almost fifty years later, on that 23rd of September, 1932, the seed of nationalism was planted in me.

6.
LARES-SAN JUAN-NEW YORK VIA CARACAS?

As soon as I graduated from high school I followed the example of my parents and moved to San Juan. Except as a day-laborer—what everyone called a "peon"—on some farm, there was no work in Lares or any other town in the mountains, and my plan didn't include being a peon on someone else's farm. Somebody, I don't recall who, told me that it would be easier to find work in San Juan. That seemed a reasonable possibility to me, because I'd taken typing and stenography classes in high school. I reasoned that those skills would qualify me for work in an office and that eventually I'd be able to register at the University of Puerto Rico. Once I finished my bachelors degree, I planned to study law.

I knew of a cousin of mine, Federico (Fico) López, who lived with his wife on Calle Luna in Old San Juan, in a very pretty top-floor apartment with a flat roof they used as a terrace. He was a salesman in La Favorita, a leather-goods shop. I contacted him, and he said he'd be glad to help me find work, and that I could live with him.

My stay in Fico's apartment lasted about six months. He tried in vain to find a job for me in the store he worked in. I, in turn, knocked on the door of many businesses, but the situation was worse than I'd thought. We were still in the midst of the Depression, and the island's economy gave no signs of improving. The fact that I had no "experience"—meaning experience working at a "real job," I learned— complicated things, too. Meanwhile, I stayed in touch with my brother Fonso, who was still watching out for my well-being from New York.

When I finished the eighth grade, Fonso had offered to have me go live with him. I asked him to wait until I'd graduated from high school. Now that I'd done that, he insisted that I go to New York. He had it all planned out. He would teach me his trade and talk to his boss about getting me a job in the tire factory, and I could go to college at night. I accepted his invitation, although with a heavy heart, because the truth was, I didn't want to leave Puerto Rico. But once the decision was made, Fonso sent me a one-way ticket from San Juan to New York City on the SS Caracas. The departure date was October 7, 1937.

The *Caracas* was a steamship of the Atlantic & Caribbean Line, which dominated the cargo and passenger service between Venezuela and New

York, with a stop in Puerto Rico. In fact, it was the company's flagship, and it had a capacity of 140 passengers. It was a luxury liner, perfect for a person who had the resources to buy a first-class ticket. It goes without saying that mine was a second-class ticket, and of that category, the cheapest. It had cost Fonso twenty-five dollars, practically a fortune in those days.

The boat sailed just before midnight. Before we were to leave for the pier, Fico and his wife threw a farewell party for me. As the hour of departure approached, we walked down toward the docks. I was dressed all in white: a short-sleeve shirt, short pants, a pair of white socks and a pair of "champions," as we called the high-top sneakers everybody wore in those days. I didn't wear underwear—I wore underwear for the first time in New York City. My entire baggage consisted of one shoebox, since I was wearing the only clothes I owned. In the box I had carefully placed my report cards from school, a few sheets of blank paper, and a fountain pen that Fico had given me as a farewell present.

Tired and a little groggy from the effects of the alcohol—I wasn't accustomed to drinking—I fell asleep the minute I reached my cabin. When I woke up, it was sometime before dawn. I went up on deck and leaned against the railing. The orchestra was playing some tropical melody. I was filled with a terrible sadness. Tears fell from my eyes as I saw in the distance—so far in the distance—the lights of my beloved Puerto Rico. If there hadn't been so much water between the ship and the shore, I'd have dived into the ocean and swum back to the little island that was rapidly disappearing from view.

The cabin assigned to me was located on the ship's lowest level, three stories under the water line. On the other side of the wall was the boiler room and the coal bin. During the five days we were at sea, I had to put up with the constant, unending hammering of the enormous machines. I was left almost deaf by them, and the noise continued to boom in my head for several days after we reached our destination.

Like the other second-class passengers, my movements on the ship were restricted: I was not allowed to enter the salons and other areas reserved for passengers in first class. At one point I tried to go up on the top deck to see what that part of the ship was like, but when I tried to enter, a guard told me I had to go back. When I asked why I couldn't go up on deck, his reply was curt: "Because you don't belong there." That experience in an American ship, in which the command—the captain, pilot, and the rest of the officers—were all white Americans, was my initiation for what awaited me in New York.

Finally, on October 12, the *Caracas* arrived in my new home. It anchored at the Brooklyn shipyard. Fonso was supposed to be waiting for me on the dock. Since we hadn't seen each other in many years, he'd come up with a way for us to recognize one another. In his last letter, he'd told me that when I got off the boat I should look for a bald man and call out, "Alfonso!" and that he'd take care of the rest.

As I walked down the gangway I found myself in a crowd of people waiting to meet the passengers. I looked everywhere among them to see if I could spot someone that looked like the Fonso I'd known as a child, but no matter where I looked, I couldn't see him. Nor did I see any head that was completely bald. I starting yelling "Fonso! Fonso!" at the top of my lungs, but no one answered. By the time almost all the passengers and their respective friends and families had left, I was beginning to feel some sense of desperation, but then I saw a bald man coming down the pier. Hopefully, I shouted out "Fonso!" and he waved and started walking faster. When he came up to me, he hugged me tight and started to cry. With tears in his eyes, he said he'd gotten to the pier early so he went into a bar nearby to have a little drink of *scotch* to celebrate the arrival of his *kid brother*, as he affectionately called me. (These were new words to me, English peppering his Spanish.) Clearly, he'd had more than one *scotch*.

Fonso lived on 54th Street and Tenth Avenue in Manhattan. To get there from Brooklyn we had to take the train. Back then, the fare was five cents. When we were seated on the train, Fonso explained to me that the stations had signs with the numbers of the streets. He told me to watch for "59th Street," which was where we'd be getting off. And at that, he lay back in the seat and went to sleep. I was surprised—"stunned" might be a better word—but I nervously watched for our station. I noticed that in some of them, the signs didn't have numbers, but names, which made me even more tense. When we reached the 14th Street station I relaxed a little. I shook Fonso to wake him, but he was out like a light and just kept on snoring. Finally, the train reached 59th St. I shook him, hard, and shouted in his ear, "Fonso, we're here! This is 59th Street!" I heard him say, "Oh, good. . . ," and when the doors opened I rushed out with the rest of the passengers, sure that my brother was right behind me. What was my surprise and horror to discover that he was still on the train.

"Now I'm really in trouble," I thought to myself. I remembered, however, that in my pocket, along with a quarter, I had a piece of paper that Fonso had given me on the pier, and that on it was his address. I climbed the long stairs out of the subway station and once outside, I realized that I had taken the wrong exit. I started walking, looking for a street sign that said "59th St." I was beginning to feel really chilled, as the clothes I had on were not suitable at all for the New York fall. Then I saw a policeman. I went up to him and showed him the piece of paper with the address on it. He said something to me in English. The only thing I was able to understand was the word lost. I nodded. He pointed to the next street and held up four fingers, to show me that I should walk four blocks that way. I said *Thank you* in my best English, which was probably unintelligible, and walked down to the corner. I then turned and walked four blocks south, until I came to Fonso's building.

Fonso's apartment was on the fifth floor. At the entrance to the building there was a list of names and a row of doorbells. I found one that said "Luiggi and Ofarril" and pressed it. Someone called out, "Who?" and I, still deaf from the ship's engines, yelled "Gilberto." Nothing happened. The voice came again—"Who?"—and I again shouted my name. Then I saw that the door opened automatically. I pushed it and proceeded to climb the creaky, rickety stairs to the fifth floor. I knocked on the door of the apartment, and there was Juana, who welcomed me with hugs and kisses. She was surprised not to see Fonso with me, and asked me what had happened to him. Very diplomatically, I told her he'd fallen asleep on the train and hadn't had time to get off when the doors opened. Juana, who knew her husband all too well, muttered, "That drunk! He was drunk, wasn't he?" I said I hadn't really noticed, but he'd told me he had a drink to celebrate my arrival. Juana left it at that. She pulled me inside and asked me about my trip. I narrated the discomforts and humiliations of my shipboard odyssey, and although she commiserated with me, she also laughed out loud.

Three hours later, Fonso appeared. He told us he hadn't waked up until the train reached the end of the line, in the Bronx. Juana read him the riot act. They fought for a while, but as they always did, it seemed, they soon made up and celebrated the arrival of the new *kid brother*.

7.
DISHWASHER AND SKULLCRACKER

As soon as I arrived in New York City, Fonso took me to see my sister Catate, who lived a few blocks away, also on the West Side. If I hardly remembered Fonso, I had even fewer memories of the sister I had been separated from when I was little more than a baby. But Catate was excited to see me, as though we'd spent our whole life together. And not just that—she had a very nice surprise for me: She'd found me a job, and I was to start right away.

Catate worked as a waitress at a well-known restaurant at 75th and Columbus. She explained that a few days earlier, a job as a dishwasher had opened up at the restaurant and she'd spoken to the owner, with whom she was on very good terms, about giving me the job. The owner had agreed. I didn't think about it a second. Next Monday I'd be working at the restaurant. The pay was fifty cents an hour, and I'd work from six in the morning to six in the evening, six days a week.

I felt incredibly lucky, because I'd hardly set foot in New York and already had a job. The happiness didn't last long, however. It turned out that the chef at the restaurant, who was Greek, had had his eye on the job for his nephew. Catate had stolen a march on him, and that was enough for him to hate me on sight. From then on, he looked for any opportunity to make my life miserable.

My station was in the basement. There, we peeled the vegetables and washed the cooking utensils, plates, glasses, and silverware. In his search for revenge, the chef would intentionally spill soapy water at the top of the stairs so I'd slip and fall and, if all went well, break my neck. Or he'd put hot pans in the sink so I'd burn my hands. I soon figured out the game and was careful not to fall for his tricks. One day, however, as I was on my way down to the basement to peel a sack of potatoes and another sack of onions I wasn't thinking and didn't realize that there was soapy water on the floor. I slipped and slid down the stairs on my back. I was bruised and scraped, but fortunately no bones were broken.

As I lay on the floor in agony, I could see the chef at the top of the stairs laughing at me and applauding. Catate, who had seen what happened, came to my aid. I was so badly banged up that I had to be taken to the hospital for tests and first aid. Catate spoke to the owner to tell her what had happened. She didn't do anything about it, however, since, as she explained to Catate, it was much easier to find a dishwasher than a good cook.

At that moment I couldn't have cared less if she lost a cook or if I lost my job—the chef was going to pay. So when I went back to work I waited patiently for the right moment. As was common at the time, the chef's uniform included an apron and a tall white toque that distinguished him from the rest of the kitchen staff. One day, I waited for him to take off his toque and when he wasn't looking—*wham!*—I brought a number 7 pot down over his head like a ten-gallon hat. I hit him so hard it almost cut off his ear. Then I grabbed my belongings, which I'd already packed up, and ran out of the restaurant like a shot, while the man was yelling in his English even worse than mine, "He has *keelled* me! He has *kee-eelled* me! Help!"

When I got back to the apartment, I told Juana what I'd done and went to my room. The situation didn't end there, though. Late that afternoon, an Irish cop came to the door with a complaint that had been filed against me by the chef—attempted murder, according to the police officer! When he explained why he was there, Juana, who was no retiring little mouse, practically ate him alive, she was so angry, and she brought him to my room so he could see first-hand what that miserable so-and-so had done to me. When he saw me all battered and banged up and bandaged, the cop agreed with Juana and Fonso that if anybody should go to jail it should be the chef. Instead of arresting me, he left. As you can imagine, I never went back to the restaurant. Catate saw my side of the situation and never mentioned that violent act of mine, which could have cost her her job. But fortunately it didn't. She continued to work in the restaurant and, like Fonso, help me all she could.

As soon as I'd recovered, I started looking for another job. One day Fonso told me there was a dishwasher's job available in a hotel called the New Yorker. On 34th St. and Eighth Avenue, the New Yorker was at that time the largest hotel in the city, with over a thousand rooms, three private dining room, three restaurants, and ten master chefs. When I arrived, I ran into a Puerto Rican guy that worked there. By one of those twists of fate, he was from Lares! When he found out we were from the same town he took me to the personnel office and helped me fill out the job application. The woman who interviewed me, who knew my new friend, asked me about my experience. I told her I'd worked as a dishwasher at a restaurant for a year, but I didn't tell her, for obvious reasons, what its name was. She hired me to wash the Jewish dishes at fifty cents an hour. I say the Jewish dishes because, as I found out, Jewish groups and families held all sorts of activities at the New Yorker, especially during Rosh Hashanah and Passover, and for those activities the hotel used special plates, glassware, and so on.

I'd hardly started my new job when I dropped a plate, which shattered into a thousand pieces. My supervisor told me I'd have to pay for it. The stupid plate cost three dollars! I had no choice but to pay, but at least I didn't lose my job. At the same time, I found another job in the same hotel, making toast and squeezing orange juice and washing the breakfast cups, saucers, sugar bowls, and so on. With it came a raise, to sixty cents an hour. I was a fast learner and I worked so hard and so efficiently that the head of the kitchen took me under his wing and taught me to prepare soups. The job as chef's assistant brought another raise. Within about year, I got a job cleaning rooms in the hotel, at a dollar an hour. My life was gradually improving. I realized, though, that the improvement was due in large part to the support I got from my coworkers at the hotel, especially those who were actively taking part in the process to unionize hotel workers.

In fact, I was one of the first to get a union card—mine was number 6—when Local 6 of the New York Hotel Trades Council started organizing the New Yorker. I worked as a volunteer organizer and was elected union delegate. On January 18, 1939, after an intense campaign, the Hotel Association of New York, which represented all the hotels in the city, agreed to sign the first collective bargaining pact with the New York Hotel Trades Council. The New Yorker was one of the first big hotels to sign the agreement.

During those first years I also devoted myself to my studies. In 1938 I started taking night courses at City College, which was on Convent Avenue on the West Side. Back then, there was a policy of free tuition for any resident of the city who met certain requirements, including graduation from high school with a certain grade-point average. I was majoring in labor relations. City College was the ideal place to go for that, since it was already a center of great intellectual and political activity, and the most advanced thinking in social issues. And that, of course, paralleled my growing participation in the labor movement in New York City.

8.
A CUP OF COFFEE OPENS MANY DOORS

The election of Franklin Delano Roosevelt to the presidency of the United States in 1933 and the consequent implementation of the New Deal created a favorable climate for the organization of the working class. In 1935, Congress passed the National Labor Relations Act, known as the Wagner Act, in honor of Sen. Robert F. Wagner (D–NY). This legislation allowed workers to organize in the private sector and prohibited employers from controlling or interfering with the formation of unions.

One of the most exploited sectors of the working class in New York City was the hotel and restaurant employees. In 1937, several unions that represented the workers in this sector joined to launch an organizing offensive in the hotel industry, and a few months later, in February of 1938, the New York Hotel Trades Council was created, under the leadership of Jay Rubin.

In 1938, while I was still working in the Greek restaurant, a union organizer invited me to a meeting with other restaurant employees who lived in the borough of Manhattan. The purpose of the meeting was to develop strategies for recruiting new union members in the area. I accepted his invitation. The sponsors of the meeting were the leaders of Local 302 of the Cafeteria and Restaurant Workers Union. This local had fallen into the control of the Mafia during the first years of the Depression. In 1935, after the Left took over the Food Workers Industrial Union, the Mafia influence was eliminated from this and other locals.

It turned out that the union organizers had been going around to restaurants, identifying potential leaders and organizers. They'd picked me out because I had several characteristics that might be valuable for their purposes: I got on well with people, by now I spoke English pretty well, and I was Puerto Rican. This last characteristic was extremely important at that moment because many restaurant employees in the city were Latin American, especially Puerto Rican, and our numbers were growing fast.

The idea of working as a labor organizer was very attractive to me, so I offered to become a volunteer. As a volunteer, I would help organize in my spare time and the union would only give me money for lunch and transportation. From the ranks of the volunteers, the union chose the best to work full time.

When the time came to assign us our duties, I was put under the supervision of a very intelligent Jewish organizer from whom I learned a great deal. In our group there was also a woman, Helen Wendel, an excellent organizer who was the ex-wife of one of the other organizers, a man named Myers. She had a two-year-old son from that marriage, Jayson, whom I came to love like my own son. For a while, Helen and I had a relationship, which ended in 1940, when I married for the first time. But the friendship between Helen and me continued until the day she died. Jayson and I were always very close, and he stood by me in many of my struggles on behalf of the Puerto Rican community. Now, in what I might call my late-senior years, Jayson, like all of my children, is always looking after me.

Once the group of organizers was, well, *organized*—there seems to be no other way to say that!—we began to meet to discuss our strategies. One night while we were talking, I remembered a piece of advice that doña Juanita Pellicier would always give me back in Lares: "With a cup of coffee, even without milk and sugar, you can get many things." I proposed the idea of a cup of coffee to the group, and they liked it.

Organizing restaurants workers was no easy task. Despite the existence of the Wagner Act, employers threatened their employees, and since there were not many jobs, the employees were afraid to sign the cards that authorized the union to act as their representative. We had, then, to show them that "in union there was strength" and that in the last analysis, the employers needed employees, not the other way around, as they'd been taught to believe.

The organizing scenario that emerged out of my "cup of coffee" idea was the following: Once we'd managed to get several workers in a particular restaurant to sign the card, we would concentrate our efforts on the restaurant itself. We organizers would arrive at breakfast time, an hour when there would usually be a lot of customers. A group of about ten of us would sit down at various tables, while another six would sit at the counter. A third group would stand in line to demand that we be given quick service, because we had to get to work. When the waitress brought the menu, those of us sitting at the tables or the counter would order a cup of coffee and a glass of water, then take our sweet time drinking the coffee. The owner, who was usually at the cash register, would be getting more and more desperate because the tables and counter would be occupied and the customers would be slow as Christmas giving their orders and drinking their coffee. Once we'd created that atmosphere, several of our organizers standing in line would loudly complain and then, "disgusted," storm out of the café while others would try to persuade the real customers to go somewhere else, where there was better service. Once enough people had gotten tired of waiting and left, those of us at the tables and counter would get up and pay for our single cups of coffee. The next day, the same operation would be carried out, with new faces. At the end of that second day, the lead organizer would go up to the owner to explain who we were and tell him that if he didn't recognize the union, we'd continue to disrupt his breakfast hour every day. In ninety percent of the cases, the owner would agree to negotiate. With this strategy, we managed to organize many restaurants and cafes in the city.

In some cases, though, we had to take more drastic measures. For example, on one occasion we confronted a recalcitrant, abusive employer who was known to physically abuse his employees. We managed to persuade the employees to sign their cards after they left work in the afternoon. When we went to claim the right to represent them, the owner tried to attack us. To convince him that we were serious, we decided to close his restaurant for a weekend.

Friday has always been a big day for restaurants. That day we poured a solution of sulfuric acid mixed with clove and a little sodium nitrate—a Puerto Rican recipe for a stink bomb—at the entrance to the restaurant. The place stank for two days, which kept even the hardiest customers at bay. Then we sent a message to the owner that we were ready to meet to negotiate whenever he was. He responded instantly. He sat down with us at the negotiating table and signed the agreement. As part of the agreements, he agreed to pay his employees for the two days of lost work.

It was after losing my dishwasher's job at the restaurant that I found work at the New Yorker Hotel. Despite the change of employment, I continued to work as a volunteer organizer for Local 302 for several months. In recognition of the work I did, the local offered me a permanent position. I considered it seriously, since I really enjoyed the work of organizing. But after analyzing my situation and discussing the matter with Fonso, I concluded that the best thing for me at that moment was to stay at the New Yorker, since there I was assured of two free hot meals a day as part of my union benefits. In addition, I was already immersed in hotel union-organization and had been elected delegate to the union.

9.
WHAT A PENNY MEANS TO ME

Whenever I see a penny on the ground, I stop and pick it up. When she was little, my daughter Marielita would always scold me for bending down to pick up pennies. Fortunately for her, and for my own happiness, Marielita has never known poverty. I still remember as though it were yesterday the times that for lack of a penny I had nothing to eat at lunchtime at Henry Clay Elementary in Lares. And now in adulthood, I've needed a penny more than once. Not having one when I most needed one helped me to better understand what the struggle for equality is about.

Shortly after I started taking night classes at City College, I had an eye-opening experience. At that time I lived in an apartment at 86th St. and Broadway, and to get from my place to the college, which was at 138th St. and Convent Avenue, I would take the subway. Once as I stepped up to the ticket window I realized that I had only four cents in my pocket. I lacked one sad penny for the fare. Naïve as I was, I explained my situation to the lady in the booth (in my not-so-great English) and asked if she'd sell me a ticket for four cents. I imagine that by my accent she thought I was a "lazy Puerto Rican," because she said so in so many words. That lady gave me what-for! "If you only have 4 cents, mister, that's your problem. I can't let you through. Move on."

It was 10:30 at night. When I left the station, I found all the businesses in the neighborhood closed, with the exception of a little bar that was full of people. I decided not to go in. It was November, and it was freezing cold. I had to make a decision: either walk home or stand around waiting for a kind soul to pass by who'd take pity on me and give me a penny. I opted for the second. Not long after, two men came along. I stopped them and explained my problem. One of them said, "Come with us, we'll pay your fare." I could feel my faith in human kindness reborn. We walked past the ticket booth; the woman looked at me as though she'd never seen me before. My good Samaritan put in a nickel and I passed through the turnstile and stepped onto the platform. I couldn't help noting that my saviors were black men, as was that woman who refused to let me pass because I didn't have a penny. At that moment, the train entered the station and the three of us got on. I thanked the men in both English and Spanish. When I reached my stop, we said goodbye. I never saw them again, but I always remember that moment of reaffirmation of my belief that the value of a person has nothing to do with his or her skin color or sex.

I never forget the pennies I lacked for lunch, much less the experience in the subway. Now I always carry a penny in my wallet. The others, including the ones I pick up on the street, I keep in a little bucket, and when I have a thousand or so I exchange them for bills or deposit them in the bank.

Speaking of banks, I remember that some time ago I received a check from Medicare for one cent. When I went to deposit it in my account, the cashier handed it back to me, laughing and saying, "Very funny!"

10.
EL BARRIO

Several weeks after my arrival in New York City, Fonso and his family moved to a more comfortable apartment on 86th St. between Central Park and Broadway. I continued to live with them for about a year. When they decided to move again, the moment had come for me to find my own place. It wasn't hard to decide where I wanted to live. The main Puerto Rican enclave in the city was on the East Side of Manhattan, in Harlem. Plus, it was close to my work, and the rents were low. We Puerto Ricans called it El Barrio; to everyone else, it was Spanish Harlem.

El Barrio covered a relatively small area. It extended from 110th St. to 116th St. and from Fifth Avenue to Morningside Avenue. On the west, it was bordered by Morningside Park. On the north was the African American neighborhood; on the south, the buildings across from the lake at 110th St., inhabited mainly by Jews; and on the east, Italian Harlem. Within those few blocks lived approximately 25,000 Puerto Ricans, the vast majority of them working-class. It was a piece of Puerto Rico in a foreign city, where everyone spoke, lived, and fought in Spanish; where there were *bodegas* instead of grocery stores, *barberías* instead of barber shops, *restaurantes de comida criolla* instead of "Puerto Rican restaurants," *cantinas* instead of bars, and *salones de baile* rather than dance halls—the Park Palace, for example. There was also a complex of small businesses, often, at the beginning, in makeshift booths and stands, that stretched from 111th St. to 116th St. along Park Avenue. We called it La Marqueta—"the market"—and it sold all sorts of products from Puerto Rico. Puerto Ricans from all across Manhattan and the other boroughs of New York City went to El Barrio to visit relatives, do their shopping, or take part in political and social activities. That was also where the brothel was located that Fonso took me to so that I could, in his words, "become a man," and from which we were forcibly ejected because my brother cheated in a card game.

While I was looking for a place to live in El Barrio, I ran into a lady named Isabel Gutiérrez. In another one of those strange twists of fate, I had met her once before, in Lares. At that time she and her husband had a little business selling coconut candy. It turned out that they had come to New York City to try their luck, and to make ends meet they rented out rooms in their apartment.

Just then there was one available. She rented it to me for $3.50 a month. And that was how I began living at 7 W. 111th St. between Fifth and Lenox.

One of the first things doña Isabel told me when she rented me the apartment was not to dare cross Fifth Avenue, because that's where the Italians lived. Other neighbors told me the same thing. For many of the Puerto Ricans who lived in El Barrio at the time, the Italian section was off-limits, and the Italians were the embodiment of the devil himself. And there was good reason for that.

The Italian section of Harlem had coalesced at the turn of the century. The Italians were a poor community, like the Puerto Rican community, and suffered a great deal from white prejudice and discrimination. In the thirties, however, they had become integrated into the city's political system and in the process of adaptation they had created their own institutions. The much-feared Mafia and street gangs zealously guarded the territory from the slow but constant penetration of other ethnic and racial groups. The gangs had established the rule that no one, especially blacks and Puerto Ricans, could enter their territory without permission. Whoever violated that rule would pay the price.

Since I was always stubborn—pig-headed, some said, and some say I still am—I ignored the warnings and decided to cross the street into the forbidden zone. It was one day in winter, and it was cold, cold, cold. I still remember the battering I took. But what hurt the most was the humiliation I suffered. They stripped all my clothes off me, including my socks and shoes, and sent me back into El Barrio practically naked. I swore that would not be the end of it. I got a group of guys together and we formed one of the first Puerto Rican gangs in El Barrio. We worked out a plan to get our revenge for the abuses the Italians had subjected us to.

We entered the Italian territory and one by one ambushed several members of the gang that had attacked me. Then we gave them some of their own medicine. With that we sent a clear message to all the Italian gangs: Puerto Ricans had to be respected. From that point on, whenever I went into Italian territory, I was armed. In the winter I carried a knife under the sleeve of my coat, attached to a rubber band. If things got nasty, I would just pull down the rubber band and the knife would slip into my hand. I don't remember, and am not interested in remembering, the times I had to use it.

That was the origin of the first Puerto Rican gangs in New York City. They were primitive organizations of self-defense. When one of our own got jumped, we would take it out on two of theirs, so they'd learn some respect. These gangs, unlike those of today, had nothing to do with drugs or other illegal business. In time I realized that this violence between two poor communities with so many problems in common was absurd, and served only to delay the development of class solidarity, but at the time it was part of our daily life and you just had to deal with it.

We Puerto Ricans also had to deal with the New York City police. The police force was controlled by the Irish, who, like many if not all Italians, tended to look down on the newly arrived Puerto Ricans. The abuse, the outrages committed against us were legendary. I'll never forget one cop, named O'Hara. He was an abuser's abuser, and he sowed terror in our community. Every time he came to a place and saw several Puerto Ricans together, he'd disperse the group with his nightstick, without a word to anyone. I was the butt of his sadism more than once. His name was engraved in the history of the community with the expressions *"cuídate de la jara"* (watch out for O'Hara) and *"aquí viene la jara"* (Here comes O'Hara, *jara* being our own spelling of the gorilla's last name, and a generic word in El Barrio for "bad cop"). Those expressions became so widespread, in fact, that one heard them in other Puerto Rican enclaves in the U.S. and even on the island, as a result of the constant traveling back and forth of Puerto Ricans living in El Barrio.

What never made it into folk history was what finally happened to O'Hara. Sick and tired of his abuses, a group of us decided to take the law, so to speak, into our own hands, and we laid an ambush for him. I gave him a terrible beating, stripped off his clothes and shoes, burned his uniform, and threw him out of El Barrio naked. We heard later that when he got back to the station house they gave him a new uniform and sent him back out to patrol our community. O'Hara wasn't too keen on that idea, so he applied for a transfer. Whether that was true or not, we never saw him again in our neighborhood. Other O'Haras, though, continued to mete out their own brand of justice in El Barrio. In the sixties, the Puerto Rican community dealt with this problem in a more effective and permanent way. But we'll talk about that later.

I lived in the little room in doña Isabel's apartment for a couple of years. Finally, I decided to make a home for myself. In mid-1940 I stopped being her boarder and became her son-in-law. I married her daughter Célida Gutiérrez, and we moved into the main bedroom. When Célida became pregnant, we moved to an apartment on the West Side. A year after we were married, my first daughter was born. We gave her the name Marisabel, after her two grandmothers. Within all the poverty and hardships of our community, I felt relatively happy.

My job situation had also been gradually improving. From housekeeping at the hotel I moved into a more comfortable and higher-paying job: cleaning the lobby. Shortly after that, they moved me into the Audit Department, where I earned three dollars an hour. And I didn't stop there. As a result of the war in Europe, New York City was experiencing a boom that benefited the hotel industry. Business agents, vendors, and collectors from the Caribbean and Central and South America began arriving in the city in larger numbers. This, in turn, generated a demand for bilingual employees in several positions in the hotels. In late 1939, a position as room clerk opened up at the Hotel Commodore, today the Grand Hyatt. I applied for it and got the job.

My job at the Commodore consisted of selling rooms. Since there was much more demand than supply in those days, I gave special attention to the vendors that came in from Latin America. They would call me, and I'd assure them I'd find them a good room. When they arrived and came up to the desk to register, they'd repay my services with a hefty tip. So that way, with the salary of a desk clerk and a ten-dollar bill here and a twenty there, Célida, Marisabel (whom we affectionately called Isa), and I lived pretty well. This situation didn't last long, though. A short time later, the United States Army had need of my services.

11.
BETTER THREE STRIPES THAN A BAR

In 1939, Germany invaded Poland, triggering what became known as World War II. The war was fought at first in Europe and Africa, but in 1940 it spread to Asia when the Japanese, who had invaded China, joined Germany and Italy to create the alliance known as the Axis. In December 1941, when Japan attacked the U.S. naval base in Pearl Harbor, in Hawaii, the United States, which had theretofore been neutral, joined the Allied resistance.

In September of 1940, the federal government instituted compulsory military service—universal conscription, or "the draft"—and required every male between 21 and 45 years of age to register with the new agency. At that time, there were no exemptions, or "deferments," as they were called in military-ese, for married men as there had been in the past and would be again, later. However, according to the civil registry I was nineteen, so the law didn't apply to me. In 1941, with America's entrance into the war, the law was amended to include married men, even those with children.

I hated Hitler and his racist ideology, but I had started a family and didn't want to be separated from my wife and especially my daughter Isa. My intention was to not register for military service, but Célida kept arguing that going into the army was better than going to jail. My heart was torn in two by this dilemma and my head ached from trying to decide what to do.

When I received the notice from the Defense Department that I was to report to the recruitment center on 44th St. and Lexington, I realized I had to make a decision. As I was discussing my dilemma with a friend, he told me about a trick that he said was the perfect solution for my problem. It consisted of inserting a clove of garlic in your rectum on the morning of your physical examination, to produce a high fever. I told myself I had nothing to lose, so I decided to try it. When I arrived at the recruitment center, I had a fever of 104 degrees. But to my misfortune, the officer apparently knew about this little trick. As soon as the medic took my temperature and saw I had a high fever, he sent me into an adjoining room to lie down. The attendants in this room medicated me and put me on a cot. After a little over an hour, they took my temperature again. By now, the fever had gone down. I passed the exam with flying colors.

Everything happened very quickly. They finished filling out my papers and assigned me an ID number: 32 998 603. They also informed me that I'd be receiving two stainless-steel tags—dog tags, they called them—that I was supposed to wear around my neck at all times. Though it was cold comfort, they told me the tags would be used to identify my body if I were killed in action. From the recruitment center I was sent directly to training camp, without even being able to say goodbye to Célida and Isa. Two days later, Célida received a letter from me explaining what had happened. The process of separation was terrible. Over the next months I wrote Célida every day, sometimes twice a day.

Since I'd scored high on the vocational aptitude test and was light-skinned and spoke English, I was informed that after basic training I'd be sent to the Army Air Force cadet school. Back then, Puerto Ricans living in the States were assigned on the basis of our skin color to either white or black battalions.

At that time, the Air Force was still a division of the regular army. In six weeks, I reported to the training camp in Miami Beach. The whole Miami area looked like a huge military encampment. The Army had emptied out the hotels to house soldiers. I was stationed there with hundreds of other aviation officer-candidates, training to go to the front. I felt tremendously out of place—we Puerto Ricans call it "feeling like a cockroach at a chickens' dance"—since there was not a single other Puerto Rican, at least that I ever ran into, in the entire camp. And that went twice for African Americans, who weren't allowed into the air force until 1943, and even then, only in a segregated training camp in the South.

The two alternatives for us were the European front or the Pacific front. If I'd had anything to say about the matter, I'd have chosen to go to Europe, since my hatred of Hitler had only grown after seeing the anti-Nazi propaganda films in basic training. But the Army decided to assign me to the 5th Air Force, which was stationed in the Pacific.

At that point in my life I was in excellent physical shape and had tested high in physical skills and vocational aptitude. So high, in fact, that I was made an instructor in calisthenics. My superiors were very pleased with my performance and considered me a shoo-in for second lieutenant, which would make me eligible to fly war planes. I liked the idea of being a pilot, until the day before the graduation exam. That day one of the guys in our group received a letter from a friend who had graduated in the first group of officers, with a rank of second lieutenant. He said that all the officers sent to the Pacific front had been shot down like sitting ducks by the Japanese. That night I wrote a letter to Célida telling her I'd decided to flunk the skills examination, because I wanted to come back to her and Isa alive. And flunk it I did. Upset at my grade, my immediate superiors questioned me pretty harshly, but I couldn't have cared less what they thought about me. And so, instead of a second lieutenant's silver bar, I was given the three stripes of a sergeant.

Later I realized that all I'd done was buy some time. I was relocated to a base in Sioux Falls, South Dakota, where I was made an instructor in radio and Morse code. I taught there for six months, when suddenly I was ordered to the front. I was given a ten-day pass, which I used to visit Célida and Isa in New York. Célida told me that I'd have looked really handsome with that silver bar on my shoulder, and I told her I agreed, but this would have been the last time she'd ever see me with that pretty little bar, because I'd almost certainly have come home in a much bigger metal box that covered my whole body.

From South Dakota I was sent to San Francisco, though I first spent almost a month and a half in a hospital in Nevada, where I was treated for a double pneumonia that almost killed me. In San Francisco we boarded a ship bound for New Guinea, the second-largest island on the planet and of great strategic value to our armed forces.

The situation in the Pacific was critical. The Japanese had invaded all the islands in the region, including the territory of New Guinea, which since 1919 had been administered by Australia. For the Allies, control of this island was essential to the campaign in the Philippines and to avoid a possible Japanese invasion of Australia. In December 1943, a few months after the Allied troops retook control of the ports of Lae and Finschafen, two Japanese strongholds on the island, I arrived in Papua New Guinea.

12.
ON THE PACIFIC FRONT

We arrived at the port of Lae, in southern New Guinea. Now in active combat, I was given the posts of radio operator and rear gunner on a B-25. It was not a plane that inspired much confidence in me; it was the same bomber used by the first graduating class at the air force officers training camp in Miami Beach, and it was the determining factor in my decision to flunk the officer's exam. I took part in several missions in the region. On one of the encounters we were shot down by a Japanese plane and had to parachute out. When I hit the ground, I injured my Achilles tendon. I was lost in the jungle for four days in the middle of monsoon season, completely incommunicado and surrounded by Japanese reconnaissance troops. Days would pass without a letup in the rain, and the terrain was covered with water. I spent most of the time up in trees, eating tubers and drinking the rainwater that collected in the huge leaves of some of the plants, until I was finally rescued by an Allied patrol. I was lucky; the rest of the crew was never found.

There was another time, on January 25, 1944, when I had another close shave. I remember the exact date because that day I celebrated, as I had for as long as I can remember, my birthday—my twenty-fifth. That night we were returning to Finschafen at an altitude of between eighteen and twenty thousand feet above a mountainous area. As almost everyone knows, the Japanese army had radio stations that broadcasted programs in perfect English; what many people don't know is that they would also intercept warplane transmissions and reply back with the coordinates of supposed Allied landing strips so Allied planes would come in for a landing and the Japanese could capture or destroy our planes. To avoid being detected, we flew in complete radio silence. I had the job of triangulating the Japanese positions so we wouldn't be spotted, and of obtaining the coordinates of a British base nearby, which sent messages in Morse code. As hard as we tried, we couldn't be sure that we'd identified the location, so we had to keep flying over the area.

At one point, the captain told me that we had fuel for just fifteen minutes more in the air, that if we didn't find the British landing field soon, we'd be forced to parachute. As you can imagine, I wasn't at all keen on that idea, since the Japanese, who had earned the reputation of being cruel, even merciless with the enemy, controlled a large part of the area, and there was the real possibility that we'd be taken prisoner. Given that scenario, I told the captain that our only alternative was to open communication and use our identification code to be picked up by friendly troops. He agreed, so I said a little prayer and called *mayday, mayday*. I did establish communication, and I explained our situation and asked for the landing coordinates. To our good fortune, we immediately found the lights, and they gave us instructions and permission to land. Thank goodness it was the Brits and not the Japanese!

After we landed, the pilot told the soldiers on the base that I'd been responsible for guiding us to a safe landing, and that it was my birthday. A while later, three or four soldiers appeared with a cake, almost frozen, and some black beers. So we celebrated my twenty-fifth birthday. I felt like I'd been reborn.

From New Guinea I was sent to the Philippines. Like Puerto Rico, the Philippines were a Spanish colony until 1898, when Spain ceded them to the United States as war compensation. From that year on, until the Japanese invaded the territory, the Philippine Islands were under the control of the United States. Faced with war, all the islands' political organizations— Nationalists, Socialists, Communists, and others, no matter their ideology— joined in a united front against the Japanese and collaborated with the Allies. One of the elements of that front was the Philippine resistance movement known as the Hukbalahap, better known as the Huk. This Nationalist-Socialist guerrilla movement was decisive in the defeat of the Japanese army.

I arrived in the Philippines after the American troops had retaken the island of Leyte in one of the bloodiest naval battles of the Second World War. Leyte was one of the major islands in the archipelago, and the Huk presence there was significant. When the American army took control of the island, it set up a provisional government. But great was the disappointment of some, including myself, when we found out that this government was made up of conservative Filipinos, many of whom had collaborated with the Japanese. As in other parts of the Philippines, the Huk were excluded and persecuted by the authorities. When the Americans made this decision, they didn't realize they were transferring the Filipinos' hatred of the Japanese to themselves.

During my stay on Leyte I made friends with many Filipinos. I was not at all your run-of-the-mill American soldier. I liked to talk to people in the villages and spend time with them. This empathy for the Filipinos was aided by the fact that even then, many of them, especially among the more-educated classes, spoke Spanish, and we shared a common history of colonization.

The Huk had its people everywhere. On one occasion, a Filipino that I'd become friends with struck up a conversation. He asked me about myself and what I had done before entering the Army. I told him my story, recounted my experiences in the United States, explained the independence movement in Puerto Rico and the figure of Pedro Albizu Campos. He then invited me to meet some friends of his, and I agreed. He took me to the leader of the Huk in the province. I was impressed by his personality. He explained who the Huks were and told me about the cause they were fighting for. Although always keeping a certain distance, I had a friendly relationship with the Huks. It was through them that I stayed abreast of what was happening in Luzon and other areas of the Philippines, since the Army didn't give us much information about those matters. I learned about the Filipinos' protests and struggles. This experience reinforced my anti-imperialist sentiments and taught me a great deal about the character of revolutionary movements, which to succeed had to know how to adapt themselves to the concrete situation of the moment. The most important lesson I learned, though, was that the struggle for freedom is innate in every people, every nation.

While I was stationed in the Philippines, I took a hard emotional blow. As happened with so many soldiers, the war had an effect on my family life. In 1944, I received a Dear John letter from Célida. She told me, first, that she had changed her name to Sally. It seemed she'd gotten the idea that I was not going to be coming home alive so she'd decided to start a new life with another person, whom she now wanted to marry. I explained the situation to my commanding officer, who had been through the same thing, and he gave me a ten-day pass to deal with the situation. After going to New York to finalize the legal aspect of the divorce and matters related to the custody of my daughter, I returned to the Philippines just as General Douglas MacArthur, Supreme Commander of the Allied Forces in the Pacific, was preparing to invade Japan.

After the U.S. dropped the atomic bombs on Hiroshima and Nagasaki in August 1945, the Japanese surrendered. This nuclear bombing, the only one in the history of humankind, which caused hundreds of thousands of deaths among the civilian population, was not necessary. I reacted strongly against that act of cowardice. I arrived in Okinawa with the army of occupation, and I remained there for three months; I was later transferred to the Japanese capital, Tokyo, where I was stationed for six months.

As a result of the atomic bombs, hatred of Americans among the Japanese people had intensified. There had been incidents, and apparently no American soldier was safe. The High Command issued an order that soldiers could not leave their military base unaccompanied. But because of my rejection of the atomic bombs dropped on their country, I had conceived a great empathy for the Japanese people, and during my stay there I came to know the other face of Japan. It was very different from what I had seen at the front, and also from the stereotype of the Japanese that I had both learned from propaganda films and posters and created for myself. Soon, I met a family that had a dye shop, and we became quite fond of one another. They lived in a suburb outside Tokyo. On my free days, I would ignore the order that prohibited soldiers from leaving the base by themselves. Sometimes I would even stay with the family. When I visited them, I would leave my pistol on the base. I would take them cigarettes, food, and beer, and they made me part of the family—the parents even wanted me to marry their daughter.

I felt so comfortable and at home in Japan that I seriously considered the idea of staying there to live for a while after my discharge. I even started learning the language. But finally I decided to return to New York. The desire to be close to Isa again was stronger than my love for Japan. Isa has always loved me a great deal. Her love for me is so great, in fact, that before she agreed to marry her husband, she told him he had to adopt the surname Gerena. He loved her so much, in return, that he agreed to do that.

So when the moment of my discharge came, I returned to New York. I took very little baggage with me, although I did leave Japan with several rolls of silk cloth dyed by my Japanese family as a farewell gift to me. Unfortunately, the cloth disappeared on the trip back.

I returned a changed man. After having seen the horrors of war, having fraternized with the patriotic freedom-fighters in the Philippines, and having come to know the true face of the Japanese people, my outlook had broadened greatly. I returned more rebellious than I had been before, and I was filled with a strong antiwar, anti-racist, anti-imperialist conscience.

13.
BACK IN NEW YORK CITY

In November 1946, after receiving my honorable discharge and four medals from the United States Army, I returned to New York City. In compliance with Section 8 of the Compulsory Military Service Act of 1940, the Hotel Commodore gave me back the same job I had when I entered the Army. As part of the arrangement, I was to be provided lodging and food. As I was now a single man, I went to live in a room in one of the hotels in the chain the Commodore belonged to. It was located at 37th St. and Lexington Avenue.

My experience in the Army and in war had transformed me in many ways. Among other things, it had taught me the horrors of war and strengthened my conviction that powerful countries use every means at their disposal, from the clumsiest and stupidest to the most sophisticated, to manipulate and control weaker countries. It had also taught me that the oppressed people of the world have to organize, and have to struggle to create a better world for themselves and society in general. If I had any resources that might aid in that effort, it was my organizational abilities, so when I returned to the belly of the beast, as I called it, I dedicated myself body and soul to organizing. I concentrated my efforts on what was nearest and dearest to me: the working class and the Puerto Rican community.

I returned to New York at a time when forces on the political right all across the country were launching a strong offensive against workers. In addition, the Puerto Rican community in the city was beginning to grow very fast, and it was becoming the scapegoat blamed for many social problems. I was seeing the beginning of what, during the fifties, was called the "Puerto Rican problem."

I began to take an active part in several radical organizations. Within the labor movement, I worked closely with leftist groups, especially with the Communist Party of the United States, whose analysis and strategies I often agreed with.

In the city's hotel industry most workers had already been organized. Local 6 represented the culinary workers—dishwashers, cooks, assistant chefs, bartenders, maître d's, waiters, and other kitchen workers—and Local 144 included the bellhops, doormen, porters, hat checks, cloakroom attendants, elevator operators, valets, floor security guards, and cleaning staff. The white-collar workers—that is, the people who did office work of any kind: receptionists, room clerks, floor clerks, billing clerks, and cashiers—were seen as part of the administrative staff; in numerical terms, they were in the minority. These workers had to be organized, and I was one of them. Jay Rubin, who knew me personally and had been aware of my organizational abilities since I worked as a volunteer in the campaign he directed to organize restaurant workers in Local 302 and the hotel industry in the late thirties and early forties, gave me the job of organizing them. The idea was that once the union was formed, we would incorporate it into the Hotel Workers International.

Once again, I worked as a volunteer, spending my free time organizing the New York hotel industry. I created White Collar Workers Local 3 of the New York Hotel Trades Council. I began with the employees of the Hotel Commodore. From there I went on to organize the Waldorf, Pennsylvania, McAlpin, Statler Hilton, New Yorker, Plaza, and Governor Clinton hotels, as well as others. Once these were organized, it was easy to bring in the smaller hotels. By 1947, we had a strong union in that sector.

When the Hotel Commodore management realized that the person behind the campaign to organize the office workers was me, they tried to buy me off. One day the general manager called me in to tell me that a position for a general manager had opened up in one of the chain's hotels and that with my knowledge of the hotel industry and my cultural background, I was the ideal candidate for it. The only problem was that I had to move to Mexico City, which was where the hotel was. It goes without saying that I rejected the offer on principle. In addition, I knew it was a trick, and that once I got to Mexico City the hotel would invent some excuse to fire me. Knowing that things wouldn't end there, I explained the situation I was in to Jay and he suggested that I resign from the hotel and go to work at once, full-time, for Local 6. They needed a good organizer and a business manager to deal with the needs of the growing number of Puerto Rican workers being hired by the hotel industry, especially in the area of the kitchen.

I was delighted with the change in my employment. In my position as organizer and business manager for Local 6, I had twenty-eight hotels in New York City under my jurisdiction. I was responsible for everything related to organizing those hotels' restaurants and receiving and processing the complaints and grievances against the employers. The work was exhausting but very gratifying; plus, it paid well. The constant one-on-one contact with the workers allowed me to create strong bonds of friendship and workplace solidarity with many of them, especially Puerto Ricans, and that translated

quite often into invitations to share a good dinner in the kitchen of a
luxury hotel, or social activities, including family parties and fiestas in the
neighborhoods where the workers lived. In that way I created a large base of
support among Puerto Rican culinary workers in the hotel sector.

14.
BLACKBALLED IN THE HOTELS

Shortly after the end of World War II, an intense process of realignment of the political forces in the United States began. In 1944, Earl Browder, secretary-general of the Communist Party of the United States (CPUSA), dissolved the organization and encouraged former members to join the Democratic Party. This unleashed a war in the CPUSA that culminated in 1946 with the expulsion of Browder and his followers from the party.[6]

Meanwhile, the political right took control of Congress and, after the death of President Franklin D. Roosevelt in 1945, launched a national witch-hunt against Communism, while at the international level there began what came to be known as the Cold War against the Soviet Union. The House Un-American Activities Committee (HUAC), the Senate Internal Security Subcommittee [SISS], and the Senate Committee on Government Operations' Permanent Subcommittee on Investigations, this last body chaired by the infamous senator Joseph "Joe" McCarthy, saw Communists behind every door. For his part, FBI director J. Edgar Hoover channeled large quantities of that agency's resources into infiltrating and disarticulating both the Communist Party of the United States and left-leaning unions. Among the principal targets of the new inquisitors were unions. From the narrow perspective of those crusaders, there were only two kinds of unions: "Communist" unions and "patriotic" unions, which were simply unions controlled by employers that sought industrial peace at workers' expense. If the Communist presence in a union was visible, the FBI would concentrate its efforts on wiping the union out, and if this were not possible, they would encourage and support the so-called patriotic unions at the "Communist" unions' expense.

In June 1947, Congress passed the Taft-Hartley Act. With the stroke of a pen, many of the labor rights granted by the Wagner Act were eliminated. In addition to being a profoundly anti-labor piece of legislation, the new law required all officials of local, national, and international unions to sign an affidavit declaring that they were not members of the Communist Party and did not support any organization that advocated the overthrow of the U.S. government by force.

One of the unions against which the inquisitors directed their greatest fury was Local 6, in which several leaders and organizers had been or were still members of the Communist Party. In September 1947, federal agents burst into the Local's offices and arrested its president, Michael Obermeier, who for some time had been the local's unquestioned leader, accusing him of having entered the United States illegally and being a member of a political organization—i.e., the Communist Party—that advocated the overthrow of the U.S. government by force. A few days later, most of the delegates to the AFL's national convention decided to sign the affidavit.

Under strong pressure from the AFL, the leadership of the New York Hotel Trades Council (NYHTC) began to cave in to the demands of the conservative wing of its membership and of Local 6. This decision generated great resistance among the more progressive members, who, among other things, were opposed to the union's officers and organizers signing the affidavit. The internal tensions exploded in 1949 when the NYHTC negotiated a contract that in the eyes of many of us was contrary to the membership's best interests, especially as it included a clause promising not to strike until 1952. The opposition, of which I was a member, organized to prevent the membership from endorsing this agreement. In a historic assembly held in the convention center next door to the Hotel New Yorker and attended by 1500 delegates, we managed to halt the proceedings by taking control of the microphones. This victory was possible in large part due to the participation of hundreds of Puerto Rican workers, who held the worst-paid jobs in the industry and who would have been most affected by the agreement's financial clauses. On several occasions the NYHTC tried to persuade the membership to endorse the agreement, but we always mobilized our followers and interrupted the meetings to prevent that from happening. Tensions reached the point that the AFL hired a private security company to deal with us. Not even those hired guns could stop us, however. At that, the AFL and the NYHTC adopted a new strategy to get rid of us.

Legally, the NYHTC had the power to negotiate the contract, which would take effect even if it were not ratified by the membership. As one might expect in that profoundly anti-labor environment, employers violated labor and union agreements with impunity. In early 1950, in open defiance of the NYHTC and AFL management, we responded with a campaign of work stoppages and other disruptive actions in hotels, including the Waldorf, the Governor Clinton, and the McAlpin. This campaign, which was very effective, forced the union to renegotiate the agreement to include raises for employees. Our actions put the leadership of the NYHTC in a very uncomfortable position, as it made them look like they couldn't control their members. At the same time, we intensified our campaign denouncing the AFL's position of appeasement. Pressured by the

AFL and arguing that the internal struggles between the Communists and non-Communists (you were either one or the other) had paralyzed the union, the hotel industry's International put Local 6 in receivership, and despite the fact that the hotel industry was not under the jurisdiction of the Taft-Hartley Act, it agreed to require all union officials to sign the affidavit.

Thirteen of the organizers of Local 6 refused to sign the document, and that gave the union the excuse it needed to begin an administrative process against us. The NYHTC proceeded to fire Martin Cody, the director of organization, and twelve organizers, including myself, and banned us from taking part in union activities for three years. They accused us of using our positions for Communist activities.

The anti-Communist campaign within the NYHTC spread to other subsidiaries, including Local 144. Among the organizers expelled was Molly West, Jay Rubin's former wife, who also refused to sign. In addition, the NYHTC sent an unequivocal message to the membership: any member who took part in the fired members' rebellious activities, including what the official communiqué called "Communist tactics," would be subject to disciplinary action.

The fact that I refused to sign the affidavit was from that point on used by my political adversaries as evidence that I belonged or had belonged to the Communist Party. In fact, one of the questions which still today is of some interest to investigators is whether Gilberto Gerena Valentín was a member of the Party. The answer is no. It was out of principle that I refused to sign the affidavit. Of course I did believe that whether I was a Communist or not was nobody's business but my own; I believed that the Constitution gave me the right to have my own political ideas and associate with anyone I wanted. Like many other coworkers of mine who were not Communists, I considered the Party to be a defender of the interests of the working class and considered its members to be citizens whose rights were being denied by their own government, in open violation of the Constitution. If I defended the members of the Communist Party, it was to help safeguard true democracy. In addition, as a firm believer in the freedom of nations and their people, I believed, and continue to believe, in the right of a people to take up arms if necessary to end colonialism.

What is undeniable, and what I have never repented of, is that beginning in the 1940s I agreed with many of the Communist Party's positions. I worked closely with men and women who belonged to the Party and I owe a great deal of my knowledge about organizational strategy and tactics to them. With many of those Communist Party members I forged a profound friendship. In the day-to-day struggle in our communities, we worked shoulder to shoulder to improve the conditions of life for Puerto Ricans. Among the Communist comrades with whom I developed a close working relationship and friendship were the brothers Jesús and Joaquín Colón, César Andreu Iglesias, Clemente Soto Vélez, Mercedes Arroyo, José Santiago, and Juan Emmanuelli. The last three belonged to the Party's radical wing and fought against Browderism head on. That cannot be said of other Puerto Rican Communist leaders, who were fully identified with Browderism and looked askance at my relationship with the radical sector of the Communist Party.

Not a few times did my Communist friends, especially Arroyo, Santiago, and Emmanuelli, try to convince me to join the Communist Party. Despite their insistence, I refused. It was, however, in large part through them that I found a political space more in keeping with my own ideological positions and from which I could work both for the improvement of the Puerto Rican community's conditions in New York, especially the working-class sector of that community, and for Puerto Rican independence. That space was the American Labor Party. . . .

15.
THE AMERICAN LABOR PARTY

When I returned to New York from the Pacific front, I found an extremely complex political situation. On the one hand, the Puerto Rico Nationalist Party (PNPR) in New York City had split and the alliance of the early forties between Communists and Nationalists had collapsed. Likewise, other internal struggles had significantly weakened it. The PNPR had become insignificant, with little or no influence in the community. The Communist Party of the United States, on the other hand, was also not an option for me since I did not agree with many of its positions. The only alternative that remained was the American Labor Party (ALP).

The American Labor Party was an independent political party. It had been created in 1936 by non-Communist leftists in New York for the purpose of defending the interests of workers in that state. Its election strategy was supporting those candidates—Democrats, Republicans, or independents—who would commit to the ALP's platform principles. For example, in 1937 and 1938, the ALP endorsed Puerto Rican Oscar García Rivera, a Republican who did not have the support of his own party's machinery, for state assemblyman for District 17. The first Puerto Rican elected to public office in New York City and the United States, García Rivera won because of the Puerto Rican vote provided to him by the ALP, defeating the Democratic machine in Harlem. However, during his term García Rivera supported legislation contrary to the ALP's positions, and so was not backed by the Party for a second term. This cost him his victory.

In 1938 the ALP also supported the candidacy of former Republican congressman Vito Marcantonio for the U.S. House of Representatives. Marc, as those of us close to him called him, was a member of Mayor Fiorello LaGuardia's political machine, a liberal Republican who did much for El Barrio. A man of socialist leanings, Mark broke with the Republican Party and became a member of the ALP in 1937. The next year he was elected to Congress with the support of the Puerto Rican residents of El Barrio. Over the next few years, and as the Puerto Rican community grew, El Barrio became Marcantonio's principal bastion of support. A decade later, in 1947, Marcantonio was invincible. In an attempt to defeat him, Democrats and Republicans passed a law that prohibited a candidate from being inscribed for election by more than one party. In this way they forced Marc to run only on the ALP ticket. Despite all that, he won the election.

It was in 1947 that I formally began working for the ALP. I started out in the Public Relations Department, writing and distributing bulletins and other electoral materials in the community. Another of my jobs was attending activities and working up the audience for Marc's entrance. In recognition of my dedication and organizing ability, in 1948 Marc made me captain of District 14, that is, Spanish Harlem. As district captain I was responsible for keeping the voting lists up to date and ensuring that each and every voter went to the polls on election day. Another of my responsibilities was keeping the district residents informed of what the party was doing and to serve as the party's ear within the community. In 1949 I took an active part in the campaign to elect Manuel Medina to the state assembly for District 14. For a long time, Medina had been Marc's personal secretary. Unfortunately, he lost by fewer than 1000 votes.

In the ALP I honed my skills as a community organizer. I learned an enormous amount in the clinics and workshops the party offered, including electoral strategies, political campaign strategies, and how to prepare petitions; I also picked up invaluable information on issues relating to health and housing. Over the next few years, I actively participated in all the activities the ALP held in El Barrio.

One of the pressing problems affecting the community at that time was a wave of illegal evictions of Puerto Rican tenants by unscrupulous landlords. In the early forties, as part of its anti-inflationary economic policy, the Roosevelt administration passed the Emergency Price Control Act. In November 1943, rents were frozen in New York City and evictions, among other things, were regulated. Although the law expired in 1947 and all new construction was therefore freed from rent controls, rent control continued on buildings built before that date. This was a blow to landlords, because it limited their ability to profit from their rents. The most unscrupulous of them, however, found ways to throw people out without due process of law, especially if they were behind in their rent.

To deal with the problem of evictions in El Barrio, the ALP created a Housing Committee that would mobilize immediately when an eviction occurred. This committee had been created in the late thirties, when evictions were the order of the day. Now that the practice had reared its ugly head again, the committee reenergized. It was composed of volunteers and included plumbers, electricians, movers, and religious leaders. On the committee, the most active members were

Jesús "Chuíto" Caballero, Francisco "Paco" Archilla, Julio Flores, the Reverend José Rodríguez, and I. There was also a group of scouts, whose job was to keep watch for evictions and immediately notify the committee.

Often, landlords would evict people on Friday afternoons, so the people they evicted couldn't immediately seek aid in court. The gorillas hired by the landlords would show up with crowbars and sledgehammers, break down the doors, take out the tenants and all their belongings and throw them into the street. They would smash the toilet and sink, cut the electric cables, and then board up the apartment. It was pitiful, seeing whole families, including old people and children, out on the sidewalk with nowhere to go, and it was infuriating, too. And the scene was even more heartbreaking in winter.

As soon as one of our scouts notified us of an eviction, the committee would go into action. We'd arrive at the address, pull off the plywood boarding up the door, cut off the padlocks if there were any, and then the plumber would repair the bathroom, the electrician would restore the electricity, and the carpenter would put in a new lock. Then we would move the tenants back into their apartment—it was quite a spectacle to see Paco Archilla, the mover, pick up a sofa on his back and carry it up three or four flights of stairs without any help!—and give them a basket of food with everything they needed while they were getting their life back to normal. A priest or pastor would usually stay in the apartment with the family for support.

When the landlord would hear what had happened, he would usually get an official eviction order from the court, but when the court officer would appear with the eviction notice, he would find one of the pastors, Bible in hand, who would give him a protection order prepared in advance by the Marcantonio legal firm. And then the Housing Committee's volunteer lawyers, many of them Jewish, would swing into action and litigate the case in court. One of the most distinguished was Manuel Medina, a Puerto Rican.

As a general rule, we won the cases. When we did, we'd sometimes sue the landlords for the damage they'd caused to the tenants' belongings, which would have been thrown in the street like garbage, and arrange to lower the rent to pay for the damage. The system worked so well that we would often be called by other Puerto Rican communities in the city to ask for our help. In addition to helping them, we would send in volunteers to show them how to set up the same operation in their borough or neighborhood.

In 1948, the American Labor Party decided to support Henry Wallace's Progressive Party in the presidential elections. One of the most progressive members of Roosevelt's administration, Wallace[7] had been thrown out of the Democratic Party for opposing the Cold War policies of Harry S. Truman. One sector of the Democratic Party left with him and created the United States Progressive Party, whose platform promised to return the United States to the common man and put an end to a number of evils: big money's control over government; racial segregation; interventionism; the bellicose American stance toward the USSR; the anti-Communist campaign; and widespread violations of civil rights. The Left, including the ALP, endorsed Wallace's candidacy. I attended the Progressive Party's constituent convention in Philadelphia as a delegate from District 18. Unfortunately, the new party did not generate the support it had hoped for and it gradually disappeared after losing the presidential election.

At that convention I met Francia Lubán, my second wife. Of Russian Jewish ancestry (her original surname was Lubinski), Francia had been raised in Mexico. Her parents had emigrated to that country to escape the terrible persecution of Jews under Czar Nicholas. From Mexico, Francia moved to New York. There she found work at the Edward B. Marks Music Company,[8] where she was in charge of the Latin American section. Her work there allowed her to make friends with many Latin American musicians working in the city, including Cubans Bola de Nieve and Machito, Puerto Ricans Pedro Flores, Bobby Capó, and Tito Rodríguez, and the Trio Los Panchos, which almost always had a Puerto Rican as its lead singer. Francia belonged to the musicians union, in which she was very active, and in fact, she attended the Progressive Party convention as a union delegate. When we returned to New York City we continued to see each other, and a few months later we married.

Marrying Francia brought yet another change to my life. I had to leave my little hotel room and find an apartment, for one thing. Some friends, Cedric and Marta Belfrage (he was English and she was Mexican), helped us find a four-bedroom place on the first floor at 206 E. 65th St. in Manhattan. It was there, in December of 1949, that the first and only child of that marriage was born, my son Joseph, who to my immense grief has just recently died. A few months after he was born, I was expelled from Local 6.

16.
ORGANIZING WORKERS
AT THE EMERSON PLANT

Those were hard times. I found myself without a job when I most needed one—my son had just been born and bills were piling up. I had been warned that the New York Hotel Trades Council would use every means possible to prevent me from ever working again in the industry. At first, I couldn't believe they would stoop so low. I tried to find work in several hotels in the city, but the NYHTC had taken upon itself to inform every one of them that Gerena Valentín was a troublemaker, and that he was forbidden to work in the industry. After several months of fruitless job-searching, I found a job with Local 810 of the Teamsters Union as an organizer in the workshops on the Hudson River and in Riverside. It didn't last long.

Finally, a job appeared at the Woodstock Hotel on W. 43rd St. near Times Square. It didn't pay much, but at least it helped pay the rent and put food on the table. I was hired in housekeeping, cleaning rooms, the same job I'd had at the New Yorker Hotel years earlier when I was beginning my career in the hotel industry. I got the job thanks to the friendship I had developed with the supervisor of Housekeeping there. She knew what had happened to me and despite everything, made up her mind to help me. But she was honest with me from the beginning; she warned me that if she got "orders from above" she'd have no alternative but to let me go.

Three or four weeks later, the hotel management received word from the NYHTC that I had been suspended from the union and that they were forbidding me to work in the hotel industry. That convinced me once and for all that my work with hotels had come to an end. At that point, a friend who was a member of Local 430 of the United Electrical Workers took me to meet Al Stern, the union business manager. As had happened in Local 6, the government alleged that Local 430 was controlled by Communists, and it did everything it could to destroy it.

Al began our meeting by telling me that he had heard good things about me. He had been told that I was a good organizer, and I wasn't afraid of anything, and—the key to the kingdom back then—that I spoke both English and Spanish. He asked me if I liked working as a union organizer. We talked about my experiences in Local 6 and I gave him my interpretation of what happened. He agreed with me, and he consoled me by saying that in the long run this Communist hysteria was bound to die out. He then asked me whether I was ready to go to work. My answer: "When do I start?"

He told me that for some time they had been trying to organize a television plant in Emerson, New Jersey, where 300 workers were employed. Most of the workers were Italian, but there were also a good many Puerto Ricans and blacks. Many wanted to join Local 430, but there were several problems that had to be overcome. One of them was that the owners of the plant, who had always been opposed to their employees' unionizing, were now supporting the entrance of a "patriotic" union. They were at that very moment in the process of gathering signatures to decide who would be representing their workers. My job was to help organize the shop, but I would have to do it from the inside. And to do that, the union would find me a job in the plant. In addition to the salary I would receive as an employee, the union would pay my transportation expenses and a fee.

The Emerson factory, which was named after the town it was located in, was on the other side of the Hudson River. Since I had a little car at the time—it rattled and wheezed, but at least it ran—it didn't take me too long to get there. When I got to the factory, I went directly to the personnel department. I spoke to the woman who was interviewing me about my job experience and my skills as a carpenter, which I had learned at Henry Clay under my teacher, Fabián Martínez. The lady told me that there was a position open in the repair shop. I took the job, although I had no idea what I might have gotten myself into. She told me, there and then, to go up to the third floor and find the repair shop supervisor, an Italian named Giuseppe.

This was the first time I had ever entered the production floor of a factory. There were three conveyor belts that moved the television cabinets along. Giuseppe asked me if I'd ever done this work before. I told him I hadn't, but that I was a fast learner; all I needed was for him to show me how to do it. He called over one of his assistants, who showed me what to do. The work was deceptively simple-looking. I had four things to work with: a bar of wax the color of the wood of the television cabinets, a spatula, a gas burner to keep the knife blade red hot, and a cloth. The job consisted of taking down the cabinet as it came down the conveyor belt and quickly inspecting it for defects. If it had a scratch or blemish, I had to put the television to one side and with the spatula and melted wax cover the scratch, shine the wood, and then put it back up on the conveyor belt again.

I was hired for a probationary period of thirty days. In order to become permanent, a worker had to show that he was strong, agile, and fast. There was a lot of pressure, because you had to maintain the same rate as the other workers doing the same job. If you didn't, you were out. My first and second days were terrible. After lifting so many heavy television sets, my whole body hurt. I didn't think I would ever be able to keep up and I was sure I was going to be fired. The third day, Giuseppe told me not to rush, that I was doing fine, and that I would soon be a good cabinet repair man. That cheered me up quite a bit. And in fact he was right. By the next week, I had gotten the rhythm and was moving those cabinets right along. I got through the probationary period, and the supervisor assigned me to the conveyor belt. Now I could start organizing.

The factory occupied three huge floors of the building. Each one performed one part of the production process. I soon won Giuseppe's confidence, and he sent me to supervise the cabinet-production line. I was supposed to be sure the cabinets were in perfect condition before they were sent to the packing area. Within six months I knew everybody in the factory.

I became friends with a group of young men and women of Puerto Rican descent, and I talked to them casually about the labor conditions in the factory. I identified their leader. He was from Ciales, but he had grown up in the United States. He was always really happy when I talked to him about the island. Little by little I started talking to him about the need for a union. In one of our conversations he told me that before I arrived, a black man had showed up at the factory to organize. He had passed out cards but he never came back. I asked him how many workers had signed the cards and he told me none of them had. He also admitted that he had gathered up all the cards, because there was something about that person that he didn't trust. I then asked him if he and his coworkers would be willing to sign cards for Local 430, which I belonged to. At first he seemed a little hesitant; he told me he'd have to see the cards first. I gave them to him one Friday. The next Monday, he brought me a pleasant surprise. All the members of the group had signed up. It was now time to take the campaign to the other workers.

The Emerson employees tended to get together at lunch hour by ethnic or racial groups: Puerto Ricans with Puerto Ricans, blacks with blacks, and Italians with Italians. Fortunately my friend had a friend, a Puerto Rican, who was in love with an Italian girl and had been accepted into the Italian group. Through him, we managed to convince many of the Italians to sign up with us.

Labor conditions in a factory affect everyone equally, regardless of the color of their skin or their language. Supervisors will pressure everyone tremendously to meet the production quotas, and that will generate anxiety, stress, and tiredness among the workers. At the Emerson plant, the supervisors were on our backs constantly, to the point that we were sometimes even forced to come out of the bathroom without having finished our business; they said we were taking too much time. Conditions were ripe for organizing a union.

When we were ready for the elections, management counterattacked. The local had to go to the Labor Relations Board to force Emerson to allow the workers to elect their union representative. The other union launched a campaign to discredit Local 430. At lunch hour, their representatives would distribute flyers among the workers, accusing us of being against the government of the United States and of being pro-Communist. Citing the Communist trials that were taking place during those years, especially in 1950, which culminated with the imprisonment of the major leaders of the Communist Party, including William Z. Foster, Elizabeth Gurley Flynn, and Benjamin Davis, our "union" adversaries alleged that our union could not defend or represent workers because all of our officers would face the same fate as the Communist Party leaders.

The anti-Communist campaign was so fierce and effective that on the day of the elections, many of those who had endorsed us in the beginning didn't even come to work. This cost us the elections. I remember that that day, the "patriotic" union brought in a truck with an open platform from which a person disguised as Joseph Stalin passed out flyers titled "God Bless America" to the Emerson workers. By that time the Emerson management was aware that I was the person behind Local 430's organizational offensive, and they fired me. We couldn't do anything about it, since unfortunately the labor laws of New Jersey were even more favorable to employers than the laws of New York. So there I was, without a job again.

17.
THE PUERTO RICAN COMMUNITY LOSES ITS STRONGEST ALLY: THE DEATH OF MARCANTONIO

Looking back, I see that 1950 was an extremely difficult year, not just for me personally but for the Puerto Rican community in New York City. Several events directly related to the island's political status would have a profound effect on our community.

In 1940, the Popular Democratic Party (PDP), under the leadership of Luis Muñoz Marín, won the legislative elections in Puerto Rico. With that victory, and in the context of the war, a process of redefinition of the colonial relationship between Puerto Rico and the United States began. As part of its economic program, the PDP promoted the massive migration of Puerto Rican workers to the United States.

Between 1945 and 1950, the Puerto Rican community in Harlem grew very quickly. First, the Fifth Avenue border was broken through. From there, the community spread over to Madison, then Third, and so on until reaching First Avenue, which was the Italian stronghold at the time. And with this expansion, the influence and political power of Vito Marcantonio increased exponentially in East Harlem.

There were two very strong ethnic groups in East Harlem. To the east, there was the Italian community, which was quite large. On the western side, we Puerto Ricans were in the majority. With the Puerto Rican vote, Marc, who was of Italian descent, was always elected to Congress. At the borough level, the Italians controlled the Democratic Party and through it, the state Senate and Assembly and the city council.

In 1949, Italian-American Carmine DeSapio became the leader of Tammany Hall, the Democratic Party machine that dominated politics in New York City during the fifties. DeSapio, who was later associated with organized crime in the city, pretty much had a monopoly on political appointments in New York City, with the exception of El Barrio. There, Marcantonio was considered invincible. He had defeated the Democrats, the Republicans, and even, in 1948, a coalition of the Republican Party and the recently created Liberal Party. This last group was led by dissidents from the American Labor Party who were opposed to the presence of Communists in its leadership. The Liberal Party was run by David Dubinsky, president of the International Ladies Garment Workers Union (ILGWU). This union was composed largely of Puerto Ricans, most of those, women, who worked in the clothing industry. Dubinsky believed that many of these workers would follow him and vote against Marcantonio. He was wrong.

Finally, in 1950, the three parties—Democratic, Republican, and Liberal— joined forces to defeat Marcantonio in the congressional election. To do that, they presented as their single candidate a reactionary named James Donovan, a drunk Irishman who was a member of the Democratic machinery of Tammany Hall. Donovan was also the candidate of the German Bund, a pro-Fascist, racist group in the district that saluted in the Nazi style and joined the campaign to defeat the protector of the "Porto Ricans."

In that united front against Marcantonio some lesser members were Luis Muñoz Marín and the Popular Democratic Party. Marc's support for Puerto Rican independence, which dated from the thirties, was still unyielding. Now, at a time when the PDP was seeking to negotiate a colonial arrangement with the government of the United States, Marc's continued defense of the island's independence in the U.S. Congress was an obstacle that had to be overcome. In 1949, Antonio Fernós Isern, Puerto Rico's Resident Commissioner in Washington, D.C., presented a bill in Congress, HR-7674, that contained the legal basis for the creation of the so-called Commonwealth, the "Estado Libre Asociado" or "Free Associated State" of Puerto Rico. In the public hearings, Marc was stubbornly opposed to the bill. He argued on behalf of his own bill, which would in time lead to independence for Puerto Rico. He also strongly protested the fact that the hearings were held in Washington and not in Puerto Rico, thereby limiting the participation of Puerto Ricans who were opposed to HR-7674. To partially remedy that situation, a group of independence advocates and I created the Political Action Committee for the Independence of Puerto Rico and we asked to be heard during the hearings. I was chosen to present our opposition to Fernos' colonialist bill. The PDP mobilized its people in New York and sent several of its leaders, including the mayor of San Juan, doña Felisa Rincón de Gautier, to aid in the three-party effort to silence Vito Marcantonio's dissident voice.

The campaign against Marc was extremely virulent. Accusations that he was a "Red," that he promoted the migration of Puerto Ricans to New York in order to strengthen his electoral base, and that the American Labor Party was a Communist front were the order of the day. His opponents also used against him the fact that he was the only congressman who had voted against the war in Korea. A few days before the election, another element was added to the campaign when, on October 30, the Nationalist Revolution broke out in Puerto Rico.[9]

Two days later, on November 1, the phone rang in Marcantonio's office in Harlem. They were calling from his office in Washington to give him the news that a Nationalist attempt had been made on the life of president Harry S. Truman. In the shootout, a police officer and one of the Nationalists had been killed. The other Nationalist was badly wounded. The dead man's name was Griselio Torresola; the wounded man was Oscar Collazo. Marc rushed to Washington. He put aside his campaign itinerary to attend an emergency session of Congress called to discuss the matter of the assassination attempt against the president. When the session opened, Marc asked for the floor. He spoke in defense of the Puerto Rican people. He explained the situation of Puerto Rico to the people of the United States and pleaded that the Puerto Rican communities across the United States not be harmed, that there be no revenge taken against them. His was the only voice raised in defense of our community in Congress.

Meanwhile, physical attacks against Puerto Ricans in New York became common. Tempers were being fired up by the sensationalist press, which insinuated that wherever there was a Puerto Rican, a bomb was being made. That "news" certainly sold a lot of newspapers! "Puerto Ricans go home!" "Puerto Ricans tried to kill our president!"

As soon as he came back from Washington, Marc created a committee to raise money for the defense of Oscar Collazo, who had been accused of the death of a police officer and the attempted murder of two other people. The jury found him guilty as charged, despite the fact that it was proven that Collazo had not fired the bullet that killed the police officer, and the judge sentenced him to die in the electric chair. At that, we decided to launch a campaign to gather a hundred thousand signatures to ask that his death penalty be commuted. Marc put me in charge of that effort.

Since it was just then that I was in the process of organizing the Puerto Rican town and city clubs, I used that organizational structure to raise support in the community. We also created a broad committee to take the campaign not just to New York City but also into New Jersey and Pennsylvania. The petition was a tremendous success. In less than a month we gathered the hundred thousand signatures we wanted. In 1952, in response to this and other demands, President Truman commuted Collazo's death sentence to life in prison. The news came one week before the date Collazo had been scheduled for execution. That same year, on July 25, Luis Muñoz Marín inaugurated the farcical "Commonwealth" in Puerto Rico.

While all this was taking place, in New York City the conditions our community faced were deteriorating even further. Prejudice against Puerto Ricans was on the rise. In the congressional elections of 1950, Marc was defeated by a coalition of reactionary forces with the support of the Popular Democratic Party. Donovan, the alcoholic Irish machine candidate, was elected. Marc's popularity in the district, however, was clear. Despite a campaign of fear and hatred run by the Liberal-Democratic-Republican coalition, and the advertising and other propaganda against Marcantonio in the city's major newspapers, he received forty percent of the votes.

Over the next four years, Marc dedicated himself to his legal practice. From his offices, he continued to struggle in defense of the poor and of everyone's civil rights. In 1953 he broke with the ALP and the next year, 1954, he decided to run again for Congress, this time as an independent. One morning in August of that year, he fell dead of a heart attack in the park across the street from City Hall. People passed by his body without even stopping, thinking he was just some drunk. Finally, a kind soul took pity on him, touched the body, and saw that he was dead. An ambulance was called and in time his body was taken to the Giordano Funeral Home on 116th St. and Third Avenue. There, our community turned out in force to pay our respects to the man who had been our leader, Vito Marcantonio.

The hatred of the far right followed my friend to the grave. Although Marcantonio had been a devout Catholic, Cardinal Francis Spellman, a rabid anti-Communist and fervent defender of Sen. Joseph McCarthy, refused to allow him to be buried by the church. Marcantonio was finally buried in Woodlawn Cemetery in the Bronx. His funeral was the largest ever seen in East Harlem.

That same year, 1954, Donovan lost the congressional election. Disgusted with his behavior, DeSapio backed Alfred Santangelo, one of his lieutenants in Harlem, in the primaries. Donovan ran as the Republican Party candidate, but he was defeated by the Democrats. District 18, the only one not controlled by the Democratic Party during the thirties and forties, had now fallen under the control of Tammany Hall. The ALP, in turn, without the charismatic figure of Marcantonio and weakened by internal strife, fell apart, and in 1956 it was formally dissolved. It was hard for us to fill Marc's shoes. Politically, we were orphans.

18.
MY RELATIONSHIP WITH
THE REFORM DEMOCRATS

Marcantonio's death occurred in the context of an intense power struggle within the Democratic Party. Carmine DeSapio was in a life-or-death struggle with Frank J. Sampson, another Manhattan Democratic leader. In 1954, DeSapio broke with the Labor Party after its crushing defeat in the 1953 elections, and like many other members of the ALP, I joined the Democratic Party, seeking alliances with the reform sector of that party as it was trying to transform the party and move it toward more progressive positions.

In El Barrio, a group of us saw this juncture as a good time to get a Puerto Rican appointed as district leader.[10] We were preparing to launch the Reverend José Rodríguez, and I think he would probably have been elected, but DeSapio moved faster, and in 1954 appointed Tony Méndez, originally from Jayuya, up in the mountains of Puerto Rico, and now the owner of a jewelry store on 112th St. and Fifth Avenue in El Barrio and president of the Club Caribe. Tony was named to replace Sammy Kantor, who had refused to support Robert Wagner, who was then DeSapio's candidate for mayor.

Once Tony was made district leader, I gave him my support. He would often go to DeSapio to ask for jobs for Puerto Ricans. He was always given jobs, but they were for janitors, or as elevator operators, or maintenance men. Some people accused Tony of being an Uncle Tom. I can tell those critics that Tony helped us a great deal in developing political leadership in El Barrio. In fact it was Tony who helped us get Herman Badillo out of the Club Caribe and persuade him to run against the machine run by Frank Rossetti, of District 16 in Manhattan. That took place in 1961.

The group trying to develop a new generation of Puerto Rican leadership in El Barrio was composed of, among other people, men and women who had worked with Marcantonio in the Labor Party. Among them were Rev. Rodriguez, Paco Archilla, Julio Flores, Gregorio Domenech, and César Ayala. Once in a while, Chuíto Caballero would attend the meetings. Caballero was associated with Tony Méndez, and he was made district captain. In 1958, I and other members of our group worked in the campaign to elect José Ramos López to the state assembly for District 14. José was the first Puerto Rican elected on the Democratic Party ticket to serve in Albany. Once there, he worked hard to eliminate the literacy test for voters.

In 1961, Mayor Robert Wagner, who had been elected in 1953 and 1957 with DeSapio's endorsement, broke with DeSapio and went into the primaries without the machine's backing. I gave him my support, since I thought the time was right to end the Democratic machine's control in El Barrio and to make room for Puerto Ricans.

One Thursday afternoon I went to the Club Caribe to visit Tony. We had a committee ready to challenge DeSapio's Democratic machine. We wanted to support a Puerto Rican with a good, solid education. Tony's position was that the person chosen had to speak perfect English. I asked him to give us some names. He told me that he didn't want to get involved in that since he was a Democrat, but that there was a kid who had just graduated from law school, a quiet kind of guy, who was helping him fill out housing applications for the Puerto Ricans in the projects. At that time, each Democratic club got a quota from the Party for apartments in the projects.

I asked him what this person's name was. He said it was Herman Badillo, and that every Monday and Thursday he came to help with the applications. He told me also that Badillo no longer lived in El Barrio; he had moved to 96th St. and was married to a Jewish girl. The next Monday, a group of us, including Caballero, Flores, Rev. Rodríguez, Archilla, and Ayala, who was president of the Club Borinsol on 116th St., showed up at the Club Caribe to talk to Badillo.

Herman was tall, light skinned, and spoke English very well. We presented our proposal to him and he said he'd have to discuss the matter with his family; he'd let Tony know what his decision was. In about a week, Tony called to tell us that Herman was willing to consider running. In our second meeting, Herman agreed to face Frank Rossetti in the primaries. As a result, Tony Méndez became a *persona non grata* with the Democratic machine.

We ran a good campaign, but we lost by seventy-five votes. Our lawyer, who was well aware of all the Democratic machine's tricks, recommended that we ask for a recount. The Congreso de Pueblos did an investigation and we found that many of the voters didn't live at the addresses they had given. We even went to the cemetery to look around, and we found some of the names there. There were quite a few names that did not match the voter list. We found enough evidence to ask the court to invalidate the primaries due to voter fraud. At first, Herman agreed. We took the case to court, which was of course controlled by the Democratic machine, and we lost. We lost again in appellate court. We decided to continue appealing, but suddenly Herman called us together to tell us that he was going to withdraw from the case, since Mayor Wagner had offered him a position in his administration as assistant commissioner in the Buildings Department, with the promise that he would be quickly promoted to the post of commissioner. It later came out that Dr. José N. Cestero, a member of the Democratic Committee for the borough of Manhattan, exerted a great deal of pressure on Tony Méndez to convince Herman to let the thing go, and that DeSapio, in turn, pressured Mayor Wagner to give Badillo a position in his administration.

Herman turned out to be an excellent professional politician. Not long after, he moved to the Bronx, where there was a rapidly growing Puerto Rican community and where Gov. Nelson Rockefeller had made a place for him in electoral politics. In 1965 he was elected president of the borough of the Bronx. From that point on, he continued to rise in the political ranks in New York City. He was elected to the U.S. Congress from District 21, which covered the South Bronx, northern Manhattan, and the eastern part of Queens; he ran three times for mayor and was named deputy mayor by Edward Koch. At that time, Badillo had distanced himself from the reform positions of before. In his last attempt to win the mayor's office, he joined the Republican Party. In early 2001 he ran for mayor against multi-millionaire Michael Bloomberg, another renegade Democrat, who defeated him handily.

The truth was, Herman never took a leadership position in grassroots organizations in the Puerto Rican community. He lent his name in exchange for political support. He took part in the creation of the National Association of Puerto Rican Civil Rights and later, the Puerto Rican Community Development Project, but he was never very active. At our urging, he agreed to be a member of the Development Project's Board of Directors. When he attended the meetings, he often left early. His campaigns were always run by an organization called "Friends of Badillo" and in it, during the sixties and seventies, the Congreso de Pueblos always played a part. We were usually in charge of mobilizing voters. When he was asked questions about organizational matters Herman always answered, "Ask Gerena." The Congreso de Pueblos was also a vital force behind campaigns urging the mayor to appoint other Puerto Ricans to administration positions. These appointments included John Carro and Judge Emilio Núñez, who, though born in Spain, was raised in the United States and identified with our community.

In the Democratic primaries of 1961, we reform-minded Democrats and other groups also endorsed the candidacy of Carlos Ríos, a young Puerto Rican, as district leader. Ríos had been a union organizer, and he was the minister of a Protestant church in El Barrio. Our work bore fruit: Ríos defeated incumbent John Merli, who ran with DeSapio's blessing. A short time later, in 1963, Ríos was elected city councilman for District 10. In time, however, he began to flirt with the Democratic machine. In 1965, in a move that took everyone by surprise, he was appointed councilman at-large to fill a vacancy that was to be voted on in the next few days. When it was learned that Ríos had lent himself to that underhanded move, the reform Democrats withdrew their support and asked me to run for the at-large seat. In addition to the Democrats, I could count on the support of many Puerto Rican community organizations and labor unions. The main opposition to my campaign within the community came from the United Bronx Organizations, a group that was led by Ramón Vélez, who had allied himself with the South Bronx Democratic machinery. I ran on a platform of civil rights. The reformers, however, made a deal with the machine and withdrew their support, which led to my loss in the primaries. I should clarify, however, that some of them, including John Langrod, did not at all like the way I'd been dealt with by the reformers and continued to support me. The sad truth was that at that time, the reform movement, composed mainly of leaders from the West Side, had changed; it had become a group that supported candidates whose only purpose was to negotiate with the machine for positions in the administration.

The defeat didn't pain me too much. What hurt the most was my betrayal by people I had been working with for years. But that's politics. It didn't keep me awake at night. I always saw party politics as a means to an end, which was to improve life in my community. That was what, in the final analysis, had brought me to where I was.

19.
AT THE ADAMS PLANT

But let's go back to the early fifties to see how I got a new job after I was fired from Emerson for my union activities in 1952 and what this change meant for me.

Despite the blow that losing the union elections at Emerson represented for the union and for me in my role as union organizer, to a certain extent I can say that it was a good thing. That commute from 65th St. in Manhattan to the little town of Emerson, New Jersey, and back was not exactly a piece of cake, especially in a car that was falling apart. The working conditions in the factory were deplorable, and my work was truly exhausting. After picking up television sets all day, I was exhausted. And if you add to that all the difficulties and obstacles I faced in my organizing work. . .

Fortunately, this time I found a new job immediately. Two days after I was fired, Al Stern found work for me in another electronic-equipment factory. My new workplace was the Adams Laboratories, and my job was on the assembly line. Located in Long Island City, this factory manufactured communications equipment. The difference between Adams and Emerson was like the difference between night and day. Unlike Emerson, Adams had recognized Local 430 as the exclusive representative of its employees, and for several years the local had been negotiating collective agreements. The leaders and organizers of the union in the factory were excellent. However, the ethnic makeup of the workers had changed, and now there were a growing number of Puerto Ricans at the plant. Members of the local needed someone who could represent their interests. Al took me there to fill that void.

Early on, during the probationary period, I didn't involve myself too much with union matters, although the Puerto Rican workers already knew who I was, since they had read about me in the city's Hispanic newspapers. In those thirty days I devoted myself to learning everything I could about the working conditions in the factory: who was who, the relationships between the various groups of workers, and management's attitude toward its employees. The Puerto Rican workers were very productive. The place itself was also very pleasant, and management treated its employees well. All of this translated into high productivity. During the time I worked at Adams, I helped the local keep the production floor well organized by dealing with, among other things, matters relating to the Puerto Rican employees.

There was a floor supervisor named Tony Salese, an ex-Communist who had been president and organizer of Local 430 and who, like me, had been a victim of the McCarthy-ite hysteria. Due to his union contacts and knowledge, the company used Tony to renegotiate whenever its contract with the union expired. Salese, who always tried to make the contract as beneficial as possible for the workers, took a liking to me and we established an excellent working relationship.

Another person that I had a close friendship with was Julie Pariser, the vice president of the company. Pariser was a liberal Jew who had been active in leftist activities in his younger days and later was a member of the Americans for Democratic Action, a liberal organization founded in 1947 on an anti-Fascist platform. Pariser had visited Puerto Rico several times and he loved the island and its people. Once in a while he would learn a word or two in Spanish, including the not-so-nice ones, and he liked to practice speaking with the Puerto Rican workers. His attitude and his cheery disposition made him very well-liked among the plant's Puerto Rican workers.

After working for a while assembling equipment, I was promoted to quality-control inspector. Shortly afterward, Pariser asked me if I would be interested in learning to be a draftsman. I said I would, so he got the company to pay for a drafting and design course at the Delehanty Institute in Manhattan. When I graduated, I was given the position of draftsman, working on drawings for the jigs on the production floor.

In 1954, the same year Marcantonio died, a group of Puerto Rican Nationalists attacked the United States Congress. The group, comprised of Dolores (Lolita) Lebrón, Rafael Cancel Miranda, Andrés Figueroa, and Irvin Flores, fired into the ceiling of the House chamber to call attention to Puerto Rico's colonial status. There was no intention to kill anyone. Four congressmen were wounded as a result of ricochets off the ceiling. The Nationalists were arrested on the spot, offering no resistance. They were found guilty in federal court of attempted murder and other crimes and sentenced to long prison terms. Later they were taken to New York, where they were tried and sentenced to more years in prison for attempting to overthrow the government of the United States by force. As in the case of Collazo, I worked actively in the campaign to free my Nationalist compatriots.

At that time, the FBI was keeping a watch on me for having refused to sign the affidavit required by the Taft-Hartley Act and because of my participation in the campaign to commute Oscar Collazo's death sentence. One day some agents showed up at the Adams offices to inform my employers of my "anti-American" activities and "suggest" that they take measures to deal with the matter. Fortunately, Pariser already knew about my situation and he explained it to the company president. That same afternoon, one of the top managers called me into his office to tell me about the FBI's visit and ask me about my view of the situation. They accepted my explanation, and the subject was closed.

The position that management took in this case did not please the FBI. In about two weeks the plant began to receive anonymous phone calls saying a bomb had been planted in the building. As a safety measure, management had to call the Fire Department, which would then vacate the building to inspect it. This happened twice a month for several months. But the owners of the Adams factory held their ground and finally the FBI dropped that strategy. This was only one small incident in the harassment I was subjected to by the FBI. When I would leave work, agents would follow me all the way to my apartment on 65th St. and Second Avenue. On weekends, a car was always parked outside my house, and when I left I was constantly followed. I bought a camera to photograph them and I eventually compiled a nice collection of agent photographs. I must say, though, that when I turned the camera on them directly, they always covered their faces.

In Julie Pariser I found a noble, sensitive man who understood my commitment to the Puerto Rican community. When he learned about the organizing I was doing and about my idea of creating an organization to defend our rights that was not connected to any political party in particular, he gave me his full support. He always let me receive telephone calls in the plant to deal with organizational matters, and even installed a private telephone for me. He let me leave during working hours to attend press conferences and meetings, especially those related to the organization of the Puerto Rican Day Parade, one of the main projects of the Congreso de Pueblos. In 1963, when Dr. Martin Luther King asked me to organize the Puerto Rican community to attend the historic march on Washington, Pariser gave me permission to use work time to do that.

Pariser was more than a wonderful ally in our struggle. He was my dear friend. When he learned that my wife Francia was also Jewish, he was very happy, and he treated me like a *landsman*.[11] After I stopped working at the Adams plant in 1964, we continued our friendship. He was always beside me, in good times and bad. I remember that when I went on a hunger strike in 1969, he visited me at the Human Rights Commission offices in the city. When he came in, I was so weak that I couldn't see, but I did recognize my good friend's voice. I was very sad when I learned of his death.

20.
THE ORIGINS OF THE
CONGRESO DE PUEBLOS

My experience as an immigrant was very similar to that of thousands of Puerto Rican workers who preceded me and came after me. Family ties and ties within the neighborhood were fundamental in the process of making a home for oneself, adapting to the new country, and developing community. In my case, my sister migrated to New York City first, and once she was established there, she sent for my brother, who later sent for me. It was my sister who found me my first job in the city, in the same place she worked. When I arrived in the city, I lived with my brother, and when I decided to move out on my own, the person who rented me a room was a woman from my hometown of Lares, whose daughter I wound up marrying. Through another fellow from my hometown, I started out in the hotel industry, and while I was working as an organizer in that industry—this was between 1947 and 1954—I began to develop the idea and structure of what would later be called the Congreso de Pueblos, the "Congress of [Puerto Rican] Towns."

These clubs, associated with the towns in Puerto Rico that people came from, were one of the institutions that Puerto Ricans developed to help them adapt to the realities of New York City. When I arrived, there were several social, civic, and cultural clubs in our communities, as well as some created by other Spanish-speaking groups such as the Spaniards. There were not, however, many clubs centered on home towns *per se*. I remember that in 1940, there was an organization in the Bronx known as the Caborrojeños Ausentes, the "Absent Cabo Rojans"; it had been incorporated in 1937. They had a space where Puerto Ricans from that town would get together and hold social and cultural activities that were open to anyone interested.

During the forties, the Puerto Rican community, especially in El Barrio, grew by leaps and bounds. As part of the natural process of settling down, people from the various towns on the island would gather in the same small area. In 1949, if somebody wanted to find a person from Lares in El Barrio, all they had to do was go to the bar between 137th St. and Broadway and there they would either find the person or find someone with information to help find him. In Brooklyn, the people who had migrated from Lares congregated mainly on Vernon Street. You could go to the *bodega* on the corner and the owner would tell you where Rafael A. Cuevas lived, or where you could find him. If the person you were looking for was Luis Ríos or Ramón "Cupído" Iglesias, you could find them around 103rd St. and Broadway, where the people from Barceloneta tended to live. And that's the way it was with all the towns. In Manhattan, people from Arecibo lived around 125th St. and Amsterdam Avenue; people from Vieques around 116th Street; and most of the people from Culebra settled in Brooklyn.

While I was working as an organizer and business agent for Local 6, I noted a similar pattern with the Puerto Rican workers. People from the same town and people from within the same family tended to work in the same hotels, which made my organizing job much easier. That was when the idea began to take shape of creating a structure that would defend the interests of our community by using a "town club" model combined with the American Labor Party's system of providing services.

I got the idea of promoting town clubs and incorporating them with the state so they would have legal standing and could buy or rent spaces for their meetings and activities. Once we had enough clubs, we would create an umbrella organization. Among the hotel workers that gradually joined the project were Ramón Sepúlveda, Jorge Rodríguez, and Grace Quiñones, from San Germán; brothers Manuel and Ramón "Cupído" Iglesias and Luis Ríos, from Barceloneta; Dámaso Emeric, from Vieques; Max Sanoguet and Carlos Cuprill, from Mayagüez; Raúl Reyes, from Isabela; and Rafael Cuevas, Oscar Colón, and Paco Lamourt, from Lares.

As early as 1949 I began to meet with small groups of kitchen workers in the hotels. In each of the twenty-eight hotels I was responsible for, I created an ad hoc committee. For example, there were various people from Arecibo at the New Yorker Hotel who showed interest in the idea. They called So-and-So, who had four cousins, and also This-Other-One and his wife and some other people from Arecibo. I looked for a place for a first meeting. We met. I explained the advantages of having a club and once they decided to create it, I helped them prepare the bylaws and, as much as I could, find a place to meet.

The Arecibo group bought a storefront on 125th St. and Park Avenue. The San Germán group started looking for a place in the Bronx. Meanwhile, in El Barrio we formed the "Hijos de Barceloneta," the Sons and Daughters of Barceloneta, of which I was a member of the board for many years. On this occasion I convinced a Puerto Rican woman named Amanda Limberg (she always used the surname of her husband, an American who was an FBI agent) to sell us a place she owned that was perfect for a club headquarters. The Barceloneta group pooled their money and bought the place. It was in excellent condition and had a spectacular kitchen. Puerto Ricans from many other towns and cities would go to the Barceloneta club, especially our friends who worked in hotels, including people from Lares, Vieques, Culebra, and San Juan. People loved the space. We would always take the opportunity to explain to those visitors the advantages of setting up their own clubs, and we offered our support.

In El Barrio we also established the Lares Civic and Cultural Association. One of the first matters we dealt with was finding a place for meetings and activities. I spoke with Mario González Levy, who was from Lares. Mario, whose father was Puerto Rican and whose mother was Jewish, was quite well-to-do. He owned a jewelry store and a men's clothing store on Lenox Avenue, and also had an unoccupied building that had once been a clothing factory on 116th St. in El Barrio. I explained to him that we were looking for a place for the people from Lares in New York City to meet and asked if he would let us use his vacant building for a while. In exchange, we would give publicity to his clothing store in the community and would pay all the costs of getting the place in shape. Mario accepted my proposal and told me we could use the building free of charge for a month or two.

With that agreement, I called my Lares friends together to help spruce up the place. We cleaned and polished the floor; one of us who was a plumber installed new plumbing and a carpenter built a wonderful circular bar; I got a permit to sell beer and wine. And then we called our first meeting, which was attended by over fifty people from Lares. We would meet there to plan activities and basically have get-togethers. On weekends we would open the meeting room and there would be dominoes, cards, and general socializing; on Saturday night we would sometimes bring in a musical group. Some of the women would cook for the members, and sometimes the men who worked in hotels would take over the kitchen. When we had dances, we would open the bar and sell beer and wine. If some member wanted to drink rum, we would let him bring his own bottle, put his name on it, and only he and his table would be able to drink it. That way, we got around the police, who would send in agents dressed as beggars to see if we were selling other alcoholic drinks, trying to find a way to close us down. Three months later, Mario asked us to start paying rent, but he finally agreed to let us go on using the place free when we showed him a picture of himself on the wall in recognition of the support he was giving the club.

We continued to create clubs throughout New York City. The Mayagüez group set up its club on the second floor of a corner building at 106th St. and Broadway. For the Vieques group we found a place to rent in the same building that the Lares group had our club. Then came a whole second litter: clubs for Ceiba, Culebra, Arecibo, Yauco, Aguas Buenas, and Barranquitas. The Hijos de Ceiba found a floor in the same building the Lares and Vieques clubs were located in. These were the first clubs to join the Congreso de Pueblos.

In 1954, we started organizing the Congreso de Pueblos. We began with a dozen clubs. Two years later, we incorporated ourselves. For many years we took turns holding meetings for the umbrella organization in the local clubs. Later, we rented a place at 254 W. 72nd St. We paid $100 a month rent to a Jewish gentleman who helped us out. We shared the expenses: one club would pay the rent one month, another the telephone, and another the electric bill. We fixed the place up really nice. Each one of us brought our own chair, and in that little office each of us did our job. We worked that way for about ten years, until 1967, when with funds from the Puerto Rican Community Development Project we were able to pay our office expenses and secretarial staff.

While this was going on, other town clubs were being created spontaneously in several other Puerto Rican communities. In some cases, more than one club for the same town was created. Often, family ties, or the reverse (long-standing fights between families that had started back in Puerto Rico), explained the duplication. In other cases, it was class differences. For example, three San Juan clubs were created. One was for *blanquitos* (the lighter-skinned and more upper-class San Juaneros), another for people "from the jungle" (which the first group looked down on as "dirty" or "ignorant" and because they came from San Juan's housing projects and slums). The Congreso tried to get the duplicate clubs to consolidate, but that was not always possible.

By 1956, there were clubs in New York City representing every one of the seventy-eight towns in Puerto Rico, most of them the result of work that we had done. That year we officially convened the constituent assembly for the Congreso de Pueblos. We held it in one of the meeting rooms in the Manhattan Center.[12] Representatives from fifty clubs attended. At the meeting, I was elected president, and we named a committee whose job would be to choose a board of directors. The next year, 1957, we held our second assembly. On that occasion, the meeting was held in the main ballroom of the Manhattan

Center. Our work had borne fruit: twelve hundred delegates attended. I was reelected president and a permanent board of directors was named. Among the members, I recall Manuel Martínez, from Ciales; María López, from Aguas Buenas; and Pedro Maldonado, Max Saguonet, and Carlos Cuprill, from Mayagüez. With the founding of the Congreso, a new stage began in Puerto Ricans' struggle in New York City for their civil rights.

21.
HOW THE CONGRESO DE PUEBLOS FUNCTIONED

In 1956, when the Congreso de Pueblos was officially created, one of the organization's explicit aims was to be an advocate for, and to defend, Puerto Ricans' interests and their civil and human rights in New York City. The only clubs that could be members of our organization were those of the towns and cities of Puerto Rico. In organizational terms, the Congreso helped find spaces for people to meet in, provided legal and organizational consulting services, and helped with everything related to the incorporation process. In that respect, we depended greatly on attorney Felipe Torres, who prepared the incorporation papers.

The Congreso was a success, and in the fifties through the seventies it played a very important role in the community, since it met some of the fundamental needs of the rapidly increasing number of immigrants who found themselves in a strange and sometimes hostile environment. Its presence spread through the city's four boroughs, wherever there was a Puerto Rican community—that is, especially in Manhattan, the Bronx, and Brooklyn, and to a lesser degree in Queens. Through our network of services, Puerto Ricans newly arrived from the island found fast help in resolving their pressing problems. If some family member lost his or her job, all they had to do was come to us and we would go to our job bank to help the person find work. If someone lost their apartment, our attorneys and the Housing Committee were there to help.

To belong to the Congreso the town clubs had to meet some basic requirements: they had to have a set of bylaws, they had to hold monthly meetings that followed parliamentary procedure, and they had to hold an annual meeting in which their boards of directors were elected. Although we did not set a specific membership fee for the town clubs, the usual amount we asked for was three dollars a month. The clubs, for their part, helped defray the Congreso's operating expenses by contributing whatever they could. In some cases, the clubs were small and their members had very little money; in that case they didn't pay a club membership fee, and that was not a reason to decertify them. What we were interested in was organizing the community and making the Congreso a vehicle for empowerment.

All the clubs had the right to send five delegates to the Congreso's annual meeting. These delegates became members of the board of directors. They had to be certified by the president of the club and recognized by the executive committee in order to vote in our assembly. The Board of Directors was charged with establishing the organization's goals and objectives for the next year. They were also responsible for electing the executive committee, which was charged with carrying out all those tasks necessary for achieving the Congreso's goals and objectives, coordinating activities, and running the organization.

As a mechanism for strengthening the clubs, we created what we called "family caucuses." These caucuses were made up of three or four families who were responsible for identifying people in New York City from their hometowns and integrating them into the club. We also created several standing committees. One of the most important was the one that picked up Puerto Ricans arriving from the island at Idlewild Airport, now in JFK Airport, in Queens.

For financial reasons, most Puerto Ricans flew in on what we all called the *vuelos quiquiriquí*—the cockadoodle-doo flights. Today they're called the "red-eye" flights because they arrive at about dawn and people stagger off them without any sleep, their eyes bloodshot. Back then, these were small propeller planes flown by Trans-Caribbean Airways, an airline established in 1945 by entrepreneur O. Roy Chalk.[13] The flights cost $45 each way; they left Puerto Rico at 11 pm and arrived in New York, as I said, at about dawn. When the plane landed, passengers had to walk across the apron to the small terminal where our committee would be waiting to welcome them. In the winter, the committee took blankets and clothes appropriate for New York's cold winter.

In some cases, there would be family members inside the terminal waiting for the travelers, and they would take them home with them. Other travelers would already know about the Congreso and the services we provided our compatriots, and they would let us know when they were arriving. Many times, the Congreso would act as an intermediary between the individual town club and a traveler. In the terminal, our committee members would call out the name of the town the passengers were coming from and the individual club's delegate would claim them. Since the Congreso's assembly room was large, we would take them to 72nd St. There, doña Carmen Colón, who was always with us, had a nice hot *asopao de pollo* waiting, since no food was served on the flights. Later, during the day, we would call all the individual clubs to tell them their fellow townspeople had arrived.

Following the model of the American Labor Party, the Congreso maintained a job bank. With a group of volunteers that gave us a hand, doña Carmen would identify available jobs in both private industry and public service. We developed a good relationship with the social workers in the New York City Housing Department, which back then was called the Public Welfare Department. When we referred some family to them, they would usually provide them with emergency funds to buy food with, and they would help us find an apartment for them. The department also provided emergency help for buying bedroom and dining room furniture and kitchen equipment, and for winter clothes.

As the Congreso grew and its activities expanded, more and more volunteers would come to us, including teachers and directors of community programs interested in helping out with our projects. As part of our community services, in 1965 and 1966 we created a summer program for underprivileged children in the Puerto Rican community. An Irishman who owned a summer camp, Camp Felicia, in upstate New York let us use the facilities free for these children. On one occasion, in 1966, he also loaned us the camp for a summer workshop to train women as activists so that they could play a role in Puerto Ricans' civil rights struggles. We also promoted Puerto Rican consciousness-raising and the formation of leaders among the growing number of young professionals in the community. For example, we founded the Wednesday Group to train leaders. I will speak more about the Ladies Committee and the Wednesday Group later.

In those critical years of the fifties and sixties, the Congreso de Pueblos was the militant arm of the Puerto Rican community in New York City. Due mainly to our efforts, the English-language literacy exam required to vote in New York state elections was eliminated; we took our struggle against police brutality to the streets and our actions spurred important changes in the police department, including opening doors for Puerto Rican police officers; and we promoted and defended the rights of our artists, musicians, and other entertainers. It was also as a result of the Congreso's work that many Puerto Ricans seeking electoral office, such as Herman Badillo, were elected, and that others, such as John Carro, were appointed to important posts in city government.

The Congreso de Pueblos was the driving force behind the creation of several organizations which at a crucial moment played an important role in empowering our community, such as the New York Puerto Rican Day Parade; the National Association of Puerto Rican Civil Rights, precursor of the National Congress for Puerto Rican Rights; and the Puerto Rican Folklore Festival of New York.

The Congreso's activities expanded beyond the city limits and even the state of New York. As our work became better known, we were invited to help Puerto Rican communities in New Jersey, Connecticut, Pennsylvania, and Illinois plan their organizational structures and establish priorities for activities.

There came a time when, due to its activism, the Congreso de Pueblos began to be a political problem, as Vito Marcantonio was for the government of Puerto Rico earlier when the government wanted to be the sole representative of Puerto Ricans in New York City. In 1958, I received a telephone call from Puerto Rico telling me that the Popular Democratic Party (PDP) had decided to organize a counterpart to the Congreso de Pueblos. It was to be called Fuerza Unida Puertorriqueña (FUP; the United Puerto Rican Force). The person charged by Gov. Muñoz Marín with putting this organization together was Josefina "Fini" Rincón, the sister of Felisa Rincón de Gautier, mayor of San Juan. Like Felisa, Fini was a PDP activist. She had been secretary of the San Juan city government. Her presence in New York politics was not new; she had taken part alongside other PDP leaders, such as Jaime Benítez, in the Mayor's Committee for Puerto Rican Affairs, the group created by the government of New York in conspiracy with the PDP in hopes of weakening Marcantonio's influence in the Puerto Rican community and unseating him from Congress.

Fini Rincón had a wonderful apartment on the ground floor of a building on Central Park West. It was paid for by the government of Puerto Rico. She used it for, among other things, political lobbying. She would call Puerto Rican organizations to meetings of that political fiction called Fuerza Unida Puertorriqueña. But we organized and made sure that Fini's organization got nowhere. Soon, it went the way it came. . . . Apparently Mayor Wagner and the PDP finally realized that that particular organization had no future in New York politics and that the community at that point was behind the Congreso de Pueblos.

There were other attempts to destroy the Congreso. Some malcontents created a group called the Confederation of Puerto Rican Organizations, whose headquarters was in Brooklyn. This group was dead on arrival, however, since its organizers made the mistake of inviting people to join who were committed to our organization, and they soon gave it the coup de grace. In the early sixties, also in the Bronx, a group emerged called the Organizaciones Unidas del Bronx (the United Bronx Organizations, or OUB); it was led by Monserrate Flores with the support of Ramón Vélez. Vélez utilized this group in his attempt to create an empire in the Bronx and weaken my influence in the Puerto Rican community. Although several organizations that were members of the Congreso de Pueblos joined the OUB, many maintained their affiliation with us. The OUB leadership was weak and indecisive. Aside from a blood drive at Lincoln Hospital, I can't recall the group organizing any major activities in the community on its own. It was not proactive in the community's struggle for empowerment.

As time went on, the first generation of Puerto Ricans born and raised in New York City emerged and a large number of professionals arrived from the island. These events, along with other factors, caused the town clubs to gradually become less important in the community's life. Although still today some of those clubs remain, they are not a shadow of what they were in the fifties, sixties, and seventies. Puerto Ricans have continued to create and join other types of organizations, but none has been as important or as militant in defense of the interests of our community as the Congreso de Pueblos.

22.
IT WASN'T ALL WORK. . .

A great deal of volunteer work was done in the Congreso de Pueblos, but we also had a good time.

In addition to promoting social and cultural activities in the various clubs that made up the organization, we took part in large-scale cultural projects such as the Puerto Rican Day Parade and the Folklore Festival, but we also had our own social and cultural programs. One of the most popular was the outings that we organized so people could get outside the city once in a while. These outings were generally on Sunday. We would rent five or six buses and head out of the city. The price was very reasonable: $7.50 per person. Among the passengers in every bus there was usually a group with musical instruments. We would leave early from 72nd Street, and by 8:30 am we would have arrived at our destination. We would usually go up into the Catskill Mountains, where there were some very nice lodges that we would rent by the day. Almost all of them had pools. As time went on, one of these lodges came into the hands of Puerto Ricans, who changed its name to the Puerto Rican Alps. Our fee for the outings also included lunch and a dance. The women of the Congreso were in charge of the cooking, and there was always a lechón on a spit. We would often have some of the very best Puerto Rican musical groups; the Johnny Albino Trio was one of our favorites. Another was the Pájaros Locos, from Long Island. People would bring their children, and they, too, would have a ball.

Always after the Congreso's annual meetings we would have a party. Sometimes we would go to the Broadway Casino, where there was usually a good orchestra playing. The owner of this place, Alfredo Gil, was an excellent host. We always filled the place up. Sometimes we would wind up at the Club Caborrojeño, which was originally on 145th St. and Broadway, but after it burned reopened on 96th St. and Broadway. Its owner, Roberto Ruperto, was also an excellent host, and when we would go there he would bend over backwards for us. Another place we often went to was the Barceloneta club headquarters; Luis Ríos was president. Located at 103rd St. and Broadway, this club was open every weekend and always had terrific music. It also had a wonderful kitchen, under the expert hand of Ramón "Cupído" Iglesias, a banquet waiter in union Local 6 but famous for being an excellent chef. Since many of our comrades were hotel workers, almost all of the male leadership in the Congreso knew how to cook.

Wednesday nights we would go to the Palladium. That was the day the bands rehearsed. After the rehearsal there was always a little dance. Our group was made up mainly of doña Carmen Colón, the secretary of the Congreso; the Maisonave Ríoses, husband and wife from Ponce; Paquito Lamourt, from Lares; and my wife Francia and I. Sometimes we would be joined by Paquita Berio, from Santurce; Max Sanoguet, from Mayagüez; and Vitín Suárez, from Ponce. When Machito y los Afrocubanos played at the Park Palace, or the Alfaraona X group from Puerto Rico, we'd put on our dancing shoes and be there in a flash. After the dancing was over, we'd go to 110th St. and Lexington to eat at a little place that was open until 3 am. There was always a crowd there, so we'd have to stand in line. But we loved it, and we always had a good time.

23.
THE CAMPAIGN AGAINST THE LITERACY TEST IN ENGLISH

In 1921, as a way to control the political participation of the growing number of immigrants from Southern and Eastern Europe, the state of New York passed legislation requiring all voters to be able to read and write English. As a mechanism to demonstrate English proficiency, a literacy test was created.

Despite the fact that Puerto Ricans were American citizens, and had been since 1917, when the Congress of the United States imposed U.S. citizenship on the residents of Puerto Rico, the state of New York required us to take the exam. It served as a barrier to the full incorporation of Puerto Ricans into the political process. In addition to being in English, a language that the vast majority of Puerto Rican immigrants did not know, the test asked questions that very few of us would be able to answer, such as "Who gave the Statue of Liberty to the United States?" The test, therefore, limited our numbers at the voting booth, and that, in turn, benefited white politicians, who were always elected.

This crass violation of our civil rights was like demanding that the Statue of Liberty throw the torch in her hand into New York Harbor. Now that I think of it, that monument was not erected thinking of us. It's located next to Ellis Island, the control point for migrants coming from the rest of the world. But the boats that arrived from Puerto Rico moored at the docks in Brooklyn, far from New York Harbor.

As part of Marcantonio's political strategy, the American Labor Party ran campaigns to register Puerto Ricans to vote. Marc was one of the first to denounce the electoral discrimination that we were subjected to. With the disappearance of the American Labor Party as a political force in El Barrio, the problem of our political exclusion became vital for the Congreso de Pueblos. In December of 1955, we created the Hispanic Voters Association. I convinced Dr. Sergio Peña, my personal doctor and a man very much loved within the community, to accept the responsibility of presiding over that organization. I was elected secretary-general. The new organization's purpose was to promote the political participation of Spanish-speaking residents, especially Puerto Ricans, in New York City and New York State. We also agreed to support the candidacy of anyone, regardless of political affiliation, who was committed to aiding our community, and to participate in any campaign that defended the interests of Puerto Ricans, inside or outside New York City and New York State—for example, in Freehold, New Jersey, about which I'll speak a little later.

It was the Hispanic Voters Association that launched an intense campaign to fight the English literacy test. The Congreso de Pueblos was once again the driving force behind that campaign, providing a cadre of men and women as volunteers. The campaign was coordinated from Dr. Peña's office at 856 Prospect Avenue in the Bronx, and it covered the city's major boroughs—Manhattan, the Bronx, Brooklyn, and Queens—where most of the Puerto Rican town clubs were located. Over the next few years, the Congreso de Pueblos religiously mounted picket lines and held other protest and educational activities during the municipal primaries and elections. Our activities were not limited to polling places; we picketed in front of the Elections Board and City Hall and we supported the election of candidates committed to eliminating the literacy test, such as José Ramos López in 1958, who ran for the state legislature.

In the early sixties, and during the most crucial years of the civil rights struggle, we also created an organization called the National Association of Puerto Rican Civil Rights. From there we continued our campaign against the English literacy test. In 1965, Irma Vidal Santaella, Herman Badillo, and I, as the Association's official representative, attended the civil rights hearings in Washington and set forth our position on the plight of Puerto Ricans in the United States.

In our visit to Congress, we were accompanied by a delegation of leaders of the Puerto Rican community, many of whom were members of the Association or the Congreso de Pueblos, or both. Apparently, at seeing so many Puerto Ricans together, the police remembered the Nationalist assault on Congress in 1954 and got nervous, since they turned the dogs loose on us when we were about to go up the steps at the Capitol building to attend a meeting with an aide to one of the congressmen who were considering supporting our demands.

Despite this setback, that same year, 1965, the Congress passed Section 4 of the Voting Rights Act. Commonly known as the Puerto Rican Amendment, this clause stated that in order to safeguard the rights of individuals educated in U.S. schools in which the predominant language was not English, the states were prohibited from conditioning the right to vote on the person's ability to read, write, understand, and interpret a text in English. It also limited the states' power to deny the right to vote to persons who had not finished the sixth grade.

As might have been expected, the white establishment opposed passage of Section 4. That same year, several Puerto Ricans in New York City were prevented from voting. The Elections Commission argued that it was not a federal matter. We took the case to federal court and in 1966 the Supreme Court declared the New York law requiring a literacy test in English unconstitutional. Four years later, the U.S. Congress amended the Voting Rights Act to eliminate all literacy and educational requirements for voting in state elections.

Following our example, organizations in other states ran campaigns to fight the literacy test. In this area, as in others such as bilingual education, we Puerto Ricans were in the vanguard of the civil rights struggle in the United States.

24.
FREEHOLD, NEW JERSEY

From the moment we conceived the Congreso de Pueblos, our idea was to work with the Puerto Rican community in New York City, where the vast majority of our compatriots lived. The rapid growth of Puerto Rican communities in other states on the East Coast, however, led us naturally to want to help solve our people's problems in other parts of the country. Our first incursion was into the neighboring state of New Jersey.

In early January 1956, I received a communication from a Puerto Rican who worked on a farm in Freehold, New Jersey. He told me that the Italian owner of the farm had shown him an editorial in the local newspaper, *The Freeholder*, reporting comments made by Superior Court Judge Frank T. Lloyd in reaction to a grand jury report on the unhygienic conditions and substandard housing in that city's slums. In his remarks, Lloyd stated that Puerto Ricans were responsible for these conditions and that we were accustomed to living in filthy, disgusting conditions. Outraged at these remarks, I called several members of the Congreso de Pueblos' board to see what we could do. We created an ad hoc committee made up of our Brooklyn comrades Ramón González, president of the Puerto Rican Businessmen's Association, Clemente Soto Vélez, public relations secretary of that organization and of the Association of Spanish Businessmen, and Antonia Denis, the well-known community leader; Roberto Torres and Raúl Ortiz, from the Bronx; and Chuíto Caballero and I, representing Manhattan. There was no representation from Queens, since at that time the Puerto Rican population of that borough was very small and there were no town clubs there that belonged to the Congreso. We also asked Francisco "Paco" Archilla to join us; Paco was a veteran New York City community leader, a comrade in the American Labor Party who had moved to New Jersey. As an experienced community organizer, Paco brought vast experience to the cause. When he moved to New Jersey, he immediately became active in efforts to organize the Puerto Rican community in Monmouth and Ocean counties. When the Lloyd affair exploded, he came to the Congreso de Pueblos for aid.

Our committee decided to create a campaign to demand that the judge be removed from office. As part of our strategy, we went to the Spanish-language press in the city and persuaded *El Diario de Nueva York* to join our campaign and to publish an editorial demanding an apology from the judge and also asking the governor of New Jersey, Robert B. Meyner, to remove him from office. This matter was definitely of interest within the community, and the newspaper became a staunch defender of our cause. We lit the fuse, and now the sparks were flying. We mobilized all the community, political, cultural, union, and professional organizations that any of us belonged to or with which we had good relations. The Society of Hispanic Voters, of which I was secretary-general and founding member, organized a campaign of letters and telegrams to Gov. Robert Meyner, State Attorney General Grover Richman, and Judge Arthur T. Vanderbilt, chief justice of the New Jersey Supreme Court, demanding an investigation.

Soto Vélez and González brought the two organizations that represented the businessmen and women of the city's Spanish-speaking community into the struggle. Paco Archilla concentrated his efforts on organizing a campaign in the Puerto Rican communities in New Jersey. Other Puerto Rican and Hispanic organizations, including the Puerto Rico Institute, the General Puerto Rican Confederation of New York, and the Puerto Rican Independence Party, New York chapter, joined our campaign, as well. Due in large part to my relationship with the labor movement, I persuaded several unions to express their support for our demands. Our committee also visited the two radio and TV broadcasters that offered Spanish-language programming in the city and asked them to publicize the matter.

The pressure began to have an effect. On January 11, Gov. Meyner sent an official letter to the Hispanic Voters Society informing us that he had begun an investigation of the case. Knowing politicians, we realized that if we didn't continue our pressure the whole thing would just get swept under the rug, so we decided to mobilize a large demonstration. We called it for January 15 at the Park Palace; it would be on behalf of migrant workers in the Puerto Rican community in the state of New Jersey. We would demand a meeting with Meyner, who had initially refused to meet with us.

Located on 110th St. near Fifth Avenue, the Park Palace was one of the major clubs for dancing and other social activities for the Hispanic community in New York City. There was space in the ballroom for about 800 people. More than 2000 people showed up for our meeting, and many had to stand outside in the cold. We improvised a loudspeaker system to inform the crowd outside what was being discussed on the floor. The meeting adopted a proposal that we had prepared: we would travel in a caravan of cars from New York City to

Freehold for a demonstration; the protests would take place the next Sunday, January 22. Among the people attending we passed out flyers with a map of the route, and we invited everyone to join us.

Meanwhile, we were continuing our pressure on Gov. Meyner, who finally agreed to meet with us. A group of us, including representatives from Puerto Rican organizations in New Jersey, met with the governor. Taking advantage of the fact that we were in a pre-election year, we gave him an ultimatum. If he wanted the Hispanic vote—it was no longer just Puerto Ricans, but also Mexicans, Spaniards, and the few Cubans who were living in New Jersey at that time—he had to get rid of the judge in Freehold who had insulted the Puerto Ricans. The governor gave in to our demands, and on January 17 he acted: he made a public announcement that he had removed Judge Lloyd for improper judicial conduct.

We decided, however, to continue with our demonstration on the 22nd. It would celebrate our victory. On Sunday, our caravan set out for Freehold. The section of Interstate 95 from New York to New Jersey was lined with state and city police officers. By that time, I had spoken with the Teamsters Union, who represented truckers, to explain what we were going to do and ask for their cooperation. The Teamsters were in complete support of our demands, and their members waited patiently while our caravan of over three hundred cars held up thousands of trucks and other vehicles traveling along that highway. When we came to the Freehold exit, more than 500 Puerto Ricans and their allies stopped us. Many of us lay down in the snow to symbolize our determination to fight to the end. That night, we met once again in the Park Palace, this time to celebrate this first victory and, even more important, to pledge to continue to promote the unity of the Puerto Rican community and Hispanic community in general, in both New York and throughout the Northeast, where most of our Puerto Rican brothers and sisters living in the United States had settled.

In order to show Judge Lloyd his error, our committee invited him to come to Puerto Rico to see how we live. He accepted our invitation and made the trip with his wife. They returned to New Jersey in love with the island. For its part, *The Freeholder* offered to publish a retraction.

25.
THE ORIGINS OF THE PUERTO RICAN DAY PARADE

When they arrived in the United States, many European immigrants created their own cultural organizations. Several of these groups, including the Italians, also founded parades to commemorate their national heritage. Spaniards held theirs on October 12, the Día de la Raza. Until the early fifties, Latin Americans took part in those activities, but with the rapid growth of the Puerto Rican community in the city, at the first annual meeting of the Congreso de Pueblos in 1954 the idea of holding a Puerto Rican parade was presented.

That same year, as president of the Congreso de Pueblos, I appointed a committee to meet with officers from the various ethnic parade-organizing committees so we could learn more about parade logistics and organization. The committee was made up of Luis Ríos, of Barceloneta; Johnny Meléndez, of Fajardo; Juan Benítez, of San Juan; and Manolo Román, of Arecibo. The committee met with the organizers of the Italian, Greek, Irish, and Jewish parades. One of the people who helped us in our efforts was Fortune Pope, owner of radio station WHOM, whose Spanish-language programming was very popular in the Puerto Rican community.

Since at this time we were encouraging the entire Hispanic community of the city to come together in a united front, we invited leaders from other Hispanic groups to join us, and we proposed the creation of a Puerto Rican parade promoting exactly that: Latino unity. The first meeting to discuss the idea of one big parade incorporating all the Latino and Hispanic population in the city was held in the home of Gregorio Domenech at 121st St. and Park Avenue in Manhattan. In addition to Gregorio, two other members of the Congreso de Pueblos were present: Dora Orta, from Arecibo, and I. Also attending were Juan Mas, a leader of the Cuban community who worked in the hotel industry; Manuel Mora, a Spaniard who owned a hardware store in Harlem; and the Basque nationalist Jesús de Galíndez, who taught international law and was completing his doctorate in history at Columbia University.

Although we were all in agreement about the importance of creating a parade, differences of opinion very quickly arose with respect to its name and composition. Mora and Galíndez argued that it should be held in October, on specifically the 12th, the Día de la Raza. Mas suggested that it be called the Hispanic Parade, and the Spaniards were in agreement with that. We Puerto Ricans were opposed, arguing that the name should reflect the fact that the Puerto Rican community was the largest and would also have the greatest possible participation in the activity. The meeting ended in a stalemate over the name for the parade. We did, however, agree to meet again two weeks later. Meanwhile, we asked Galíndez, who was a columnist for *El Diario de Nueva York*, to write an editorial in support of the idea and urging all Hispanics in the city to join our enterprise. We also agreed that the Congreso de Pueblos would be in charge of mobilizing people for the event.

The next week, Galíndez had his editorial ready. As we had agreed, he gave it to me beforehand to look over. After discussing it with Domenech and Dora Orta, I reorganized it a little. The next day, as I had agreed with Galíndez, I went to his apartment on Fifth Avenue in Greenwich Village to take him the revised document. When I spoke to the doorman, he told me that Galíndez wasn't at home, but that he was probably up at Columbia University. So I went uptown, but I was told that Galíndez had called in sick. Given this situation, I went back to his apartment. Since Galíndez had not come in yet, I gave the envelope with the document to the doorman, who promised to give it to Galíndez personally.

But Galíndez never returned to his apartment. His disappearance was reported to the police, but no one could find him. A short time later, there began to be rumors that he had been kidnapped by agents of Dominican dictator Rafael Leonidas Trujillo and flown to the Dominican Republic, where he had been assassinated. The rumors turned out to be true. Galíndez had lived in Santo Domingo for several years before moving to New York City. In New York, he had become an outspoken critic of Trujillo. Two weeks before his disappearance, he had completed his PhD dissertation, which was titled "The Trujillo Era: A Casuistic Study of Dictatorship." Years later, we learned that he had been tortured and thrown to the sharks. (He was granted his doctorate posthumously.)

Galíndez' disappearance was cause for great sadness among us, and a blow to the Hispanic community. We lost an excellent public-relations man and a force for consensus. But his loss did not stop our project. *El Diario de Nueva York* published his editorial, which was brief, to the point, and convincing. It was very well received in the Spanish-speaking community. Many people joined our cause, and that, in turn, forced us to find other places to meet, since Domenech's house was too small for the growing number of people interested in the project.

With Galíndez' disappearance, the unity among the Hispanic groups began to weaken, and the debate over the nature and name of the parade intensified. One group, which I was in, wanted to call it the Puerto Rican Day Parade of Hispanic Unity, while another, led by Víctor López and Chuíto Caballero, and with the support of well-known Puerto Rican columnist Luisa Quintero, argued for the Puerto Rican Day Parade, period. To try to achieve the unity of the Puerto Rican community that we all wanted, we met in the Alamarc Hotel to try to reach an agreement. Attorney Oscar González Suárez represented the López-Caballero group, while lawyer Felipe Torres represented our group, the Congreso de Pueblos. After two days of discussions, we finally reached an agreement: the parade would be called the Puerto Rican Day Parade. In April 1957, the Committee for the Puerto Rican Day Parade, Inc. was registered in Albany with the aid of the two attorneys.

The Parade was sponsored by the Congreso de Pueblos. Archilla and I were in charge of coordinating it. We coordinated that first parade with absolutely no idea of how to do such a thing. When we went to request a permit to march along the traditional route used by the Irish, Italian, Greek, and Jewish community—starting at 43rd St. and running to 86th St. along Fifth Avenue, and ending at Third Avenue—we met another obstacle. The administration of Mayor Robert F. Wagner, Jr., refused our request. After a great deal of lobbying on our part, they gave us a permit to march through El Barrio along Fifth Avenue from 116th St. to 96th St. Then it turned out that no one wanted to contribute money for the parade's expenses, which included the cost of materials and labor for the dais, banners, ribbons for the grand marshal, and then money to pay assistants. All the money eventually came out of the organizers' pockets.

Finally, on April 15, 1958, the first Puerto Rican Day Parade was held. We dedicated it to Jesús Galíndez in recognition of his part in organizing the activity. Tony Méndez, who was our political leader in El Barrio, was the Grand Marshal. Over 15,000 Spanish-speaking people marched in the parade, the vast majority of them Puerto Ricans. There were very few floats, but lots and lots of automobiles belonging to the poor people in El Barrio, full of family members and friends and decorated with crepe paper.

That day we faced a series of problems. It started pouring rain on Saturday and didn't stop until Monday. Since the banners hung across the streets were made with water-based paint, the paint ran, and when we arrived at 96th St. we found that the main banner was just a long piece of white cloth running from one side of Fifth Avenue to the other. Then, everybody wanted to be on the dais.

Built by Paco Archilla out of recycled wood donated by Mora, since we didn't have any money to buy new wood, the platform collapsed. Then Tony Méndez arrived late and had to run like crazy for three blocks to get to the head of the parade, which he finally did at 113th St. He was totally out of breath. But despite the rain and all the other problems, the people would not be prevented from having their day. They marched in the rain as happy as larks. Somebody said it was the baptism that God gave the parade as a sign of his blessing.

In 1959 we held the second parade. This time, the board of directors, which was controlled by the Congreso de Pueblos, decided that Víctor López would lead the parade and Chuíto Caballero would be the treasurer. Manuel Martínez was the coordinator.

That year, 1959, was the year for the Democratic primaries. Unfortunately, the divisions within the party were clear for all to see. Mayor Wagner needed the vote of the Puerto Rican community if he was going to win. He asked for my support, and I told him that in principle I had no problem supporting him, but he had to give us a permit for the parade to take the official parade route, that is, up Fifth Avenue from 43rd St. to 86th St. and Third Avenue. We also asked him to attend a press conference called by the Congreso de Pueblos to announce that we'd been given the permit. Wagner accepted, and from that year on, the Puerto Rican Day Parade has taken the same route as the ones for the Irish, Italians, Greeks, and Jews.

Not everyone was pleased that we Puerto Ricans were going to march along Fifth Avenue. The day before the 1959 parade, I received an urgent phone call telling me that I needed to get over to Fifth Avenue immediately to see what had been done to the shop windows. When I arrived, I found that practically all the store windows along the avenue, from 43rd St. to 80th, were covered with plywood panels, and that many had signs reading "Puerto Ricans, go home," with the Puerto Rican flag upside down. I called Paco Archilla and told him to find a pickup and a helper and, starting at midnight that day, to take down the panels. We took down every single business's plywood panels. The next day we marched without having to face that insult, which was intended to provoke the parade's participants and create a situation that would discredit the event. But that was not the only hiccup. To make our event look bad, laxative was given to the police horses, which were marching at the front, so they would dirty the streets we were going to march down. At the end of the parade, the Health Department came in with fire hoses to clean the streets, and they soaked the people along the route. We pulled Mayor Wagner aside and gave him an ultimatum: "If this situation is not taken care of, you will not have the Puerto Rican vote." Wagner knew we were serious, and he ordered those provocations to stop.

Meanwhile, López and Caballero's management proved ineffective. There was growing discontent among the members of the parade committee since they were not called to meetings or informed about the use of the money we had collected. In a meeting held in 1960, López and Caballero were forced to resign. With the backing of the Congreso de Pueblos, Manuel Martínez took over the parade management and I became coordinator. We democratized the processes and set all the finances straight. In 1963 I was elected president of the parade, and I coordinated until 1974. By that time, the Puerto Rican Day Parade was one of the main ethnic activities in New York City.

26.
FIDEL'S VISITS TO NEW YORK CITY

One of the great political events of the late twentieth century was the Cuban Revolution. With the coming of Comandante Fidel Castro to power in 1959, a new stage began in the history of Cuba, Latin America, and, indeed, the United States. The overthrow of dictator Fulgencio Batista by forces under Fidel was cause for concern in the U.S. government, since Fidel's radical program of socioeconomic and political reforms, including nationalization of the properties of large American corporations, especially sugarcane plantations, were a threat to U.S. interests in the hemisphere.

In 1959, four months after the triumph of the Revolution, Fidel was invited by the American Society of Newspaper Editors to visit the United States. A welcoming committee was created in New York City for this event. As president of the Congreso de Pueblos and coordinator of the Puerto Rican Day Parade, I was invited to take part in a meeting to organize the welcome and help coordinate security for Fidel. Among the group that was to participate in the welcoming activities were Cubans, Puerto Ricans, Spaniards, and Mexicans. Although I must recognize that our Cuban comrades were in charge of coordinating the activities, the fact was that the pro-Fidel Cuban community in the city was small, and most of those who took part in the welcoming activities were Puerto Ricans.

During the visit, President Dwight Eisenhower refused to meet with Fidel, sending Vice President Richard Nixon in his place. Nixon, as you remember, had become famous (or infamous) for his part in the witch-hunt led by the House Un-American Activities Committee during the fifties. Despite the U.S. government's negative attitude, Fidel's popularity in the Hispanic community and in progressive circles was at its height. The activity's organizers agreed that the welcome would take place in Central Park in Manhattan. From both the logistical and political point of view, I think that was the correct decision, since Central Park is near El Barrio, the principal concentration of Spanish-speakers in New York City.

The celebration in Central Park was to be in the open, which meant that the event had to be carefully and minutely organized, especially with respect to the Cuban revolutionary leader's security. Many Puerto Rican comrades worked hard on that aspect of the event. The activity was amazing. Tens of thousands of spectators, especially Puerto Ricans, came to the park to greet Fidel.

A year and a half later, in September 1960, Fidel returned to New York City to attend the annual meeting of the United Nations General Assembly. Once again I was invited to be part of the welcoming committee and, along with a group of members from the Congreso de Pueblos and the Puerto Rican Day Parade, of the security committee.

By that point, relations between Cuba and the United States were at the breaking point. Fidel had implemented his agrarian reform, which meant, in part, that land could not be owned by foreigners—read: American capitalists— and he had begun a rapprochement with the Soviet Union, which at that time was the other great world power. In response, the U.S. government had begun to take actions to remove Fidel from power.

From the moment the Cuban leader announced his visit, his enemies began a campaign to discredit him. The yellow press was especially active in that effort. Almost every hotel in New York City, responding to pressures from the U.S. security apparatus, refused to allow Fidel and his delegation to stay with them. Finally, arrangements were made for him to stay at the Hotel Shelburne, on 37th St. and Lexington Avenue near the Cuban Embassy and the United Nations Building. The Cuban delegation was going to be impressive. In addition to several dozen escorts, Fidel was bringing his own cooks and all the food he was going to eat during his stay in the hotel.

When I found out that he had decided to use the Shelburne, I let my Cuban comrades know of some concerns I had: The area the hotel was in was very vulnerable, since it was in the middle of a relatively racist community. The leader of the Cuban group in New York City was Juan Mas, a hotel worker, whom I had known for some time. When my concerns were acknowledged to be well founded, I communicated with the Black Muslims, led by Malcolm X, to ask for their logistical support with regard to the Comandante's security. They readily agreed. In the end, the Cuban delegation moved to the Hotel Theresa, located in the heart of Harlem, at 125th St. and Seventh Avenue. The Theresa was the largest and best hotel managed by blacks in New York City. The delegation took an entire floor, so they could be safe and comfortable.

Once Fidel and his entourage arrived, the entire area became a beehive of activity. The streets were closed to traffic, and only identified pedestrians were allowed in. The security set-up was huge. Our black comrades, specifically the Fruit of Islam, the self-defense group of the Nation of Islam, were in charge of security around the hotel and inside it. In our group we had a quasi-military organization of about fifty Puerto Rican men and women. On that occasion, I had the opportunity to speak with Fidel.

After his speech at the United Nations, at which he denounced the campaign run by the American imperialists against the Cuban Revolutionary government, Fidel returned to Cuba. A few months later, in October of that same year, the United States imposed the embargo on Cuba and followed that up in April of 1961 with the Bay of Pigs invasion, which was orchestrated and supported by the Central Intelligence Agency. That same year, Cuba officially became a socialist republic, as it still is today, despite all attempts by the United States to strangle it economically and assassinate Fidel.

In the late seventies, the possibility was discussed that Castro might visit the United Nations again. On that occasion, in my official capacity as a member of the city council, I sent an invitation for him to visit the South Bronx and see with his own eyes the miserable conditions of life for his Puerto Rican brothers and sisters in the belly of the beast. I likewise extended an invitation for him to attend a baseball game at Yankee Stadium, which was in the Bronx. I am sure that had he made his visit, Fidel would have visited our community and gone to the game, because he is and always has been a great fan of the sport.

27.
MARCHING WITH
MARTIN LUTHER KING

During the fifties, the black civil rights movement began to strengthen in the United States. In 1955, Rosa Parks, one of the leaders of the movement in Montgomery, Alabama, defied the segregationist laws of the state and refused to give up her seat on the bus to a white man. Parks's arrest was the catalyst for a protest movement that spread all across the nation. A young minister named Martin Luther King became the leader of the movement within the state, and in the process became the best-known leader of the civil rights movement in the entire United States.

In the early sixties, the tensions and conflicts in American society intensified, fueled in part by the unpopular Vietnam War and the wars of national liberation in other parts of the world, including Cuba. During that period we saw the emergence of a radicalized student movement, and new groups within the black, Chicano, and Puerto Rican communities began to openly question the status quo.

In 1963, several black leaders of the civil rights struggle, among them Rev. King, decided to lead a march for work and equality on Washington, D.C. At that moment, we Puerto Ricans in New York City were engaged on several fronts in a struggle for our civil rights, as well, including the full right to vote and a decent education. Several black civil rights leaders were active in the fight against racial segregation in the city's schools, among them the Reverend Milton Galamison of Brooklyn and Bayard Rustin of Manhattan, who were also working with Rev. King in organizing the march. The black leadership gave me the responsibility for mobilizing Puerto Ricans, as I was the president of the Congreso de Pueblos, the only organization large enough to deal with all the complexities of that task. My assignment was to organize Puerto Ricans in New York City and also in New Jersey, Connecticut, Pennsylvania, and Massachusetts.

During the first six months of that year, we worked very, very hard on that important organizational project. The labor movement helped me tremendously with transportation and expenses. At that point I was working full-time at the Adams factory on Long Island. My boss, Julie

Pariser, was incredibly supportive, giving me time off to attend meetings and other activities related to the activity. On August 28, over 250,000 men and women from all parts of the United States went to Washington, D.C., among them more than 30,000 Puerto Ricans.

It was an extremely emotional moment for me when the organizers of the event told me that I would be one of the speakers at the March, and that I would be speaking as a representative of the Puerto Rican community in the United States. I addressed the public in Spanish. When I stood at the lectern that had been set up in front of the Lincoln Memorial and faced the thousands and thousands of faces looking up at me as the representative of my community, I became very nervous. But I immediately recovered my composure and, having memorized my speech, I spoke for fifteen minutes. Although I know that most of the people there didn't have any idea what I was talking about, they very respectfully and affectionately applauded me when I was done. It was on that same stage that the Reverend King gave his famous "I Have a Dream" speech.

28.
THE SCHOOL BOYCOTT

One of the major problems that faced the children of Puerto Rican immigrants arriving in New York City was their lack of knowledge or limited mastery of English and the American culture. The solution offered by schools for this problem was the same as that offered for immigrants from other countries: they were given placement exams that they could not possibly pass due to their linguistic limitations and were then sent down to lower grades or put into classes for "special needs" students, meaning students with learning disabilities or with low IQs. Fortunately for me, when I arrived in New York City in 1937 I didn't have to go through that traumatic experience, since I had already graduated from high school. I was, however, witness to the way schools could destroy the lives of many of our youngsters.

During the sixties, within our communities there emerged an increasingly strong movement aimed at reforming the school system and making it respond better to the needs of Puerto Rican boys and girls. In the South Bronx, the movement was led by Evelina López Antonetty;[14] in Brooklyn, among many strong advocates one of the strongest was Antonia Denis.[15] At the same time, the black community and the city were engaged in an intense struggle to integrate the schools. The main leader of that movement was Milton Galamison,[16] of Brooklyn, a pastor in the Presbyterian Church and a tireless fighter for minority civil rights.

I began to work with Galamison in the early sixties. Ewart Guinier,[17] a friend of many years' standing who had been a union organizer, a member of the American Labor Party, and a civil rights leader in Manhattan, introduced me. Galamison and I immediately developed a close working relationship. Like Guinier, Galamison understood the need for blacks and Puerto Ricans to join in a common front against the racist, insensitive school system, and he always treated Puerto Ricans as equal partners in the struggle; he also recognized our leadership. In fact, it was those two men who invited me to attend the meeting in Atlanta with Martin Luther King to discuss the organization of the March on Washington. Other black leaders, such as Bayard Rustin and Rhody McCoy, were not very interested in our position and always treated us like an appendage in the struggle. They talked about the needs of blacks and Puerto Ricans, but always tried to minimize the role of Puerto Rican leaders. Not a few times did I have to push my way to the microphone in a press conference in order to show that we Puerto Ricans had our own leaders and our own problems.

In 1963, the Reverend Galamison began to develop the idea of a huge boycott of the New York City schools by blacks and Puerto Ricans. The idea was to show our strength by closing the schools for one day; in order to do that, we had to convince the parents of our children not to send them to school. Galamison invited me to attend the meetings for the boycott. I took the matter to the Congreso de Pueblos and our organization agreed to join the effort.

The coordination of the boycott was in the hands of Rustin. At the meeting called to create the organizing committee, Rustin offered us two seats on the committee, which was made up of twelve members. Aware of the fact that without us Puerto Ricans the boycott would be a failure, I refused his offer and demanded parity in all decision-making. The black leaders accepted my counter-offer and we launched the project. Within the Puerto Rican community, there was some resistance to joining the boycott, as some people feared that our image as obedient citizens would be damaged. Others were opposed simply out of racism. It was in that context that a short time later, one faction of the Puerto Rican Day Parade board of directors tried to remove me as president. They opposed me because I was pushing to get the Parade, the Congreso de Pueblos, and the National Puerto Rican Association of Civil Rights to forge coalitions with blacks.

In our efforts to organize this boycott all of us on the boycott committee worked very hard within our communities. We met with school officials to try to reach an agreement, but they refused to negotiate, so on February 3, 1964, in a clear show of support for our demands, more than 465,000 schoolchildren were kept home, between 100,000 and 150,000 of them Puerto Ricans. As part of the activities that day, we set up Freedom Schools at community centers and churches where we talked to students about civil rights. We also picketed at many schools and in front of the Board of Education. Despite the boycott's success, the black leadership could not decide what strategies to follow next, or what the specific solutions to the problems should be. Tensions between Puerto Ricans and the black leadership intensified when one sector of the black leadership resisted recognizing the particular needs of our community.

The fact was, our decision to join the boycott was in large measure a tactical one. I saw our participation as an opportunity to throw light on the problem of discrimination against our children within the school system. In El Barrio, few Puerto Rican children would have been helped by a special project to desegregate the schools that the black civil rights movement was advocating. Our parents would never have agreed to bus their children outside the community, especially not their daughters. Even more important, we were aware that our children would be discriminated against no matter whether they were sent to black, white, or mixed schools, because both blacks and whites treated us as foreigners because we didn't speak English. Discrimination against Puerto Ricans was rampant. We were truly between a rock and a hard place.

Our participation in the boycott did, however, call national attention to the problem, and that's what we had been seeking. As soon as the first boycott ended, the National Puerto Rican Association of Civil Rights, of which I was the president, called several Puerto Rican organizations to a meeting in the Manhattan Center to discuss a Puerto Rican educational agenda. Among our demands were including Spanish in elementary school curriculums; requiring all teachers to have a basic knowledge of Spanish; and including courses presenting a positive vision of Puerto Ricans not just to Puerto Rican students, but to the entire student population. We also agreed to have a citywide activity to present our demands and show our strength. In another meeting, this one held at La Ronda, a restaurant on 116th St. between Lenox and 7th avenues, at representatives of over fifty Puerto Rican organizations, among them the Congreso de Pueblos, the Parade, the Civil Rights Association, and the Puerto Rican Forum, we decided to hold a silent march.

On March 1, 1964, more than ten thousand Puerto Ricans marched at 2:30 pm from City Hall in Manhattan to the Board of Education offices on Livingston Street in Brooklyn, a distance of two miles, to present our demands. In addition to the demands mentioned above, we asked that aptitude exams be eliminated, because since they were in English they were biased against Puerto Rican children, whose dominant language was Spanish. We also asked that a Puerto Rican be named to the city's Board of Education and that more counselors, psychologists, and remedial-education teachers be recruited. That march was the first mass demonstration by Puerto Ricans in New York City, or anywhere in the United States, as an independent group, in defense of our civil rights.

A firm believer in education as a tool for personal and collective improvement, I took an active part in the years that followed—in fact, until I returned to Puerto Rico—in practically every organization created to promote educational rights for Puerto Ricans in New York City. I was part of the city's school decentralization movement and in the struggle to appoint Puerto Rican school principals in our communities. I was one of the few leaders in the community to openly support the occupation of City College by Puerto Rican students, and I also supported their demands that a Puerto Rican Studies program be established at the City University of New York (CUNY). I also took part in the movement that culminated in the creation of Hostos Community College, the first bilingual college in the United States; I issued demands and picketed to support the appointment of Puerto Rican professors in the CUNY system; and I supported the founding of the Center for Puerto Rican Studies.

29.
STRETCHING PUERTO RICANS TO MAKE THEM COPS

One of the most difficult problems we had to deal with during the civil rights struggle was the almost total absence of Puerto Ricans on the New York City police force. Of course there were almost no blacks, either. The fact is, blacks became accepted in the department after Puerto Ricans. Before we made our inroads, the police force was dominated from top to bottom by the Irish. Almost all cops were white, tall, good-looking. They looked like Hollywood actors dressed in blue.

In addition to prejudice and racism, one of the subterfuges used to restrict access by Puerto Rican candidates to the police force was their height. At that time, to become a cop you had to pass not just a written exam, but a physical exam, as well, which included a requirement that you be at least 5'8" tall, and not an eighth of an inch less. That requirement in itself disqualified many Puerto Ricans, since we tend to be on the short side.

Our communities were patrolled, then, by white cops. They were not familiar with our customs and did not speak Spanish, so they thought they needed to use their night sticks to make themselves understood. You could be Albert Einstein, and if a cop didn't like the way you looked at him, it would go bad for you. Sometimes they would hit you in the head on purpose, to crack your skull. Many of us were incapacitated or wound up with Alzheimer's as a result of this abuse, and many even died. The Congreso de Pueblos fought against police brutality and demanded that the issue be dealt with.

In fact, one of the reasons that led us to create the National Puerto Rican Association of Civil Rights was the problem of police brutality. This problem was so extreme that in 1963, police officers shot and killed two young Puerto Rican men—Víctor Rodríguez and Máximo Solero—on 96th St. and Riverside Drive. The Association, along with the Congreso de Pueblos and members of other organizations, picketed precinct stations all across New York City simultaneously, demanding among other things that action be taken against the police linked to the murders and that an independent civilian commission be created to deal with police brutality. Until that moment, the commission charged with investigating police brutality was made up of members of the police force. It was like the fox guarding the hen house. Police officers accused of excessive force were always acquitted or given a slap on the wrist. Faced with the authorities' foot-dragging in response to our demands, we made a complaint to the city's Human Rights Commission.

While this was going on, a police officer named O'Brien, a friend of mine, an Irishman who worked in the administrative section, offered to help me increase the number of Puerto Ricans on the police force, specifically by ensuring that they passed the physical.

Let me pause here to clarify that not all Irishmen are racists. I had good friends who were Irish, comrades that worked with me shoulder to shoulder, who understood our struggle, who supported what we were doing and who on many occasions volunteered to help us. For example, when I was working on the Human Rights Commission, I became very good friends with the director of public relations, an Irishman named Murphy. We had lunch together almost every day, and he kept me informed about everything happening in City Hall. He was one of the good Irishmen.

But let's go back to the issue at hand. To my question as to how O'Brien was going to get more Puerto Ricans to pass the physical exam, his answer was, "We're gonna stretch 'em."

At first I resisted the whole idea of integrating Puerto Ricans into the force. I've never had much love for cops, since so many of them are abusive. But I finally agreed that we owed it to our community. O'Brien then invited me to the Police Department gym in Manhattan and explained how he was going to do it. The candidate would have to be at least 5 feet 7 1/2 inches tall, and for the procedure to work, he would have to be "prepared" before the day of the physical. He would be laid on a stretcher and strapped down by the shoulders, and then weights would be put on each leg and pulled. After the first youngsters passed the physical, word spread in the community that Gilberto Gerena Valentín was stretching cops. Many young men came to me. I would assign them a day. We had to coordinate the stretching so it would be as close as possible to the date of the exam. Kids came not just on their own, but sometimes their mothers would come to me and say, "Gerena, my son is not doing so well— make a cop out of him."

And that is the true story of how Puerto Ricans born or raised in New York City began to enter the Police Department in larger numbers. Later, in the seventies, as a result of the amendment to the 1964 Civil Rights Act prohibiting discrimination on the basis of height, the Police Department revised its requirement. Also, they began to recruit police officers in Puerto Rico and include women on the force. Meanwhile, though, a lot of young men got stretched. Although some of them forgot how they came to be cops and behaved as badly as the racist white cops, if not worse, others remembered their origins and maintained excellent relations with their community.

30.
HOW THEY TRIED TO TAKE THE PRESIDENCY OF THE PUERTO RICAN DAY PARADE AWAY FROM ME

I had returned home tired but happy with the work we were doing in our fight against discrimination against Puerto Rican children in the city's school system. Just inside the door I found a message from Virginia González, one of the secretaries of the Congreso de Pueblos' board of directors. Virginia was a founding member of the Congreso and belonged to the organization's Ladies Committee, which was a network of women committed to the Congreso's programs. She was also a delegate from the Lajas Club to the Puerto Rican Day Parade committee, and as such had helped found and coordinate the parade. The message was brief; she was asking me to call an emergency meeting of the board of directors.

At the meeting, Virginia reported that the president of the Parade's Board of Directors, attorney Irma Vidal Santaella,[18] had called an extraordinary meeting to be held that Sunday. The purpose was to strip me of the presidency of the Parade's organizing committee. According to Virginia, my work in solidarity with the black community had alienated the most conservative faction in the Parade's governing body. The group taking this action against me was composed of Irma Vidal; Ángel M. Rivera, who represented an organization in Queens; María López, the president of the Aguas Buenas club; and José Lumen Román, a journalist with the *Diario La Prensa* and an announcer on radio station WHOM.

According to Virginia's informant, Lumen Román had told Vidal Santaella that he had come into possession of certain documents—a report from the House Un-American Activities Committee—that named me as a member of the Communist Party of the United States, and in the meeting on Sunday he intended to accuse me of having deceived the Parade organization by not providing them with that information. He also told her that his group could count on eight of the fifteen votes of the board of directors.

In my absence, Virginia had started mobilizing the Congreso's delegates to the Parade general committee, which helped. On Saturday we used our telephone banks to speak to all the remaining delegates. Every one of them promised to attend the meeting, and that put us in a more favorable position. Meanwhile, we looked carefully at the memo calling for the assembly. Among the members of the board who had signed it there was one person, whose name I will not mention, who had always in the past stood firmly beside me. We went to his house and his wife told us that he was asleep. We insisted on talking to him. He got up—a little groggy, since he had been drinking—and came out to talk to us. We showed him the memo calling the meeting and asked him if that was his signature. He said it was, but he admitted that he wasn't very clear as to the purpose of the meeting. It turned out that he had been asked to sign it while he was drunk. When we told him that it was to strip me of the presidency, he said he couldn't agree to that—he was my friend. He gave me a big hug, apologized, and asked what he could do to make things right. We asked him to go to the assembly to revoke his signature and, in addition, sign a document that would also be signed by the seven members opposed to calling the meeting. This second document was basically a motion that a new assembly be called and that I, as president, run it.

We arrived an hour before the meeting was to start. It was held in a meeting room in the Barceloneta town-club headquarters at 103rd St. and Broadway in Manhattan. There were over three hundred delegates—since the other side had also mobilized their people—and tempers were running high. We let Vidal Santaella open the meeting. She announced that the Board of Directors had called the assembly as per the bylaws. You should have seen her face when Monserrate Flores, a member of the board and president of the San Germán club, raised his hand and declared that in order to take over the Parade, the board needed eight votes, while they had only seven. At that point, a roll call was held and the names of the members who had authorized the meeting were called out. When my friend's name was called, he stood up and said he withdrew his signature from the petition. Immediately, we presented our motion that a second meeting be held with the delegates present at that time and that I, as president, should run the meeting. The motion passed. As soon as the second meeting was opened, a motion was presented to ask for Vidal Santaella's resignation as president of the Parade board of directors. That motion, too, passed.

Then Lumen Román asked for the floor and moved that I be stripped of the presidency of the Parade committee. At that moment I was holding in my hands the document which, according to him, accused me of being a Communist. I proceeded to read to the delegates the paragraph that stated that I was to be called to testify at a hearing before the House Un-American Activities Committee, and I explained that I was never called to testify and that if I had been, I wouldn't have gone. The boos and catcalls directed at Lumen Román were so loud that he had to leave the meeting. He was followed by Ángel M. Rivera, Irma Vidal Santaella, María López, and several others.

A few days later, the board of directors met. The group led by Vidal Santaella presented their resignations. We asked that they reconsider their decision and remain on the Parade committee for the good of the community, but they stood firm.

We managed to survive that crisis. A new board of directors was elected, and the Parade was held the next year without further problems. In fact, it was a great success. I continued in my position as president until the next elections, which were in September, when I endorsed the candidacy of Monserrate Flores as president of the next Parade. He was elected. He worked very hard and earned the affection and respect of all the participating organizations. From that point on I coordinated the event every year until 1970. Four years after that, in 1974, I coordinated the Parade for the last time.

In 1983, years after the events that I have just narrated, Vidal Santaella was elected to the New York Supreme Court. Long before, María López had stepped down from the presidency of the Aguas Buenas town club and Ángel M. Rivera had apologized for the incident and returned to join our struggle. Rivera told me he'd spent a small fortune on the campaign to throw me off the Parade committee. Lumen Román retired a short time after these events and went back to Puerto Rico to live in Arecibo. I think he is still alive.

31.
THE PRETTIEST FLAG IN THE WORLD MEASURES 50 FEET BY 35 FEET

I learned to love the Puerto Rican flag, my flag, when I was just a little boy. It was, in fact, on that September 23, 1932, when Pedro Albizu Campos planted the tamarind tree in Lares that my heart throbbed with emotion for the first time as I saw hundreds of Puerto Rican flags waving in the hands of Puerto Rican men, women, and children proud of their nationality. And although I lived, in total, more than half my life outside Puerto Rico, I never lost that love for my flag. On the contrary, those years in the United States taught me to love it even more. And even today, almost thirty years after my return to Puerto Rico, I still love it and defend it with all my strength and power.

During the time I lived in the United States I cultivated wonderful friendships with Americans of all races and ethnic groups. They were men and women proud of their nation but respectful of my rights, my beliefs, and my flag. Most of them supported my causes, and many of them struggled right alongside me to fight racism and prejudice against our community. Among them, some were like family, as is the case of Donald Rubin, whom I helped raise and whom I have loved like a son since he was barely two years old. Two other great, dear friends were Julie Pariser, whom I've spoken about earlier, and Don Goodman.

Like Julie, Don was a liberal Jew who helped found the Americans for Democratic Action. From the moment we met one another, he supported the projects I was involved in, including the Congreso de Pueblos, the Puerto Rican Day Parade, and the National Puerto Rican Association of Civil Rights. He always looked out for me and made sure nothing happened to me.

Don owned a textile factory in what's known as the Garment District in Manhattan, which at that time ran from 42nd St. to 23rd St. on the West Side. Located at 28th St. and Sixth Avenue, Don's factory was in an old two-story building that was in excellent condition. Most of Don's employees were Puerto Rican women, and a very special relationship that went beyond the mere job had developed between Don and his employees. Whenever he visited Puerto Rico, which happened quite often, he would carry gifts for his employees' families, and when some relative of one of them died, he would help pay the funeral expenses. The workers loved him like a father.

In March 1963, a few years after assuming the presidency of the Puerto Rican Day Parade, I received a call from Don's secretary, who was also Puerto Rican, to tell me that her boss wanted me to find a Puerto Rican flag for him, and that the color of the triangle should be sky blue. In the Congreso's offices we always had Puerto Rican flags available, so I quickly sent one to Don. Knowing him, I figured he was preparing a flag for the escort that leads the Parade, to fly alongside the flags of New York State and the United States.

A week later, Don called me personally to tell me that he had a surprise for me. He invited me to visit the factory on Friday to show it to me. If I wanted, he said, I could bring as many friends as I liked. I told myself that if I took him at his word, we wouldn't all fit inside the building. Finally, I decided to take my secretary, two members of the Congreso, and two members of the Parade organization.

We arrived at the factory at noon that Friday. The receptionist, dressed as though for a wedding, asked me to wait a moment. In a few minutes a group of Puerto Rican workers appeared. They welcomed us and took us to Don. He was arranging the tables for a buffet lunch. After greeting us warmly, he led us into an immense room. What was our surprise and emotion to see an enormous Puerto Rican flag hanging from high up on the wall and draped over a row of tables. It measured 50 feet by 35 feet!

We then went into the dining room, where the presentation ceremony was to take place. Don's entire workforce took their seats at the tables he'd set up, while he seated me and my colleagues at the head table. At that, a Puerto Rican musical group entered with guitar, cuatro, güiro, and maracas. One of the employees made the introductions. There was a great deal of applause. Then somebody asked the musicians to play the Puerto Rican anthem, "La Borinqueña." Always the wise guy, I asked which one, the official one or the revolutionary one. Everyone shouted in unison, "Both!" Unfortunately, the musicians didn't know the song, but the guitarist strummed along as everyone sang the "official" national anthem, with lyrics by Manuel Fernández Juncos. As we began the second version, I realized that I was the only person that was singing Lola Rodríguez de Tió's lyrics to the "revolutionary" anthem. Nobody else knew the words to that one.

That done, I stood up to speak; as this all came as a complete surprise to me, I improvised a eulogy to the flag. I talked about Mariana Bracetti, the revolutionary who sewed the Lares flag in 1868, and told the story of how that flag originated. Then I addressed the factory workers.

"You," I said, "have made history today by sewing the largest Puerto Rican flag in the world. On Sunday, June 1, that flag that you ladies have made, with the best cotton and linen fabric on the market, with its perfect hem and nylon cord, will dazzle everyone on Fifth Avenue."

My speech earned a huge ovation. One lady stood up teary-eyed and spoke of how proud she felt at this moment to be Puerto Rican and how much she wanted freedom for our island. More applause. I looked at Don out of the corner of my eye. He had a huge smile on his face as he applauded.

I invited Don and the ladies who had sewn the flag to attend the parade and share the dais with us. Right on schedule, the Parade kicked off at noon that Sunday. It was led by the flag carried by dozens of Puerto Rican men and women. Thousands of Puerto Ricans viewing the event wept with emotion to see such a glorious, enormous flag carried down Fifth Avenue in the middle of New York City. People would break through the security cordon to touch it. There was constant applause, from 43rd St. to 86th St. and Third Avenue. I marched proudly before the flag until we reached 69th St., where the dais had been erected. There, I went up to greet the guests of honor: Mayor Robert Wagner, the city commissioners, and my dear friend Don Goodman, who was accompanied by his family and some of the women who had sewn the flag.

In the collective euphoria something completely unexpected happened. People spontaneously began to throw money onto the flag, from pennies to bills of various denominations. The weight of the coins was such that the flag started almost dragging along the ground, so we named an ad hoc committee to gather the money every ten blocks. At the end of the parade, we counted the money; there was over ten thousand dollars.

From that year on, the flag was an inevitable presence in the Puerto Rican Day Parade. It was also carried in various activities sponsored by the Congreso, the Parade committee, and the National Puerto Rican Association of Civil Rights. It went with us to the demonstration against the U.S. Navy's presence in Culebra that we held in Washington in 1970, and to many other demonstrations in New York City, Washington, and Puerto Rico. After my return to the island in 1985, the flag was always there when we marched against the Navy; it was there in 1993, to support making Spanish Puerto Rico's official language, and in 1996 at the protest demonstration at the Governors Convention held at the Hotel El Conquistador in Fajardo.

In these demonstrations, the flag saw its share of rain. Sometimes, people would take shelter under it, open their umbrellas, and push the flag up, causing rips and tears and holes which, as the years went by, became more and more visible. Finally, in 1996, we had to take it out of circulation. But we didn't bury it or burn it; we separated its five stripes along the seams, cut the stripes into pieces five feet long, and stored them, with the triangle and star, in a transparent plastic box. Since then, every morning when I get up I pray beside it, and I kiss it to honor the service it rendered for its country.

In 1997, I got a surprise that almost killed me, but with happiness. José Rivera, my dear friend and comrade in so many political and union struggles and city assemblyman for the Bronx, brought me another 50-foot by 35-foot flag. Just like the original, this flag has accompanied me in the parades and on marches for just causes that I have attended since then.

32.
BOYCOTT AS A WEAPON

Don Moncho had a bodega in El Barrio. Everybody in the family worked in it, and they kept it open until late at night. When the Congreso de Pueblos needed soft drinks, don Moncho would donate them. He would also donate ham and cheese for sandwiches. He always supported our groups, and we reciprocated with our business.

One day I was in don Moncho's *bodega* when the driver of the truck that distributed Schaefer beer in El Barrio came in. The driver, a young, strong Italian no more than 30 years old, spoke to don Moncho disrespectfully, saying, "Hey, chico, come get your beer." At that time, white racists used the name "chico" when they spoke to Puerto Ricans. They would call blacks "boy." Don Moncho, an older man who was not in good health, took his hand cart and had to walk about three blocks to pick up twenty cases of beer. When he brought the beer back in, I asked him if it was always like that. He said it was, and explained that the Schaefer drivers always left the merchandise down on that corner for him to pick up and take back to his bodega himself. If he didn't go pick it up, they wouldn't bring it at all, and he would lose those sales. The soda-truck drivers did the same thing. Don Moncho had to go to wherever the truck parked to pick up his sodas. This was a common practice in El Barrio at the time, although not in the white communities, where merchandise would be taken right to the door of the store, in back or in front.

I left the *bodega* disgusted by what I had seen happening to Puerto Rican business owners. I took the matter to the Board of Directors of the Congreso de Pueblos. We discussed the matter for a good while and finally came to the conclusion that the cause of this treatment of our *bodega* owners was the prejudice and discrimination that Puerto Ricans in general were subject to. But we also knew we were increasingly important to the city's economy as consumers of goods and services. The truth was, we Puerto Ricans were excellent consumers of beer, soft drinks, other products such as canned soup, and even ice, since at that time almost no one had a refrigerator. But despite being good consumers, there were practically no Puerto Ricans working in food-distributing companies. We decided to discuss the matter in a meeting to which we invited many *bodega* owners.

It took us two meetings to draw up a program of action. We decided unanimously to mount a selective boycott against three of the companies that were making the most money from our purchases but were giving nothing back to the community in return. The businesses we originally singled out were the Schaefer brewery, Coca-Cola, Campbell's Soups, and Pan American Airways. Schaefer was far and away the beer most consumed in the Puerto Rican community in New York City. At home and in the parks, especially during the summer, it would be in everyone's hand. Coca-Cola dominated the soft-drink market, and Pan Am was the main airline between New York and Puerto Rico. It was only later that Eastern Airlines arrived.

We created several committees charged with presenting our arguments and demands to those companies' management. We were specifically asking for jobs for our people. As might be expected, our demands fell on deaf ears. At that, we informed the TV stations that those corporations mainly advertised in that we would be launching a boycott and mounting picket lines. *La Prensa* and *El Diario de Nueva York* also supported us. We launched a vigorous campaign to convince Puerto Ricans not to buy the products and services that those companies were selling. The community and the *bodega* owners supported our initiative. In the specific case of Schaefer, we distributed flyers throughout the community and even outside it—for example, in Yankee Stadium—saying that Schaefer would give you diarrhea and that you should drink Miller instead. Miller, in turn, agreed to deliver its product to the *bodega*'s door, and they launched an intensive advertising campaign on Hispanic radio and TV to advertise the product as the "Champagne of Bottle Beers." Schaefer's sales plummeted. At the same time, we would watch for the Schaefer trucks, and when they arrived we would demand that the drivers deliver the merchandise directly to the bodegas.

Don Moncho took an active part in the boycott. When the Schaefer driver came to tell him to go pick up his beer, don Moncho told him to forget it, he could take them back. The guy got very upset and left, but not without a threatening phrase: "I'll be back." In a while, he returned with four or five buddies, but we were ready for them. When they came in, we backed them into a corner and gave the truck driver a good beating. He left bruised and battered and carrying a clear message to the Schaefer management: From now on, we would not allow that beer to be distributed in El Barrio. It was then that the company reacted and called us to a meeting. We went straight to the point. We explained that we wanted jobs for Puerto Ricans in the company. Not long afterward we received the management's answer in the form of a list of professional jobs. We had to deal harshly with this tactic. Those were not the jobs we were interested in. We wanted jobs for the people who lived in our neighborhood—that is, for truck drivers, office workers, salespeople, and supervisors. They then offered us jobs in maintenance, as janitors and cleaning staff. We accepted those menial jobs, but we continued our boycott. We gave them a list of fifty acceptable positions. Schaefer finally folded and gave in to our demands. They also agreed that the truck drivers would deliver the merchandise to the door of the bodega and unload it off the truck.

The boycott against Campbell's Soup and Coca-Cola was also effective, and we persuaded them to offer jobs to Puerto Ricans. In the case of Coca-Cola, our boycott included a campaign to promote their competition, Pepsi-Cola. We visited the warehouses that distributed those products, including Goya Foods, Metro Co-op, and the Melrose Food Corporation, and we won a few jobs for Puerto Ricans, although I must admit that in the case of Goya and Metro Co-op, their whole labor force was already Hispanic, especially Puerto Rican.

With Pan American Airways we followed a similar strategy. We ran a campaign accusing the airline of discriminating against Puerto Ricans in their recruitment and hiring, and we recommended that travelers use the other airlines that flew to Puerto Rico at the time. To force Pan Am to negotiate with us, we closed down several flights. We did this with the support of Raúl Ortiz, who had a travel agency in El Barrio. Raúl would give us the list of passengers traveling to Puerto Rico, and the evening before the flight we'd call all the people who had bought tickets and tell them the flight had been canceled. We would also fill flights with reservations that we'd cancel at the last minute. At the same time we were doing this, we would urge our community to fly on Trans Caribbean Ariways, which in 1971 was bought by American Airlines. The boycott of Pan Am was the least effective of all. In fact, they never called us to negotiate, although not long afterward they went bankrupt. I can't say that our boycott was a determining factor in that, but some of us thought it might have been.

On another occasion, we boycotted the Alexander's department store chain. During the fifties and sixties, Alexander's was the leading department store serving the middle and lower classes in New York City. It had two enormous stores in the Bronx: one on 152nd St. and Third Avenue and one on Fordham Road and the Grand Concourse. In 1965, they opened another huge store in Manhattan, between 58th and 59th streets and Lexington and Third avenues. In this case, we found ourselves in exactly the same situation as with the other companies: Puerto Ricans were among the main purchasers of merchandise in the Alexander's stores in the Bronx, but their presence in the work force was practically nil. Our strategy for dealing with the department store was a little different from the other companies; we combined picket lines in front of the stores with other actions. Initially, we concentrated our attention on the Bronx stores. There, the Congreso de Pueblos, with the support of other organizations, picketed. Meanwhile, one group of women and another of men would go into the stores' clothing departments at peak shopping hours. After we had selected merchandise for a total value of approximately fifty dollars, we would go to pay. When the bill was added up, we would take out a bag with fifty dollars in pennies. Imagine the problems that caused! The cashiers had to count out five thousand pennies one by one. That meant that the waiting time in the lines to pay became interminable, and many customers would leave without buying. Invariably, the cashiers would call the store managers, since they didn't know how to deal with the situation. The manager, in turn, would also be in a difficult situation, because there was nothing he or she could really do, since our argument was absolutely irrefutable: Pennies were "legal tender for all debts public and private," to quote the line on the dollar bill. After arguing for a while, the manager would usually tell the cashier to take the money without counting it. Others, though, would make the cashier count every single penny.

At any rate, the Alexander's management knew that sooner or later they would have to deal with us. It took two picket lines to get them to call a meeting. As we had with the other companies we boycotted, we asked for jobs, and they presented us with a list of positions available for professionals, especially engineers, buyers, and so on. Disgusted with this insensitive response, I threw the list in the face of the person who was negotiating with us and told her that if we weren't offered the jobs we wanted we would continue with our pickets and boycott. I also seized the occasion to recommend that they cover their store windows, since I couldn't guarantee that someone upset by the situation might not throw a brick through the window. To put even more pressure on them, we mounted a picket line at the Manhattan store, where the clients were mostly white upper-middle-class. While outside there were over two hundred Puerto Ricans picketing the store, inside we were following our "penny strategy." Many customers, especially the older ones, didn't even dare enter; others simply dropped out of the lines to pay because of all the hullabaloo that was going on.

We didn't have to picket again. Finally, management negotiated with us and presented a list of two hundred jobs, among them elevator operators, salespeople, and office workers. In the case of the Bronx, we forced them, as part of the arrangement, to install a swimming pool for the community near the store on 152nd St.

The success we had in these campaigns shows once again that in unity there is strength and that you've got to know how to use unity to achieve your objectives.

33.
COMMISSIONER OF HUMAN RIGHTS IN NEW YORK CITY

Although I worked in another department, at lunchtime I always got together with Pepito and his wife Annie, both of whom worked on the assembly line, to talk about this and that—issues related to the union, the latest events in our community, and, of course, gossip about the factory. One Monday in mid-December 1965, a little while before the first bell was about to ring to go back to work, Julie Pariser approached me and with a very serious look on his face said, "Gil, when the second bell rings, stop by my office, please. I have something to talk to you about." I said I'd be there. As soon as Julie left, Pepito and Annie started kidding me, saying the boss was going to fire me. Pepito said I should ask for severance pay—a week of salary for every year I'd worked there. Imagine, I had started at Adams Laboratories in 1952, after I was fired from the Emerson plant, and this was 1965. They started figuring out the money I'd have to be paid under that agreement. Then they added the three weeks of vacation, my sick days, and holidays. Wow! According to them, I'd be leaving with a sackful of money.

I told them I didn't think that was why Julie had called me to his office. I had been working for twelve years in the factory. Management thought of me as a good worker; I had done well for myself. Plus, they knew that I was a bona fide member of the union and that the collective agreement clearly set forth the procedures for firing an employee. And I knew that better than anyone, since for several years I had been a member of the union's negotiating committee. And just to make sure they didn't take their own joke seriously, I reminded them that the Adams management was not anti-union, in fact quite the reverse. Not only were the owners progressives, they understood the benefits that a good collective agreement brought to the company.

Even so, I kept trying to figure out why Julie might have called me in. What was this sudden meeting all about, and why the serious expression on his face? The only thing that occurred to me was that it might be related to the project I was working on at the time: some perspective drawings of the cabinets we were designing for an intercom system in several hospitals.

When the second bell rang I went to Julie's office. I found him sitting at his desk, smoking a huge cigar. He offered me one and I took it, but I saved it for later. He went straight to the point: "I'm really sorry to have to lose you."

So it looked like Pepito and Annie had been right! Totally confused, I asked, "Why? What's happening? I thought my work was all right."

I sighed with relief when he told me to relax, the meeting had nothing to do with the quality of my work. He then went on to tell me that Friday he'd had a visit from Dr. Frank Arricale, who'd been sent by Mayor John Lindsay to ask about me: whether I was a good worker, how long I had been at Adams, whether I was responsible, that sort of thing. It seems, Julie explained, that I'd been recommended for a position on the city's Human Rights Commission.

"I told them the truth," Julie proudly said, "that you were one of my best workers and a good man, and he was very pleased."

At the end of our conversation, Julie gave me his opinion about all this. It would be a win-win situation, he said, since Lindsay would be getting a person with lots of experience in the area of civil rights and I, with all the connections I had established in the community and with the city's civil rights groups, would be very effective at the work. Then, with a smile, he said, "You don't want to work in a factory for the rest of your life, do you?"

At first, I wasn't particularly keen on the idea of accepting a political appointment. Plus, Lindsay was a Republican, and I had always, and still do, have a "thing" against that party. Lindsay had won the election on the Republican ticket with the support of the Liberal Party. He had beaten Abraham Beame, the candidate of the Democratic machine and of Robert Wagner, Jr., the outgoing mayor, who had never really wanted to recognize our community's leadership and preferred to work with the representatives of the government of Puerto Rico. Aside from appointing a few good leaders from our community to positions in his administration, including Herman Badillo, he had done very little for us. In addition, his inability to deal effectively with the problems of the Puerto Rican community, including the thorny matter of police brutality, had cost him a great deal of support. The Congreso de Pueblos and the National Puerto Rican Association of Civil Rights, for example, had both strongly criticized his inaction. As a result, the majority of our community had voted for Lindsay in the previous elections, in a break with our traditional support for the Democratic Party.

But despite his party affiliation, Lindsay was a liberal, and he was more aware of the Puerto Rican community's problems than his predecessors had been. In

November 1963, when the police shot Víctor Rodríguez and Máximo Solero at point-blank range on 96th St. and Riverside Drive, Lindsay publicly asked for the police commissioner's resignation. He had also supported our boycott in 1964 against the Board of Education and had come out in defense of the right of every person to be taken to their residence, no matter where they might live, by yellow cabs, which had been refusing to drive passengers into certain neighborhoods. Lastly, he had just now started asking the Human Rights Commission to get tough; the municipal legislature had given the Commission jurisdiction over discriminatory actions based on race, color, national origin, and religion in the workplace and in housing, and he fully supported that measure.

When I got home, I consulted with my wife Francia about the appointment. Like Julie, she thought I could do a lot of good on the Commission. The next day, I met as usual with Pepito and Annie at lunchtime. I decided to give them a little of their own medicine, so I told them, but with a very serious demeanor, that to my great surprise I'd been fired. I thanked them for their suggestion that I ask for a week of pay for every year I'd worked there, and told them that today would be our last lunch together. I don't really think they believed me. . . . Anyway, after I'd pulled their leg a while I told them about the conversation I'd had with Julie, and they said I shouldn't think about it twice if I was offered the position. In fact, Pepito said, "Today we're going to gather signatures in the factory and ask the shop chairman to give you the union's support." I appreciated that show of confidence, but I explained that we couldn't make this public, since the conversation between Julie and the representative from Mayor Lindsay had been confidential. They understood.

The next thing I did was call a meeting of the executive committee and the board of directors of the Congreso de Pueblos to discuss the matter. I did the same thing with the boards of directors of the Puerto Rican Day Parade and the National Puerto Rican Association of Civil Rights. They all agreed that if the mayor offered me the position of commissioner, I should accept it, since it would be a great step forward for our cause. After weighing all the pros and cons, I put my reservations aside, convinced that the position would, in fact, allow me to advance the causes of the community that was so dear to me and that I had always wanted to represent.

About a week later, Dr. Arricale came to see me to ask if I was interested in the position. I told him that in principle I was, but that I wanted to meet with the mayor before making my final decision. I asked him if Lindsay would meet with me, and he told me he would. A few days later I received a letter from Lindsay inviting me to meet with him to discuss the matter. At the meeting, the mayor told me that he was aware of my career as an activist on several fronts in behalf of human rights, and that I was the kind of person that he wanted on his team. The chairman of the Commission was William Booth, a well-known black leader of the civil rights movement that I had worked with before and with whom I had an excellent relationship. I think he was the person who'd recommended me for the job. I went straight to the point and told the mayor what my position was on several issues related to human rights for Puerto Ricans. I reiterated that the police seemed to think they could get away with anything in our community, and that as part of the solution to the problem of police brutality I insisted on the creation of a civilian review board appointed by the mayor to monitor the police force's actions. I also told him that I had discussed the matter and my plans for the position with the organizations I represented, and that they were totally behind me. Bottom line, if he wanted me to be part of his team, he had to commit himself to support my work in these matters. Lindsay said he was in full agreement.

Finally, on May 1, 1966, International Workers Day, Booth issued a public statement to announce my appointment to the Human Rights Commission. I was assigned to chair the Business and Employment Division, whose job was to bring minorities into the city's economic life and ensure that the anti-discrimination laws in those areas were complied with. With something of a heavy heart, I said goodbye to my friends and coworkers at the Adams factory at an emotional reception that Julie Pariser helped organize at lunchtime, and I drove to my new office in City Hall. I was beginning my career as a public servant.

The change in my work was like night and day. Instead of starting work at 8 am, I started at 9, but there was never a set hour for leaving work; sometimes I'd be there till very late. I had my own office with a secretary, a Puerto Rican woman. My coworkers on the Commission knew me, and several of them had stood shoulder to shoulder with me in the struggle against discrimination and racism. I can say that in general, there was great enthusiasm on the commission. When I was introduced, James Murphy, an Irishman who had been a journalist for the *Daily News* and was now in charge of public relations for the Commission, told me how delighted he was because finally that bunch of lazy bums in City Hall was going to see what work was. Murphy and I became good friends and would sometimes have lunch together to exchange information and seek advice. He kept me informed of all the palace intrigues in Lindsay's court.

The fact was, I was not at all interested in being part of that world of constant intrigue in City Hall. I tried to stay at arm's length from all of it, and I focused my attention on my work as commissioner. Even so, my job demanded that I learn who was who, and I did have to fraternize with the various courtiers. When it was part of the job or I thought it might help, I would attend parties, dinners, and cocktail hours, especially during the Christmas holidays. If my presence weren't absolutely necessary, though, I preferred to spend my time with my own people, with whom I always felt at home and happy.

PHOTOGRAPHIC COLLECTION

Voting in the elections for the Puerto Rican Day Parade in 1963. Over 1200 delegates voted.

Copy of the pass from the Sioux Falls Army Air Field (1943).

After discharge from the army (ca. 1945).

Room clerk in the Commodore Hotel in Manhattan (1946).

Organizer for the New York Hotel Trades Council,
Local No. 6 (1948).

With my son Joey in New York (1954).

During the campaign for the elimination of the literacy test as a voting requirement. In the photo, I am surrounded by employees of the Migration Office of the Puerto Rico Department of Labor in New York (ca. 1955). Collection Justo Martí, Center for Puerto Rican Studies, Hunter College, CUNY.

Supporting José Erazo in his campaign for district leader in El Barrio (ca. 1960). From left: Juan Manuel Más, Oscar Rosa, Manuel Martínez, José Erazo, Ralph Rosa, Gilberto Gerena Valentín, Luis Maysonabe Ríos, and Carlos Cupril.

At Victor's Café (Columbus Ave. and 71st St, Manhattan) with Local 6 organizer Alberto Sarmiento and singer-composer Bobby Capó (ca. 1960).

Figures on the dais at the Puerto Rican Day Parade in 1963.
Above, from left: Inés Mendoza de Muñoz Marín (First Lady of Puerto Rico); Luis Muñoz Marín (Governor of Puerto Rico); José Erazo (Grand Marshall of the Parade); not identified; Gilberto Gerena Valentín (President of the Parade Committee); Samuel R. Quiñones (President of the Senate of Puerto Rico). Below, from right (speaking into the microphone): Robert Wagner (Mayor of the City of New York); Gilberto Gerena Valentín; Samuel R. Quiñones; Santiago Polanco Abreu (Speaker of the Puerto Rican House of Representatives); not identified; Joseph Monserrat (National Director of the Migration Office of the Puerto Rico Department of Labor). Collection of the Office of the Government of Puerto Rico in the United States, Center for Puerto Rican Studies, Hunter College, CUNY.

As Grand Marshall, with my wife Francia Lubán, walking ahead of representatives from the Congreso de Pueblos in the Puerto Rican Day Parade, 1964. Collection of the Office of the Government of Puerto Rico in the United States, Center for Puerto Rican Studies, Hunter College, CUNY.

In the home of Caridad López, Queens, NYC (1964). Standing, from left: Sonia (first); Angelito Egozque (fifth); Gilberto Gerena Valentín; Virginia González; Caridad López; her husband Felipe; Estel and Joe Erazo. Seated at left, Nelly Santiago.

Celebrating with members of the Congreso de Pueblos at the Broadway Casino (ca. 1968).
Collection Justo Martí, Center for Puerto Rican Studies, Hunter College, CUNY.

G. Gerena Valentin

FOR THIRTY YEARS:

► FIGHTER FOR HONEST GOVERNMENT
► LEADER IN THE PEACE AND
  CIVIL RIGHTS MOVEMENTS
► LABOR ORGANIZER
► FIGHTER FOR COMMUNITY CONTROL
► LECTURER AND WRITER

Vote Primary Day - Tuesday, June 17, 1969 - 3-10 P.M.

/ F(
C
O
U
N
C
I
L
M
A
N

A
T

L
A
R
G
E

M
A
N
H
A
T
T
A
N

Flyer for the campaign for
city councilman at large for
Manhattan (1969).

Celebrating my victory after the hunger strike at the Human Rights Commission (1969).

At the Puerto Rican Day Parade (ca. 1971) with Herman Badillo.

FBI photo after being falsely arrested for attempting to hijack a plane to Cuba (1972).

In the office of the Congreso de Pueblos at 254 W. 72nd St, Manhattan (ca. 1975).

On the picket line at a Canadian bank on Wall St protesting the imprisonment of Humberto Pagán in Canada and his possible extradition to the U.S. (ca. 1975).

Poet Juan Antonio Corretjer and I in Canada in support of Humberto Pagán (1976).

Puerto Rican leaders meeting with Mayor Edward Koch (1978). "The mayor didn't want me to sit next to him because he was afraid I'd put a bomb in his pocket." Above: from right, facing the camera: Mayor Koch; N.Y. Assemblyman Angelo del Toro; N.Y. Assemblywoman Olga Méndez; N.Y. Assemblyman José Serrano (image partly obstructed). Back to camera: second from left, N.Y. Assemblyman Roberto Rodríguez; not identified; N.Y. Assemblyman Armando Montano; not identified; City Councilman Gilberto Gerena Valentín; N.Y. Assemblyman Víctor Robles; U.S. Congressman Robert García.

Campaigning as the New Alliance Party candidate for city councilman on Southern Boulevard in the Bronx (June, 1981).

With my daughters Gilmari (in my arms) and Marielia, and Taita Rodríguez (1982).

In my position as Special Secretary for Migrant Workers, with Governor Mario Cuomo (1983).

In Vieques with my daughter Gilmari (ca. 1995).

Farming in Lares, with a stalk of plantains (ca. 1995).

On my farm in Lares with a soursop (ca. 1995).

The tamarind tree, descended from the tree under which the Liberator of the Americas, Simón Bolívar, would rest, that is growing in Lares' Plaza de la Revolución. Seeds of this tree were brought to Puerto Rico in 1931 by poet Gabriela Mistral, who in solidarity with the struggle for Puerto Rican independence presented them to Pedro Albizu Campos.

34.
MAYOR FOR A WEEKEND

John V. Lindsay turned out to be a disappointment as mayor. He started out with tremendous drive and desire for change, but he wound up bending to pressure from big political interests. At first, he tried to include members of his cabinet and staff in the formulation of public policy. Or at least he gave that impression. On one occasion, he decided to make several of us mayors for a weekend. My turn came the weekend of August 5 to 7, 1966. When I got the memo that this was going to happen, I felt a mixture of delight and fear. For me, this was a totally new experience. I asked my wife Francia what I could do in one weekend as mayor of the largest city in the United States. She looked at me and said, "Remember how many days it took God to make the world," and she told me to make a list of the things that might make the most impact.

We started half jokingly to make the list, but we were half serious about it, too. It included visiting the homeless, declaring New York City independent from the state, and buying the New York Mets so the city could run the team and make the games more affordable for the fans. We also wanted to visit the city's jails and declare a Puerto Rican Day in City Hall. I told Francia that I especially liked those last two. I didn't think the mayor would go for them, and I figured his aides would say I was *loco*, but I decided to go for it.

I prepared a list of things I would like to do as mayor-designate with respect to the jails. I would have liked to open the cells so that every prisoner could take a weekend off to visit his or her relatives. It was a good idea, but hard to implement, and it represented a certain degree of risk. I consulted the Reverend Rubén Darío Colón, a good friend of mine and the chaplain of the jail in the Bronx. We prepared an agenda and a calendar. We wanted to visit at least three institutions: the Tombs in lower Manhattan, Rikers Island in Queens, and the Bronx correctional facility, but we finally decided we could also visit the jail in Brooklyn. Just as I had imagined, Lindsay at first was a little doubtful about my plans, which were unquestionably risky from the political point of view, but he finally gave his go-ahead.

The idea of declaring a Puerto Rican Day in City Hall was easier to swallow. I'm sure Lindsay thought the activity, like his decision to appoint me Commissioner of Human Rights, would win him a lot of votes in the Puerto Rican community if he decided to run again. Getting the Puerto Rican vote was not easy, since our community tended not to vote for Republicans, while Lindsay had won the elections on the Republican and Liberal Party ticket. What the mayor and all the other politicians, whether Republican, Democrat, or Liberal, never understood was that Gerena Valentín's loyalty was solely and exclusively to his community.

Once I got Lindsay's okay and the support of the members of the Congreso de Pueblos, I began preparations for that weekend. My coworkers in the Congreso worked hard, as they always did, but I think this time they did so with even more pride and dedication. I called my friends in show business to put a show together, and I found two musical groups and a group of Puerto Rican *trovadores*. Several bodega owners in El Barrio who were personal friends of mine donated the ingredients for *frituras, pastelillos, bacalaítos,* and other Puerto Rican "goodies." Newspapers gave the event a lot of publicity.

Astute politician that he was, Lindsay didn't want anybody to get the idea that they could actually replace him as mayor. So from the beginning he declared that the "mayor for a weekend" couldn't sit in the mayor's chair on the first floor. We were assigned an office in the basement. Not that I cared.

To give the event a little more solemnity, I invited the mayor of Lares, Antonio Oliver, who had been a respected friend of mine for many years, to come in from Puerto Rico, and I was delighted that he accepted my invitation. He arrived on Thursday, August 5, and we went to JFK Airport to welcome him in a moving ceremony.

That Friday we celebrated Puerto Rico Day in City Hall. It was quite an event! Doña Carmen, my secretary for seventeen years, organized everything. I was the host. At six in the evening, City Hall came alive with Puerto Rican music and food. People ate and danced until almost dawn. I saw faces that night that I had never seen before. It looked like the whole Hispanic community in New York City had turned out. And although they were decidedly in the minority, many American friends came, too.

My friends on the Lower East Side told me that the smell of frying bacalaítos and coffee inundated the whole neighborhood. And everything was free of charge. It was a tremendous fiesta. We had a really enjoyable night, filled with celebration. The Spanish-language press gave it full coverage, and Spanish-language television and radio were also there to report.

Our visits to the jails began on Saturday and continued through Sunday. I had invited the chaplains to go with me. Two accepted my invitation; the others said they were not available. Ninety-five percent of the population of the city's penal institutions were young men, mostly blacks and Puerto Ricans. Racism was rampant; the administrators and guards of most of the jails were lily-white.

I went first to the jail in the Bronx; my chaplain friend, who visited that institution often, went with me. The warden knew we were coming, and he was waiting for us. First we held a religious ceremony, and then we met with some of the inmates. My visit had been announced, and they had asked to see me. We met with a group of spokesmen for the inmates—all this, of course, under the conditions established by penal regulations. We heard the prisoners' complaints about the jail's terrible conditions, and they spoke harshly against the justice system. As a result of this meeting, we organized a committee of inmates that would meet whenever necessary with the jail authorities, with the chaplain as an invited guest. We agreed that the chaplain would make a report on the meetings and would get in contact with me whenever he thought my intervention was needed in some issue. That meeting gave us the chance to develop the dynamic that we used in our other visits—we followed the same pattern in the Tombs, Rikers, and the Brooklyn jail. We arrived at the Brooklyn institution a little late but the warden was very understanding and allowed us to meet in the chapel with some of the inmates.

In all the jails, the complaints were the same: The inmates complained of bad food, the filth they were forced to live in, and the pathological aggressiveness of the jailers with their night sticks and pistols. But the biggest complaint the population in general voiced had to do with the unsatisfactory defense provided by their court-appointed attorneys. These lawyers would often convince their clients to plead guilty in order to get a shorter sentence, but they were almost always surprised to be handed long jail terms. Naturally, they felt betrayed. Those most affected by this practice were the Puerto Ricans, most of whom hardly spoke any English.

In personal terms, my visits to the New York City penal institutions only reaffirmed my conviction that prison in the capitalist system is not there to rehabilitate anyone. Prisons are seen as a place to park undesirables and misfits, something like a Nazi concentration camp or an Indian reservation. If the money invested every year in maintaining these inhumane institutions were used to develop a decent educational system that helped human beings adapt themselves to the needs of society, it would be another story. But unfortunately, that's not the way it is, and we continue to waste a fortune on these institutions from which most of those eventually freed are graduates of the school of crime.

Like the rest of Lindsay's aides who took part in this program, I had to prepare a report on our activities. I think my report was the one that made the greatest impact on Mayor Lindsay. He expressed his admiration for the agreements we had reached with the inmates and jail authorities, especially with regard to the role the chaplains would play as witnesses and intermediaries in conflict resolution.

35.
A SHORT BUT FIERY VISIT
TO THE WINDY CITY

In 1964, in many urban black and Puerto Rican neighborhoods wracked by poverty and desperation, certain people, reacting viscerally to the police brutality against their people, began to destroy and vandalize the businesses in their neighborhoods. That year there was a violent riot in Harlem that spread into El Barrio. The next year, the black community in Watts, in Los Angeles, rioted for several days. In the summer of 1966 the unrest spread to the Puerto Rican community in Chicago.

The immigration of Puerto Rican workers that initially concentrated in the Northeast soon spread to the industrial area of the Midwest, and especially Chicago. There, the Puerto Rican community grew quickly during the 1950s. By the mid-sixties, the largest Puerto Rican neighborhood in Chicago was on the northwest side of the city, around Division Street, an area of the city abandoned by the city authorities where poverty and hopelessness were the order of the day. As in New York and New Jersey, prejudice and racism against Puerto Ricans went hand-in-hand with police brutality. As in New York City, the Chicago Police Department was lily white and the height requirement excluded Puerto Ricans from the department. Unlike in New York City, however, the police department was controlled by the Poles, who were on average even taller than the Irish.

In Chicago, the situation for Puerto Ricans was worse than in New York City, since there was also a Mexican community in the city made up in part of undocumented workers and the police would detain anyone that looked Mexican to them and ask for papers. Obviously, many Puerto Ricans were among those detained in that way. Police harassment against our community was constant.

That summer—on June 12, 1966, to be exact—the first Puerto Rican Day Parade was held in Chicago. During the event, a fight broke out among some young Puerto Rican men. The police stepped in, and a white officer shot and wounded one of the youngsters.

At that, all the accumulated frustration in the community erupted. Puerto Ricans living along Division Street were furious, and the destruction began.

Somebody threw the first rock at a supermarket window, and from that point on, the disturbances went on for two days. There was not a business whose windows were intact, and fires began to be set. Firefighters arrived to try to put out the flames, but it was hard, since many of their hoses were punctured or cut through by the demonstrators. Hundreds of police officers surrounded the area and entered the community with dogs they would turn loose on anyone in their path. This, obviously, inflamed spirits even further. At that moment, people lost their fear of the police; they confronted them with anything they could get their hands on, and several patrol cars were burned.

When the disturbances started, a group of Puerto Rican religious leaders sent a message to us asking for our help. At that moment we were working night and day on implementing the Puerto Rican Community Development Project, which was chaired by the Reverend Rubén Darío Colón, an Episcopal minister active in the civil rights movement in our community. I was vice chairman, while Manny Díaz, another community leader who did a great deal for our community, was the executive director.

As soon as we received the message, Rubén, Manny, and I decided to go to Chicago at once. As we were about to leave, we received another communication. It seems that someone had told the city authorities that our group was going to Chicago to support the Puerto Rican community, and the mayor, a racist Irishman named Richard Daley, had ordered that we be arrested as soon as we set foot in the city. Given that situation, we decided that each of us would go separately. To avoid being recognized, Díaz and I disguised ourselves as priests, with a Bible and everything. When we arrived we were taken directly to the home of Claudio Flores, who I believe was the publisher of El Puertorriqueño, a community newspaper. There, we met with several religious leaders. We discussed the situation and decided that the community had to be informed of the implications of what was happening: those most affected by the destruction and vandalism were we ourselves, who worked in those businesses and bought the products they sold.

As a means of calming tempers, we decided to hold a mass meeting in Humboldt Park. We persuaded a number of singers and musicians, craftspeople, and soft drink and food vendors to entertain the crowd and set up booths for food and refreshments. We took to the streets and in our most priestly voices, always invoking the Lord, we mobilized a good-sized group for our assembly in the park. Other people joined us, little by little. Once assembled, we held an improvised "town meeting." One group wanted to get back to the streets to "finish off those sons of bitches." Most people, however, listened intelligently, and the Chicago leadership was outstanding that day. A committee was created that met with the mayor, who agreed to make a series of concessions to the Puerto Rican community. Once we had made our small contribution, Darío, Díaz, and I returned to New York City the next day to our own projects.

Almost no one ever knew about our visit except the religious leaders, who were very appreciative. We went back to New York with no fanfare, but with a profound sense of having helped our Puerto Rican brothers and sisters in Chicago.

The riots on Division Street were the baptism of fire for the Puerto Rican community in Chicago. They immediately began creating and developing community organizations that fully acknowledged their nationality, and a militant cadre of leaders, respectful of our cause, began to be trained. Among these, we might mention José López, an educator and strong advocate of social justice. In part as a result of that process, a gang called the Young Lords transformed itself into a militant left-wing organization committed to its community. The Lords served as an example to many young Puerto Rican men in New York City, where the organization established a chapter. And from New York, in turn, several programs that we established in the city were taken back to Chicago, such as the educational program Aspira. It was a very fruitful exchange.

Today, the part of Division Street where the riots occurred is known as Paseo Boricua—Puerto Rican Way. As you enter that stretch of the avenue, you pass under a Puerto Rican flag made of steel 59 feet long; in the neighborhood there is a high school named for Pedro Albizu Campos and a cultural center named for Juan Antonio Corretjer.[19] Our culture, as I never tire of repeating, makes us strong.

36.
FROM THE FIRES OF CHICAGO TO THE FOLKLORE FESTIVAL IN NEW YORK

One of the things that most impressed us during our visit to Chicago was the tremendous willingness shown by the Puerto Rican community, when we called that meeting on Sunday, June 14, in Humboldt Park, to celebrate a day of much-needed rest, calm, and relaxation to find their center again through their culture.

As soon as we were back in New York, Rev. Darío, Manny Díaz, and I prepared a report for the board of the Puerto Rican Community Development Project on the events in Chicago and our part in the process. As a result of our evaluation of what had happened, and the part that the festival in Humboldt Park had played in forging Puerto Rican unity and soothing spirits, we suggested to the Project that we organize a grand Puerto Rican fiesta in Central Park. Conceived as a complement to the Puerto Rican Day Parade, this activity would be not just an instrument for promoting unity and pride in our community, but also educating the other residents of the city and state of New York about Puerto Ricans. It would be an exciting cultural activity open to everyone. The idea met with tremendous approval. Six months later, in January 1967, several members of the Congreso de Pueblos, among them my wife Francia Lubán, incorporated a new nonprofit corporation under the name "Puerto Rican Folklore Fiesta, Inc." Dámaso Emeric, president of the Vieques town-club, was elected president of the new organization.

Unlike what had happened a decade earlier when we created the Puerto Rican Day Parade, we easily got the city's permission to hold our activity. In fact, the authorities, including Mayor John Lindsay, were delighted with the idea. It was a novel idea, as no events of that kind were held in Central Park at the time; the park was used mainly for music events and theater. Of course, it's also true that the mayor knew he needed the Puerto Rican vote, which was traditionally Democratic, and that the Congreso de Pueblos was the only organization capable at the time of mobilizing the number of votes he needed.

During the next year and a half, we worked on the concept, brought other people into the project, and, finally, on the last Sunday of August in 1968, we held the first Folklore Fiesta in Central Park, Manhattan, in the area of the bandshell.

The event was a shining example of good organization and unified action. All the member-clubs of the Congreso de Pueblos, without exception, set up booths with decorations and their respective flags. It was like a mixture of patron saint's festival and picnic. There was food and more food, much prepared on the spot. Behind the booths, people would be roasting pigs on the spit, while in front there would be groups of musicians, including trovadores, to entertain the people. It was impressive to see how the people from each town patronized their particular booth.

The Miller Brewery, which was running a campaign at the time to win over the Puerto Rican market, sponsored us for several years by hiring well-known orchestras to give a show. The Fiesta continued to grow until it became, after the Parade, the second-largest event in support of Puerto Rican culture in New York City. Later, Johnny Torres, president of La Metro, the first Puerto Rican business cooperative in New York, saw the value of this activity and offered us his financial support.

Originally, the Folklore Fiesta offices were located at 173 E. 116th St. in the heart of El Barrio. They provided services to all organizations that came to them seeking help for holding cultural events. They were also the site of many celebrations of Mother's Day, Father's Day, and private birthdays.

The Folklore Fiesta's leadership included many women; a woman was almost always president. I can say without fear of contradiction that it was a wonderful experience that helped Puerto Ricans in New York City to cultivate and reaffirm their culture and to struggle, as a people, for their rights.

Among the people taking part in the New York Folklore Fiesta was doña Rafaela Balladares, who, like I, had been a union organizer and community activist. It was doña Rafaela who, after retiring and returning to Puerto Rico, organized the famous Fiestas de San Sebastián in Old San Juan.

As happens with many organizations, in time the Fiesta's founders retired, while internal jealousies and backbiting tended to weaken it and drain its energy. Two years ago, the New York City Parks Foundation, which administers Central Park, revoked our permit to hold the Fiesta there because it "bothered" the white folks who lived around the area. They gave the date on which the event was traditionally held to another organization, one willing to pay more for use of the space.

37.
THE PUERTO RICAN COMMUNITY
DEVELOPMENT PROJECT (PRCDP)

By the early sixties, the civil rights movement had grown tremendously. Across the United States, with the blacks leading the way, other minority groups, especially Puerto Ricans and Mexican-Americans, organized our respective communities to demand—it was no longer a question of requesting—that racism· and poverty, the fundamental problems facing us, be dealt with. The writing was on the wall that if the authorities did not take action, the nation was going to explode into a thousand pieces. President John F. Kennedy's attempts to deal with the problems were interrupted by an assassin's bullet in November 1963. His successor, vice president Lyndon B. Johnson, followed in his footsteps and, once he became president, officially launched what came to be known as the War on Poverty. This was 1964.

Since 1963, the federal government had been assigning funds to community projects aimed at helping the black neighborhoods in New York City. We Puerto Ricans were overlooked, supposedly because we did not suffer as much segregation and discrimination as the blacks.

At that time there were, in addition to the Congreso de Pueblos, other Puerto Rican organizations trying to improve our community's conditions. One of these was the Puerto Rican Forum. Under the leadership of Antonia "Tony" Pantoja,[20] the Forum was an organization composed mainly of professionals, most of them born and raised in New York City, that sought to develop leadership within the community itself, independent of the Puerto Rican government's Migration Office, which kept insisting on directing the affairs of Puerto Ricans in the diaspora. It goes without saying that I agreed entirely with the Forum's view of things, so I became friends with Tony Pantoja.

In 1965, Tony proposed a new program—the Puerto Rican Community Development Project (PRCDP)—which would contract existing community organizations, including the town-clubs, to provide services to their respective communities; she promised that each of them would be autonomous. A board of directors was created and an executive committee was named. The board was made up of representatives from over seventy community organizations, many of them town-clubs. The executive committee was composed of, among others,

Tony, María Josefa Canino, Dr. Francisco Trillas, Joseph Erazo, Max Sagonet, Monserrate Flores, and me.

We presented the project to the city, and finally, after many months of lobbying, meetings, and demonstrations, funds were approved. Of course, as often happens, no sooner had the funds been assigned than a tug-of-war ensued for control of the organization. The group led by Tony wanted the PRCDP team to be controlled and managed by her professional people. The Forum did not see the importance of recognizing the people's inborn leadership. In addition, Tony's group stressed channeling the funds to small businesses and professionals. It was a good idea, but the problem lay in the fact that our community was organized in a different way. I, in turn, insisted that the project be a community-action enterprise, aimed at offering services to our people, and that community-based organizations should have control of the Project.

The Forum eventually backed out of the Project. Community leaders, the majority of whom were members of the Congreso de Pueblos, comprised the executive committee. Rev. Rubén Darío Colón was elected president; I was vice president. In June 1967, we opened our offices at 1502 Lexington Avenue. We also invited two well-known Democratic leaders in the reform wing of the party to join the new board; these were attorneys Herman Badillo and Joseph Erazo, who had an excellent relationship with the Congreso de Pueblos. At that moment Ramón Vélez also joined the Project. Ramón was a social worker who had arrived in the city not long before, and who quickly began to establish a base of support in the South Bronx.

We recruited Manny Díaz, who was an excellent administrator and a person committed to the community, to be the PRCDP's director. Manny was a community activist who had helped me organize the Puerto Rican contingent that took part in the March on Washington in 1963 and then worked with me on several matters related to education. With Manny, the project took off. He surrounded himself with a group of serious, committed professional people and developed new proposals that brought in more funds. Unfortunately, Manny resigned in late 1966 to take over the regional office of the federal Equal Employment Opportunity Commission, the EEOC.

New tensions emerged in the PRCDP. The group led by Ramón Vélez seized control. Ramón, who was very astute, had allied himself with the Democratic machine to undermine my influence in the community. He was seeking to turn the PRCDP into an organization that generated jobs in the community, despite the vision that had inspired our urbanization. Later, Ramón realized his mistake.

A war also broke out between the blacks and Puerto Ricans in the city over the funds from the War on Poverty. In 1968, Mayor John Lindsay named Major Owens, a black leader, who turned out to be an Uncle Tom, to the position of Commissioner of the Community Development Agency in New York. Owens, who clearly favored his own people, soon cut the PRCDP's budget. Despite our internal divisions, the PRCDP organized a demonstration in front of the Community Development Agency. I led it, and it got results. Over a thousand Puerto Ricans, many with our trademark wide-brimmed straw hats, the *pava*, lay down in the street at Broadway and Canal and stopped traffic. We refused to meet with Owens, demanding to negotiate directly with Mayor Lindsay, who was forced to restore our budget. For our part, we found additional funding for other programs.

Unfortunately, the internal struggles in the PRCDP continued. Many of the organizers had now stopped working as community activists. Nepotism and political favoritism became inevitable parts of the decision-making process, and accusations emerged that several of the organizations that made up the Project were diverting funds. On a number of occasions we tried to straighten out things that had been messed up by Ramón. Finally, the situation exploded. In the spring of 1978, the newly elected mayor, Edward Koch, the most racist mayor in New York City history, took advantage of the situation to try to destroy the Project.

Aware of Koch's maneuvers, in May 1978 a group of us decided to act. The group was made up of some of the project's coordinators and organizers and several presidents of town-clubs. We unanimously agreed to enter the Project's offices and shut them down. We occupied the headquarters for several days. Once again, we denounced the project's poor administration and its leaders, who had control of the board, although they had resigned a year earlier in order to try to avoid the storm that was approaching. We also demanded that the board be reorganized. Koch, however, was adamant. Herman Badillo, in turn, who had been Koch's opponent in the election, surprisingly accepted a post in the new mayor's administration. In his eagerness to undermine Vélez, his longtime enemy, Badillo only timidly expressed his disagreement, while the racist we had as mayor spoke loud and long against the Project.

During the summer of that year, Koch persuaded the city's budget board to vote, 20 to 2, to cut the project's funds. Councilman Olmedo and I, the only two Puerto Ricans on the board, insisted constantly that the right thing to do was restructure the Project. Koch gave the Project's funds to a black organization in

Brooklyn. Early the next year, the PRCDP closed up shop. It was a sad moment for our community.

The importance of the PRCDP was enormous. With almost a hundred town-organizations, each one with an organizer, a secretary, and the necessary staffing, we could hold many activities and offer many very necessary services within our neighborhoods. Infighting, meddling by politicians, and the siphoning-off of money finally brought down one of the best projects that had ever been developed in our community.

38.
THE "WEDNESDAY CLUB"

In 1965, in response to demands from the civil rights movement, the federal government created the Equal Employment Opportunity Commission. Under the increasing oversight by that agency and constant monitoring and pressure from our base organizations, it seemed that public agencies, private industry, and non-profit organizations were beginning to show greater diligence in recruiting our people, and jobs began appearing for professionals, skilled laborers, accountants, administrators, social workers, teachers, counselors, and various kinds of supervisors in addition to the positions for unskilled, semi-skilled, and skilled day-laborers that we had had before.

One of the functions of the Puerto Rican Community Development Project was helping to train white-collar workers and then recommending them for jobs within our communities. One of the problems we had been facing for some time was how to give continuity to the struggle to empower our people. The fact was that as the years went by a new generation of young people had emerged. These young men and women were the children of those who had come to New York during the great migration of the forties and fifties, and they found themselves in an uneasy position because they weren't sure which of the two cultures they belonged to. Some of them didn't know Spanish, which was fundamental for working with many of the new immigrants. Others were interested only in being able to get out of the community and live the American dream.

At that moment we had already begun to see that the Congreso de Pueblos, which had played such an important role in our community and was still providing many services, was slowly losing relevance, since those young people for whose future we were struggling were not identifying with the organization, which by its nature continued to be an institution of immigrants.

In conversations I had with Frank Espada and Jack Agüeros at one of the PRCDP meetings, we decided to create a group that we called the "Wednesday Club." It was, as Jack once noted, a kind of informal think tank. We made a list of young Puerto Ricans who had been born or raised in our neighborhoods and had the potential to become leaders. The idea was to develop in them, and through them, a sense of cultural identity, and also to give them training in "underground" techniques, including how to organize demonstrations and other militancy activities and how to formulate political strategies; in basic ideas as to parliamentary procedure; and in general leadership. The main focus of the cultural program would be to teach what it meant to be Puerto Rican in the United States, especially for that generation that had never set foot on the island. It would also include sessions on Puerto Rican history and culture, discrimination, race, identity, self-respect, morality, and dignity. The group would discuss our community's problems, but also problems of the black community and other ethnic groups. Each week the group would select someone to lead the debate for the next Wednesday.

In total, some forty young people took part in the program. Almost all of them had graduated from college or were about to. Several of them were about to begin their doctoral dissertations. Although we tried to make sure there was a strong presence of women in the group, we could only recruit five females. During the time the program lasted, about two years, the group met every Wednesday (which explains the name) at 10 pm. Our meeting places changed each week. We were very disciplined. Everyone had to arrive on time; if you arrived even a minute late you couldn't take part in the discussion that was going on. From time to time the possibility of admitting one or another new member was discussed, and we would take a vote on the matter. If there was opposition, even from a single person, the candidate was not accepted. Almost every member of the group lasted throughout the program, and in the base organizations people knew and talked about the group's existence.

The Wednesday Club was a success. Many young people born in New York City to Puerto Rican parents began to learn Spanish, to identify with their community's problems, to organize and lead protest actions, and to inculcate a sense of "Puerto Rican-ness" in others. Many directors of programs who worked in the community, and several New York City elected officials, came out of our Wednesday Club.

39.
MY RADIO PROGRAMS
IN NEW YORK CITY

In the early sixties, our community was growing at a very rapid pace. However, there was a lack of mass media—newspapers, radio and TV stations—to keep the community informed. The commercial newspapers we had were *El Diario de Nueva York* and *La Prensa*, which merged in 1963 to create *El Diario-La Prensa*. For a short time there was another newspaper, *El Tiempo*; I wrote a weekly satirical political column for this paper that I titled *"Por dentro y por fuera,"* Inside and Outside. As for television, it wasn't until the mid-sixties that Channel 47, a multilingual channel founded in 1960, began to offer programming mainly in Spanish. There was Channel 41, which began in 1968 with bilingual programming, but it wasn't until 1970 that it began to broadcast all its programs in Spanish. Unfortunately, the programs were not very good in either language.

In radio, the change came much earlier. Since 1947, radio station WHOM, whose studios were on 52nd St. on the West Side, had been offering an occasional program in Spanish. As the Puerto Rican community grew, WHOM's Spanish-language programming expanded, until in 1960 all its regularly scheduled weekly programs were in Spanish.

In the late sixties, the manager of WHOM, Ralph Constantino, asked if I would meet with him. As was my custom, I went with a group of colleagues from the Congreso. He had called us in to tell us that the station was willing to give us an hour in prime time, and that they'd already spoken to the makers of Wonder Bread, who were interested in entering the Puerto Rican market, about sponsoring the program. Naturally, we accepted the offer. The Board of Directors of the Congreso agreed that I would be the host.

We decided to do a program offering information on Puerto Rico and we called it *Conociendo a Puerto Rico para quererlo más*, "Getting to Know Puerto Rico to Love It More." It was broadcast every Thursday from 6 to 7 pm. Since I was president of the Congreso and had many contacts with the base organizations, it was easy for me to program it. It was mainly a historical and cultural program.

The show always opened with the song "No des tu tierra al extraño" ("Don't Give Your Land to a Stranger") performed by Davilita and the Sexteto

Borinquen. We would have guests from each town on the island. We started with Arecibo and ended with Yauco, right through the alphabet. Wonder Bread was our sponsor for a year and a half. After that, we didn't have a sponsor. In time, we changed the program's name and focus. We called the revamped program *Lucha*, "Struggle." We played protest music from Central and South America and the Caribbean, and especially from Puerto Rico. Like the earlier program, this one was a hit, so much so that in El Barrio some of the businesses would put speakers out on the street so people could listen to the program.

In 1975, the owner of WHOM sold the station to the San Juan Racing Association. The new management changed the name to Radio WJIT and turned it into a commercial music station. Overnight, and with absolutely no notice, they moved Lucha to 3 am Sunday night-to-Monday morning. We quickly responded to that low blow.

As was our habit in these situations, we formulated a plan of action. We requested a meeting with the new management. When we arrived at the station we found that the management had sent in a "spokesman" who had absolutely no power. There were about fifty of us, so we occupied the offices and studios and refused to leave until the real management met with us. Someone called the general manager and explained the situation. Meanwhile, our supporters continue to arrive, and we paralyzed the elevators to the third floor. When the station manager finally arrived, he found a demonstration of about a hundred people. In case our negotiations failed, everyone had been given their assignments. When the general manager and the president of the company that owned the station saw so many Puerto Ricans so angry, they got very upset. The president of the company said he wouldn't meet with such a big group and he asked us to appoint a committee. We rejected that idea, so he had no alternative but to meet with us all. I was the spokesman.

We explained that the decision to move our program, which had tremendous support in the community, to 3 am on Monday morning was an error, and more than that, an insult, and we told him we weren't leaving the station until he moved the program to a time when it might actually find an audience—and an audience might find *it*. After discussing the matter, we reached an agreement. The program remained at its original hour on Thursday evening, but we changed its name to *Controversia*. In addition, it would now be a program in which the problems affecting our community would be debated and brought to the public's attention. We also agreed that I would remain as moderator. Management tried to impose a sponsor on us, but we were opposed.

The new program was a complete success. Many people came in to debate or be interviewed. I prepared myself well for the interviews and debates and had help from many comrades in doing the research that needed to be done. Management behaved very well toward us. All the station's announcers were very cooperative. We received a great deal of correspondence congratulating us on the program. Finally, in 1977, I left the program in order to run for city councilman for the South Bronx.

40.
"SAUL'S LADIES"

One of the most valuable lessons I learned from my mother was that women must be respected. I might be accused of many things, but never of being *machista*. Experience always showed me that aside from the biological differences, men and women are fundamentally the same, with all the virtues and defects that human beings are born with.

Both before and after the founding of the Congreso de Pueblos, and both inside and out, women played a central role in the struggle to empower our communities in New York City. Among the women best known for their leadership were Antonia Denis, Mercedes Arroyo, Evelina López Antonetty, Antonia "Tony" Pantoja, Irma Vidal Santaella, Miriam Colón, and Carmen Colón. As in every political situation, I had some differences with them, occasionally profound differences, about tactical, strategic, organizational, and ideological issues, but I've always felt profound admiration and great respect for them.

There were many others, less well known, whose names have not entered the history books, who also made great efforts and dedicated a great deal of time to improving our community's conditions. Many of the town-clubs were presided over by women, and in the founding and day-to-day administration of the Congreso de Pueblos some were absolutely essential. I am thinking, for example, about Francia Lubán, my second wife and comrade in the struggle for many years, and Carmen Colón, the Congreso's secretary and organizer since its founding, and, to boot, the aunt of Sila Tirado Colón, my present wife.

One of the Congreso's standing committees was the Comité de Damas, the Lady's Committee. The women who belonged to it were in a certain sense the backbone of the organization. Many of them, in their positions as organizers and secretaries, fulfilled an important role in publicizing and coordinating activities, and they were very active.

In 1965, while we were holding an event, Carmen Colón approached me to tell me that a man named "Sal" wanted to speak to me. She'd misunderstood his name, as I saw when she handed me his business card, which read "Saul Alinsky."

Saul was a kind of living legend in the non-Communist left in the United States. Of Jewish origin, he had begun as a union organizer in the 1930s. Later, he organized poor communities throughout the United States: in the urban centers of Detroit and Chicago, where he worked with our Puerto Rican brothers and sisters, in Mexican neighborhoods and black ghettos in Southern California, and so on. In the 1960s, he concentrated his attention on New York City. He had heard about the Congreso de Pueblos and wanted to offer his services.

As we spoke, Saul told me he wanted to support the Congreso's efforts. I asked him what he had in mind. He suggested developing a program to train a group of women as community organizers and activists, including offering workshops in self-defense. He thought that with this program and the workshops, women would be less fearful.

In those days, as I mentioned earlier, I had a good relationship with the management of Camp Felicia in Westchester County, and they agreed to let us use the camp several weekends for this program. With the help of Carmen Colón and other female leaders of the Congreso, we enrolled thirty women. For four weekends, the group took part in intense training that included watching films and discussing organizational strategies developed by Saul in his famous manual *Rules for Radicals*. There were also classes in karate and self-defense, taught by one of Alinsky's assistants.

When they graduated, these women were ready to take on anybody. Over the next few years this group of women, all of whom were members of the Ladies Committee, was always present at our activities. If somebody had to confront a policeman and give him a slap in the face, or lie on the ground to stop traffic, these women would do it without a second thought. They attended many activities very well dressed, with their chignons and nice hats held in place by long hatpins that they would use, if necessary, to prick the mounted police officers' horses when the riders used them to push us up against walls or prevent us from moving forward, or if they tried to make the horses rear up and threaten us with their hooves.

My relationship with Saul was one that I felt truly enriched me, and I often put into practice the many things I learned from him. I should mention that Saul volunteered to implement a similar program for a group of men. Both the women who had graduated from the program, and I tried to convince some of the men to enroll in it, but it was tough. Puerto Rican men tend to be *machista*. Many of them scoffed at the idea; they said they weren't afraid of anything, that karate and self-defense classes were for women, and they could duke it out with anybody. They missed a tremendous opportunity. What they did quickly learn was that you had to watch out for those "ladies"—everyone had a healthy respect for them.

41.
MARCHING AGAINST FEAR
IN THE SOUTH

If the way Puerto Ricans were treated at the voting booth in New York was discriminatory, the blacks in the South faced a much worse situation; what we suffered in New York State with the literacy test was a cakewalk in comparison with what blacks had to deal with in the South. As in New York, in the South the lack of knowledge of the written language was used to disqualify many potential voters. In the South, registration officials, who were usually white, required potential voters to read and interpret parts of the state constitution. But it didn't end there. If a black voter somehow managed to pass the exam, he or she then would have to pay what was called a "poll tax." Unemployed or underemployed, living in extreme poverty, many black people and poor whites in the South simply couldn't pay the poll tax. Those who tried to change the law became the object of harsh repression by white paramilitary organizations like the Ku Klux Klan. Some were lynched, others tarred and feathered or burned alive, while others were crippled or otherwise maimed for life by the beatings they underwent. The local and state police—those so-called "agencies of law and order"—as often as not took part themselves in these barbaric acts, or in the best of cases looked away. In this way, racist whites perpetuated their political control in the South.

As part of the movement against racial discrimination and segregation, the black community, led by the Reverend Martin Luther King, carried out a campaign against literacy tests and the poll tax. In 1965, these efforts by blacks, joined by Puerto Ricans, led Congress, against the staunch opposition of Southern congressmen, to pass the historic Voting Rights Act. This legislation did not just declare illegal those practices that prevented minorities from voting; it also gave the federal government the power to register voters when the state failed to meet its responsibility in this regard. This did not, however, create an immediate change in the real situation for blacks in the South.

In June 1966, to promote black voter registration across the South, James Meredith began a one-man march from Memphis, Tennessee, to

Jackson, Mississippi. He called it the "March against Fear." At that moment, Meredith became a hero in the black community. In the early sixties, with the support of the National Association for the Advancement of Colored People (NAACP), Meredith had won a legal battle to allow him to register at the University of Mississippi, which until then had been only for white folks.

The day after beginning his March, Meredith was wounded by a sniper.[21] When they learned what had happened, several of the major black civil rights leaders, including Martin Luther King of the Southern Christian Leadership Conference and Stokely Carmichael of the Student Nonviolent Coordinating Committee, decided to continue the march in solidarity with Meredith and they invited all lovers of peace to join them.

The black leadership in New York City, specifically Milton Galamison, invited us to take part in the activity. In mid-June a group of almost thirty Puerto Rican activists, tested by struggle, left New York. We joined a contingent made up of members of unions and civil rights organizations in Alabama, near the Mississippi border. From there we set out for Sunflower County, where we joined the march. When we arrived, we were told that the Deacons for the Defense of Justice, a black paramilitary organization created to defend voter-registration officials in Louisiana, would be accompanying us on the rest of the march.

We marched for four days and nights. The heat was terrible. We stopped in several little towns along the way. While we were marching, volunteers would mobilize in the towns near our route to register voters, and in many of these towns, the black community would have food, soft drinks, water, and some entertainment for us. I remember one town, called Yalobusha, where we were joined by many young Negro men and women. I, who had been born and raised in poverty, had never in my life seen so much desolation and misery: people with no shoes and children with bellies bloated by parasites. The most inhumane aspect of this situation became clear to me when all along the route I saw enormous stretches of well-tended land under cultivation. Who were the owners of this land? Rich white men.

Along the way I met several young blacks who eventually became national political leaders, including Stokely Carmichael.[22] It was during this march that Carmichael, in a historic speech in Greenwood, made his now-famous call for "Black Power," thus beginning a new era in the black struggle for freedom. Carmichael put me in contact with leaders of a black self-defense group in Alabama called the Lowndes County Freedom Organization/Black

Panthers Party, out of which arose the inspiration for the creation of the Black Panther Party in October of that same year in California. I recalled that in my conversation with them, they offered me their support in creating a similar group in New York. The young men were very well intentioned, but they knew almost nothing about the Puerto Rican situation.

Southern white racists who were in power referred to poor whites as "white trash." A poor Puerto Rican living in the ghetto would be called "Puerto Rican trash." If the Puerto Rican were black-skinned, he would be called a "Rican nigger" or "nigger-Rican." Regardless of the color of a Puerto Rican's skin—white, black, or brown—to a white man, they were all the same. And if it was a Puerto Rican protesting, the whites would treat him the same as a black man.

In the towns where groups of people gathered to watch the march, we often encountered provocation from resentful whites. On one occasion when I was at the head of the march, one of these whites shouted at me mockingly, "Hey boy, what's that flag you got on your funny hat?" The "funny hat" that he was talking about was the *pava* I was wearing to protect me from the sun—a broad-brimmed woven straw hat worn by the Puerto Rican *campesino* and iconic of Puerto Rican identity. In open violation of the directives we had been given not to allow ourselves to be provoked and not to respond to insults, I shouted back angrily, "This is the Puerto Rican flag," to which he shot back, "Same shit." I had to make a superhuman effort to restrain myself, but I realized that I'd been provoked and that I could not respond any further. Later, a comrade from the Black Panthers told me that that guy was one of the leaders of the Ku Klux Klan in Tuscaloosa County, Alabama.

When the march was over, our comrades in charge of the organization gave us transportation back to New York City. We traveled in an enormous bus. The black leadership in New York thanked us for our participation, and Rev. Galamison publicly recognized our contribution in that historic march.

42.
MARCHING WITH THE POOR
IN WASHINGTON, D.C.

I don't recall the exact date, but I think it was in early March 1968 that I received an invitation from the Rev. Martin Luther King to attend a meeting in Atlanta, Georgia. The meeting's purpose, I was given to understand, was to create a broad movement that would include all the minority groups in the United States—blacks, Mexican-Americans, American Indians, Puerto Ricans, and poor whites—and would demand that the U.S. Congress pass a bill of economic rights, among which would be the right to full employment, decent housing, and a guaranteed annual income.

My relationship with Dr. King dated from early in that decade, when the Congreso de Pueblos had coordinated a contingent of Puerto Ricans from the East Coast to take part in the 1963 March on Washington. Now, five years after his famous "I Have a Dream" speech, Dr. King had become more radicalized, and his perspective had broadened. He wanted to join together all the struggles, such as the opposition to the Vietnam War, not just those related to the "Negro problem." He was seeking to create a multiracial and multiethnic coalition that would go straight to the root of the problem: the unequal distribution of wealth.

On March 14, several dozen leaders of different races and ethnic groups met for twelve hours in a motel in Atlanta. Representing the Puerto Rican community were several community activists who had worked in the civil rights movement in New York, including Grace Mora, José Ortiz, Mario Abreu, Rosalina Reilova, Ted Vélez, and me. In the meeting, I explained the situation of Puerto Ricans in the United States and stressed the need for dealing with our particular and rather unique problems. I listened to Dr. King's proposal to organize a "poor man's march" on Washington. The project would include setting up a camp, which would be called Resurrection City, in front of the Lincoln Memorial. The idea was to pressure Congress to pass a bill of economic rights. I agreed with the concept and joined the march's organizing committee. I pledged to take between fifty and a hundred buses full of marchers. Dr. King put me in charge of organizing the Puerto Rican contingent in the Northeast: New York, Connecticut, Pennsylvania, and Massachusetts.

I returned to New York and threw myself into the job. Barely three weeks after my return, the terrible event we are all familiar with occurred: On April 4, Dr. Martin Luther King was assassinated in Memphis, Tennessee, by a white racist. Despite the grief caused by the loss of this great leader, we decided to continue with our plans. The Reverend Ralph Abernathy, who replaced King as president of the Southern Christian Leadership Conference, took on the leadership of our march.

The activities that would take place in Washington, D.C., would run from May through June. For us, the Puerto Ricans of New York City, those were not the best dates, since the Puerto Rican Day Parade had been scheduled for June 2 and in May there was an incredible amount of organizing work to be done for it. In addition, there were very thorny problems to be overcome. In the black community as well as the Puerto Rican community, those who saw things from an "exclusivist" point of view were not particularly happy with this multi-sector project. In fact, as I mentioned earlier, my policy of working with the black community was one of the reasons that two years earlier people had tried to remove me as president of the Parade. But the same thing was going on in the black community. Among the leadership in charge of mobilizing their people, there were still—now perhaps even stronger— differences of opinion as to how to deal with the matter of Puerto Ricans in the city. While Galamison continued to see us as equal partners in the struggle, Rustin and his group, who were in the majority, wanted to keep us at arm's length, as minority partners. Another issue that created problems for the organization was that from the point of view of the black leadership, some of our demands, such as the question of the political status of Puerto Rico and bilingual education, were too narrow. To this, if you added the struggle that had started in New York City between Puerto Ricans and blacks for access to federal War on Poverty funds, the idea of "everyone pulling together" seemed a little over-optimistic.

In that context, then, the Congreso de Pueblos decided to go on with the project, while insisting upon our particular needs and problems. The activity gave us the opportunity to take our demands directly to Washington and to present our cause to the rest of the nation and the world. On May 27, 1968, in Central Park, we held a massive activity to mobilize people for the march. At this event, we declared our solidarity with all the poor people of the nation.

43.
OPERATION *JIMMY SHINE*

In mid-November of 1968, around 11:30 at night, Carmen Ventura called me at home to tell me that they had caught two more mice. I was delighted, but I insisted the mice couldn't be too big, because the big ones have a very well-developed sense of direction. We needed little ones, since the little ones run like crazy in every direction. I also told her she should feed them corn. Oh, and keep them in the bathtub for the moment. To keep them from escaping, I told her, she should rub cooking oil on the sides of the tub, although sooner or later, she'd have to find a cage for them.

Not long before this, I had gotten a call from Rosa Centeno to tell me that she had caught two, but they were too big. Now, with Carmen's two mice we had the six we needed for the operation we were planning. I was relieved because this assignment was a little behind schedule—the darned mice would come into apartments sometimes but other times would make themselves scarce.

Catching mice was just one of the many things we were doing to prepare for the debut of the musical *Jimmy Shine*, directed by and starring Dustin Hoffman, who not long before had become a star in the movie *The Graduate* (1967). The musical would be opening in late November of 1968 in the Brooks Atkinson, a top-of-the-line theater located on 47th St. between Broadway and Seventh Avenue.

After several rounds of auditions, Carla Pinza, a young Puerto Rican actor in New York, was hired to play the role of a prostitute. Carla, who had worked in off-Broadway productions and as a supporting actress in one movie, was excited, since she was finally going to get to perform on Broadway. At that time, Broadway was a hostile world, as it still is, for many Puerto Rican actors. You had to be extraordinary, like Chita Rivera, Rita Moreno, Miriam Colón, or Raúl Juliá, to be able to work on Broadway, even as an extra.

It seemed, however, that Carla was expected to play the role of a prostitute both on and off the stage. One of the producers made a pass at her, and Carla rejected him. After several weeks of rehearsals, on September 24 she was told that she was fired, because she didn't "meet the requirements," and that she was being replaced by an actress of Greek origin. Carla took her case to Miriam Colón, one of the major promoters of Puerto Rican theater in New York. A year earlier Miriam had created a company called the Teatro Rodante

Puertorriqueño (Puerto Rican Traveling Theater), whose goal was to perform plays free of charge for poor Puerto Rican communities in the city. Miriam took Carla's complaint to the Congreso de Pueblos' board of directors. We interviewed the young actress, who explained in great detail what had happened. Naturally, we considered it an insult to our community.

The Congreso de Pueblos took on Carla's defense. We tried in several ways to persuade the directors to hear us out, but they held their ground. They argued that the writer had made changes to the script, that the role now was for a Greek prostitute, and that Carla was no longer suitable. We told them, at that, that we considered it a case of discrimination. Given the producers' attitude, we decided to mount a protest at the play's premiere. We agreed that that Thursday we would picket the Brooks Atkinson. To make our denunciation more dramatic, we decided to extend our protest into the theater.

In addition to the committee charged with catching mice, we had one to prepare eggs filled with paint and another to prepare stink bombs. The men responsible for the eggs were Roberto Napoleón and Marcelino Pagán, while Miguel Coss was in charge of the stink bombs. The group from the Bronx led by Carlos Bracero was given the task of making a casket. Miriam Colón was mobilizing her friends in show business and trying to get fifteen tickets, ten in the orchestra and five in the balcony. She was also in charge of the Public Relations Committee, which included newspaper reporters and television and radio announcers, plus representatives from other organizations that had joined our crusade, such as the Puerto Rican Day Parade, the Folklore Fiesta, and several unions and churches. We would have a car with loudspeakers out front playing Puerto Rican music, plus a group that would explain the purpose of our activity to passers-by.

Carmen Colón was in charge of mobilizing members of the Congreso de Pueblos. Each town-club had to ensure that ten of its members showed up at the protest. Jorge Vargas, a graphic artist who worked in the Office of the Government of Puerto Rico in New York, volunteered to get paper and make ten thousand flyers, plus the posters and signs that we would need. Efraín Rosa was in charge of putting up the posters and pasting up bills.

Since it was "as cold as a witch's tit" that winter, we also had a hot-coffee brigade. *Bodegas* in El Barrio donated coffee, milk, sugar, and paper cups. The kids from City College promised to bring two megaphones, while a friend of ours from Long Island would bring firecrackers. We also appointed a committee to get all the necessary permits, plus to deal with the security, since there were often *provocateurs* sent in by the police to create situations that would make us look bad and justify using force against us.

We met four or five times to plan the activity. The last meeting took place on 45th St. between Eighth and Ninth Avenue in the Commonwealth offices. Everybody, but everybody, came. As always, José Monserrat[23] was like our own four-star general, taking charge of everything we could ask of him. The list of organizations that joined our cause was impressive. In addition to the Congreso and the Teatro Rodante, there were the Puerto Rican Day Parade, the Puerto Rican Folklore Fiesta, the National Puerto Rican Association of Civil Rights, the Brooklyn Businessmen's Association, several unions, including District 65, and several churches.

When we went to request a permit for our picket, the police wouldn't allow us to have it on the sidewalk in front of the theater; it had to be on the other side of the street. We didn't object too much because we knew there were going to be so many people that the demonstration would cover the whole block. And so it did.

December 5, the day of the premiere of *Jimmy Shine*, arrived. By six o'clock that afternoon, the whole block was full of angry Puerto Ricans carrying Puerto Rican flags. There were people there not just from New York but from other states, as well, including New Jersey and Connecticut. In addition to actors and others show business people, we were joined by Catholic priests and Protestant ministers. By the time the ticket office closed there were over seven hundred people picketing. There were so many people that the police were forced to close 47th St. from Broadway to Seventh Avenue. We had occupied two full blocks, and at eight o'clock that night there were still Puerto Ricans arriving with flags and posters. The Police Department mobilized officers from almost every precinct in Manhattan to guard the perimeter, because "those crazy Puerto Ricans were mad at somebody." The much-feared mounted police were also there, ready to run their 2000-pound horses into us in order to make way for the limousines bringing society ladies with their mink and ermine coats. We were prepared for that eventuality: a group of women trained by Saul Alinsky were wearing big hats with two long hat pins each. Their mission was to prick the horses so they would rear up and throw off their riders.

As soon as we arrived at the picket line, the precinct captain, a cop named Riley, who knew me, came over to me and said very sternly, "Mr. Valentine, I don't want any trouble." I simply answered, "You won't get any unless your boys give us trouble, captain," and I kept walking.

While the picket was going on, fifteen Puerto Ricans entered the theater, supposedly to see the show. A friend of Miriam Colón's had gotten us tickets in the orchestra and the balcony. The seats had been strategically distributed around the theater so our action would be as effective as possible. Well-dressed, perfumed, and well-equipped, the women sat in the orchestra. In their large handbags, each one had two mice and some flares. The men were seated in the balcony. Like the women, they were well-dressed, in coats and ties. One of the guys even wore a tuxedo. In their pockets they had firecrackers, flares, and stink bombs.

Outside, we had a coffin, painted black, that weighed about two hundred pounds. It was carried by several Puerto Rican actors, including Bobby Capó, Daniel Santos, Raúl Juliá, Miriam Colón, Carla Pinza, the boys from the musicians' Local 802, and several presidents of the Congreso's town-clubs. The famous Latin jazz musician Machito was also there. Born in Cuba, Machito had moved to El Barrio in the late thirties, married a Puerto Rican girl, and felt thoroughly Puerto Rican. We handed out our flyers to the people passing by the theater. It had been done in both Spanish and English and explained in great detail what had happened to Carla Pinza. We expressed our profound indignation at the discrimination shown against our community. Meanwhile, on the other side of the street, we strategically stationed several other protesters. Their instruments of protest were eggs filled with red paint.

When the lights in the theater went down and the curtain began to rise, one of our people shouted, "Viva Puerto Rico!" Immediately, the women turned their mice loose and lighted their flares. The men in the balcony tossed their stink bombs and firecrackers. The audience started running out of the theater, while several society ladies climbed up on the seats to get away from the mice. Outside, the protesters started throwing the paint-filled eggs at the theater building. Some smashed into the lighted marquee, splattering the people coming out of the theater, including some of our own.

Meanwhile, following our plan, Carmen Colón, the Congreso's secretary, threw herself to the ground. We wrapped her in the Puerto Rican flag and started singing the Puerto Rican anthem, in the official version. "I saw you push her!" screamed a woman at a police officer who had stepped in to disperse the crowd. The women in the group told Carmen to moan and groan louder, so it would look like she'd been injured by the cop. I called for an ambulance to take doña Carmen to the hospital, while others were demanding that the police officer, who was surrounded by us, give us his name and badge number, since it was a common practice of the "agents of law and order" to take off their badges at protest activities so they couldn't be identified when they committed their abuses. A short time later, an ambulance arrived to take the "injured" woman away. Two women from our group went with her to St. Clare Hospital on 52nd St. Not long after that, the hospital released her.

In the chaos that followed, the police arrested four protesters—the guy in the tuxedo, Carmen Ventura and another lady, and a young man from the Arecibo town-club. They were all carried to the precinct house on 54th St. We were prepared for that eventuality. We'd spoken with one of the lawyers who provided us with legal assistance to represent us in night court. In addition, through our contacts on the police force we already knew what precinct we would be taken to. In all this, I was told that Capt. Riley was looking for me so they could arrest me for disorderly conduct. He couldn't find me, since a friend of ours on the police force kept us informed as to the captain's movements.

While the ambulance was taking doña Carmen to the hospital, a group of us went to the 54th St. precinct and waited outside while two or three of us went in to post bail. Capt. Riley was there, but he made no move to arrest me. He knew he couldn't do anything there; he had to have done it at the site of the "crime." When we tried to post bail, we were told that people who'd been arrested had to be processed first, with mug shots, fingerprints, and so on.

We were also prepared for that part of the arrest. When the police started questioning the people they'd arrested, the detainees all said, "I don't spic Inglish." And of course, as we knew, since the precinct was located in a whites-only area, none of the officers there spoke Spanish. So they asked our group if any of us could act as interpreters. We refused, arguing that none of us worked for the police. They called police headquarters asking for an interpreter. There was not one available there, either, but they were told they could find one up in Harlem. Finally, an interpreter arrived. When the processing started, one of the women said her name was Mariana Bracetti and another, Blanca Canales. The men, in turn, identified themselves as Pedro Albizu Campos and José de Diego.[24]

While all this was going on, Carmen Ventura, who was quite a character, said to one of the cops, "Amigo, mi pipi." He understood that she was saying her name was Pipi, and he said, "So! You speak English!" Carmen said to me, "Mr. Gerena, dígale a este zángano que lo que yo quiero es ir al baño"—*Tell this fool that what I want is to go to the bathroom.* The cop, who apparently knew a few words in Spanish, jumped back, as though he were insulted, and shouted,

"Mi no zángano!" At that, she whispered, "Watch out for this guy. He's playing dumb, but he knows Spanish."

Processing the detainees was completed by about three o'clock in the morning. From there, we left to go to the night court on Lafayette St., on the Lower East Side. Our lawyer, Silverman, was waiting for us down there. Our people filled the courtroom. A white female judge was seeing the cases that night. She immediately asked for the accused to be brought in. When our comrades entered, our people almost brought down the roof with their shouting and applauding. The judge rapped the bench angrily with her gavel and told us if there was another outburst like that, she'd have the courtroom cleared. When I saw the judge's attitude here at the very beginning, I thought to myself that things were not going to go very well for us during the rest of the hearing, because when the names of Albizu Campos and Mariana Bracetti were called, there were going to be shouting and catcalls like you've never heard. I mentioned this to Silverman, who answered me calmly, "Just let me handle it."

When "Mariana Bracetti"'s name was called, it was just as I feared—howls of laughter, shouts of derision and hilarity. The judge jumped up, her eyes blazing, and if she'd been a cat she'd have hissed and arched her back and puffed up her fur. She banged her gavel so hard I thought she was going to break the desk down the middle, and she warned us again. They then brought in the guy in the tuxedo, alias Albizu Campos, and the audience erupted again! Before the judge could speak, though, Silverman asked to approach the bench. Outraged, the judge warned him, "I'm tempted to expel you with the rest of this wild bunch, Mr. Silverman," but she told him to approach.

Silverman, who spoke a little Spanish and knew the history of Puerto Rico and Pedro Albizu Campos, calmly explained what had happened, why we were there, who Pedro Albizu Campos and Mariana Bracetti were. He also explained who I was and asked that I be called as a witness. The judge agreed, but at that very instant, the courtroom filled with police officers. I think the judge, in her nervousness, had hit the button she had under her desk for emergencies. However, nothing really happened. After hearing the city attorney's allegations, Silverman called me to testify. I very respectfully told the judge my version of what had happened. She then asked the defendants to give their real names. Eventually, she dismissed one of the charges but let the charge of disorderly conduct stand. Silverman agreed. We then paid a fine of $25 for each defendant, and the group was freed immediately. We were all exhausted.

The next day we picketed again, but there weren't as many people as the night before. In fact, there were more cops than people on the picket line. But it seems that our action had been successful, since attendance at the musical was also substantially down. The next picket was to be on Thursday. On this occasion, over a hundred people took part, which for a workday could be considered a tremendous turnout. During all the rest of December, we continued to picket in front of the theater, in that bone-chilling cold.

Although we did not manage to get Carla Pinza back into the show, our pressure was effective. The American League of Theaters and Producers, an organization that represented the interests of theater owners and producers, asked for a meeting with the organizers of the activity. A broad-based committee was created, composed of representatives from the Puerto Rican theater world, the Congreso de Pueblos, the Puerto Rican Day Parade, and the Puerto Rican Community Development Project, and we met with the Producers League and Actors Equity, the union that represented theater actors. In our meeting, we agreed that equal opportunity would be given Puerto Rican actors on Broadway. It was decided that Miriam Colón, a member of Actors Equity, would be the liaison person between the two sides for this effort.

It took beatings, arrests, getting pushed around, and jail, but we sent a clear and convincing message: even if only for a supporting role, including a role as a prostitute, the right of Puerto Rican artists had to be respected

44.
RED EGGS AND STINK BOMBS

Many of the Puerto Ricans who took part in the demonstration against *Jimmy Shine* wanted to know how an egg, filled with its yolk and white, could suddenly turn red. My very great friend Roberto Napoleón had the recipe. He told me, "*Compay*, it's the easiest thing in the world," and he explained the process to me, stressing that the yolk and white shouldn't be thrown out, since it was such excellent food. "For the picket," he said, "we used two dozen eggs, and we drained the yolk and white out of them, which we later used to make a dynamite *tortilla española*.[25]

"The recipe is simple. You have to prepare the eggs the night before, because if not, they split open. You submerge the eggs in white vinegar, or any other kind, until the shell gets soft. Then, with a big needle like for vaccinations, you suck out the yolk and white. Then with another needle you immediately fill the egg with whatever color paint you want to use. Oil-based paint is best, by the way, but you have to be careful because it's heavy, and the egg might break. Then you put tape over the hole you made in the shell and put the egg in the refrigerator. You take it out the next day and put it back in the little carton it came in, and there you have a dozen perfectly nice eggs."

While I'm at it, let me take a moment to give the recipe for stink bombs. Stink bombs are very useful for closing down businesses and breaking up activities that go against the people. All you need is sulfuric acid, zinc, and bicarbonate of soda. You mix the ingredients and pour the liquid into a test tube. I learned to make them in chemistry class in high school in Lares. The first time I used them as a tool in the struggle was during a student protest. Since I was an expert at making them, I was given the assignment of preparing our arsenal. We used them to interrupt a lecture called by the school principal to announce a new school policy. I don't remember what the specific issue was that we were protesting, just that our stink bombs worked.

45.
FROM CITY HALL TO THE JAIL
ON RIKERS ISLAND

While I was working with the Human Rights Commission, I always maintained contact with my base in the Puerto Rican community: my comrades in the Parade and Folklore Fiesta organizations, the Civil Rights Association, and the Congreso de Pueblos. I continued to take an active part in the struggles to create a civilian review board for the Police Department, to seek justice for the gypsy cabs in the city, and to decentralize the school system. With respect to this last issue, a second round of school boycotts was being discussed, and my name was associated with that project.

In 1969 it was clear that Mayor John Lindsay had given in to the interests of big business and reneged on his promises to find a quick and lasting solution to the problems of police brutality and persecution of the gypsy cab-drivers. In addition, Lindsay had make it clear that he was not interested in decentralizing the school system. Given all this, my criticism of his administration grew more and more pointed. Lindsay let it be known that he wouldn't hold it against me, since I had told him from the start that my first and only loyalty was to my people in the barrio. But the straw that broke the camel's back for the Mayor was the decision by a group of Puerto Rican community leaders, including yours truly, to make several public statements slamming the Mayor's inaction on these fronts. Of course there was also my decision, which I made public, not to endorse Lindsay for re-election. The Mayor responded with a memo telling me that my criticism was incompatible with the position I was holding on his staff. It was an indirect way of asking for my resignation, but I ignored it.

While William Booth (who I found out later was the person who'd recommended me for the commissioner's post) was presiding over the Human Rights Commission, he always stood up for me. But in 1969, Lindsay decided to remove him from the Commission and appoint him to a judgeship. In Booth's place the Mayor appointed Simeon Golar, who had been the Liberal Party candidate for attorney general in the last election. Golar was an unknown in the civil rights movement in New York City. He had held several bureaucratic positions and was another Uncle Tom and, as became clear later, an exploiter of the worse kind, since after he left the Human Rights Commission he became a slum landlord in the black ghettos. As soon as his appointment was announced, word spread that his agenda included doing all of Lindsay's dirty work that had so far gone undone. I figured that meant getting rid of me. . . .

The excuse to kick me off the Commission presented itself that summer. I was running again in the primaries for the city councilman-at-large spot in Manhattan. I lost by a thin margin. It was an exhausting campaign, so I decided to take some early vacation days. I asked for time off and was given it. As I often did, I went down to Puerto Rico to recharge my batteries. When I tried to fly back to New York, I found that TWA, the airline I was flying on, had suspended all its flights due to a strike. I tried to change airlines, but there was no way to get back to New York on the day I'd planned. Golar took advantage of that to require me to report to work immediately—he sent a telegram to that effect—but a return was, of course, impossible.

I made it back to New York three days later. On Monday, July 7, 1969, when I arrived at the office, Golar informed me that I'd been fired. I immediately got in touch with several Puerto Rican comrades who always supported me to plan a strategy for countering this low blow. On July 8, a group of approximately a hundred Puerto Ricans arrived at the Commission's offices. I went upstairs to my office with one of them, while the rest awaited instructions downstairs. In my office I found my secretary, her eyes wet with tears, who told me, "Oh, Mr. Gerena, I'm so sorry for what's happened. They want you to resign immediately." She said she'd been told that as soon as I came in I was to go to Commissioner Golar's office to sign the letter of resignation he'd prepared for me. I told her to tell the Commissioner that if he wanted my resignation he should come to my office personally.

Barely a minute passed before Golar stormed into my office. He was over six feet tall and more than a few pounds overweight. Without even saying hello, he said in a hoarse voice, "I ask that you please sign this letter. The Mayor wants your resignation."

I calmly replied, "I'm not going to resign. You're going to have to fire me. I'm not moving from this office. Now, do what you have to do."

"Then I'll call the police," he answered threateningly.

Seeing what was going on, the fellow who had come upstairs with me went downstairs to tell the rest to come up. The group arrived en masse, carrying chains and padlocks, and took over the Commission's offices. They put a strict guard on Golar in his office, but left one telephone line open so he could communicate with the Mayor's office. They rest of the staff, including the employees that supported me, were asked to leave. My secretary left with them. Meanwhile, other supporters of mine arrived to set up a picket line.

We had already notified the press of what was going to happen at the Commission offices. We allowed reporters into the building and after they took our statements, including my decision to go on a hunger strike until I was given my job back, they were ushered out. We then put chains on all the doors and pushed desks into place against them.

In our group there were members of the Congreso de Pueblos, the Puerto Rican Day Parade, the Lower East Side Council of Organizations, the Young Lords, and several other organizations from the Bronx and Brooklyn. The Mayor sent messages ordering us to vacate the premises, but we ignored him. I continued my hunger strike, drinking only water with salt and sugar. On the seventh day of my strike, I was already feeling much thinner, and my eyesight seemed to be going.

Meanwhile, we kept Golar with us. We fed him well, despite the fact that some members of the group wanted him to go hungry, too. The group asked Lindsay to agree to speak with me before Simeon Golar fell out of a window in that eight-story building trying to escape. The Mayor sent several professional politicians, including Herman Badillo, to speak with us, or threaten us, rather, since they assured us that the police would be sent to arrest us. Unfortunately for them, our fear of that had disappeared days earlier. The message we always sent back to Lindsay was that he had to come see me.

By the tenth day, I had lost over thirty pounds, my knees no longer worked, and I could barely see. Julie Pariser, my dear friend, visited me. He went away very sad, and without a word. My children Isa and Donald tried to persuade me to end the strike, but I refused. At Donald's request, Dr. Frank Suárez examined me and informed the committee that if I refused to eat for one more day I could have a massive heart attack, which might kill me. The committee decided to take me out so that Dr. Suárez could transport me to the hospital. Golar was released; he ran like a man chased by the devil.

On July 18, I was taken out of the building on a gurney provided by my dear friend Roberto Napoleón. In a demonstration of support by the community, Lafayette Street was filled with people. Loudspeakers had been set up, and people thronged to the street to see me. Lindsay gave an order to take me away from the front of the Commission building. That same day, the police arrested me and another person, Rosalina Reilova. I was accused of illegal trespass and interfering with government operations. I was transferred to the jail on Rikers Island, where I was put into the infirmary. On my file, somebody had written that I had attacked a policeman, which was completely false, since I was so weak I could hardly move. According to the medical report, I was dehydrated and on the verge of a heart attack.

As soon as we arrived at the jail, one of the guards commented threateningly, "Well, well, look here, this turkey is a cop hater." The female police officer who seem to be in command ordered him to leave me alone, because I was a "Puerto Rican bigshot." If not for that, I would have been given a beating, starvation and all. The next thing I knew, they were trying to give me a shot, supposedly to calm me down, but I didn't allow it. I remembered what had happened to César Chávez, the leader of the Agricultural Workers Union in California, whose brain was damaged when he was injected during a hunger strike. Seeing that I resisted, the female police officer intervened and told the guards that if "the son of a bitch wants to die, fuck him, leave him alone." At that point, they all laughed, leaving me chained to the bed. I lay there for three days.

On the second night, they brought in a TV for me. It was between 7:30 and 8:00 at night when I saw on the news that a group of Puerto Ricans had caused a disturbance at a meeting of the New Democratic Coalition, a reform-minded group within the Democratic Party. The NDC had been meeting in the Hotel Woodstock to endorse the candidacy of John Lindsay for a second term. The demonstrators, including several delegates to the convention, tried in vain to present a motion that would postpone endorsement of Lindsay until he had given me my job back. Soon, a disturbance broke out and everything went to hell in a hand basket. I saw chairs flying and mirrors shattering while Marta Sánchez, one of the women who had been with me during the demonstrations in front of the Commission building, brought the master of ceremonies to the floor with a left to the jaw. According to Marta, she acted in response not just to the fact that they refused to consider the motion, but also that some of the people in attendance had referred to Puerto Ricans disrespectfully.

For my part, I was willing to take my hunger strike to its ultimate consequences. Worried about my failing health and lack of adequate medical attention, my doctor insisted that I end the strike. Stubborn as I am, at first I rejected the idea, but my children Isa and Donald convinced me that I had to stop. We put up bail so that they could take me to the hospital. Isa made arrangements for me to be taken to Trafalgar Hospital, on 90th St. and Second Avenue.

I had a very nice private room there. My dear friend Minerva González stayed with me all the time. As soon as I was admitted, the head of the kitchen, who was a Puerto Rican woman from Loíza and had taken part in our struggles, sent me a pitcher of fresh orange juice. Berta Bermúdez, a friend of mine who belonged to one of the town-clubs, came in from Brooklyn with food for me: *mondongo* and fresh baked bread. I was not supposed to eat any solid food, but I couldn't restrain myself, and I wolfed down that *mondongo!* Suddenly, I felt like I was kind of floating, and I fainted. They called Dr. Schaefer, who after stabilizing me scolded Berta for that well-intentioned but foolish action that could have cost me my life. Berta, for her part, took a Bible out of her purse and read me several psalms to comfort my spirit.

That night was unforgettable. It was July 20, 1969, a memorable day in the annals of human history. Prostrate in bed, unable to move, I watched on television as astronaut Neil Armstrong set foot on the moon. In about a week, I was released from the hospital. I went directly to court, where the judge dismissed the charges against me after hearing my lawyers' arguments.

As soon as news of my firing got out, I asked my union, the Union of Municipal Workers, to provide me with legal assistance in a suit against Simeon Golar, Mayor Lindsay, and the City of New York. My friends thought I was crazy, because nobody won against the city. After months of depositions and statements, the court, with the approval of City Hall, designated an arbiter to hear the case. The person chosen was a tall, ruddy man named Solniker who apparently drank too much—he had the bloodshot eyes and veiny nose of a drinker. I didn't like him, and I said so to Julius Topol, the union lawyer. Although Topol tried to calm me by arguing that this guy was the best of the three available candidates, I still didn't trust him. After several months, Solniker handed down his decision. Topol sent for me. When I arrived at the union offices, he told me, "I've got bad news." I shot back, "I told you I didn't like that arbiter, and I know he didn't like me, either." "No," Topol said, "that's not the bad news. The bad news is that you're going to have to go back to your job."

And he handed me the decision, in which Solniker found that the city hadn't proven its case, and that the commissioner had dismissed me unjustifiably for having been absent for three days. My secretary had testified that I had called in to say I couldn't get back, and the evidence showed that my airline had indeed been on strike at the time. Based on those facts, the arbiter ordered that I be given my job back, and that if I wasn't willing to go back to it, the city government would have to find me a position of the same rank, at the same salary, plus pay me all the salary increases and other benefits, retroactively, that had been granted during the two years I'd been out of work.

The arbiter's decision was final; the city could not appeal it. I thanked Topol and Victor Gottbaum, the president of the union, and left the building happy, as I'd been vindicated. That night we had a celebration in the Congreso de Pueblos office, which filled with people coming in to congratulate me, including my friends from the Adams plant. Mrs. Colón and a group of ladies from the Parade committee prepared a delicious *asopao*, and we had a terrific time remembering the various episodes of that chapter of my life.

Despite the difficult moments and the poverty I experienced during those years, the process taught me a lot. Among other things, I learned the hard way how political machines work and how politicians are willing to prostitute themselves for money. But the main lesson I learned was the importance of being firm and consistent. I learned to take control of my body, and today I can fast for long periods. In addition, I learned the fine art of responding quickly but conscientiously in moments of crisis. Although it was painful, I also learned to separate the wheat from the chaff with regard to friendships. Just as I had gotten rid of the old ugly fat on my body, I got rid of the ingrates and the disloyal in my life.

In compliance with the arbiter's order, the city paid me what they owed me and gave me back my job. As soon as I was reinstated, I turned in my resignation, which I promised was irrevocable. As you can imagine, in the mayor's race that year, I campaigned against Lindsay. He lost.

46.
A HUGE HEALTH-CARE CORPORATION

Health Insurance Plan (HIP) was a medical-insurance company founded in the forties to offer services to the middle class. In the late forties, the corporation opened a health-services center in the South Bronx, on 149th St. But as that area deteriorated, the quality of the services at the clinic did, too. This represented a grave problem for the Puerto Ricans who lived in that neighborhood, because our community had a high incidence of disease and illness.

During the late sixties and early seventies, our community's struggles were successful in attracting much better medical services. On 149th St. near Park Avenue, modern facilities were built for Lincoln Hospital and the Hostos Community College was established. Despite these advances, though, the HIP was reluctant to improve its health services in what they called the "ghetto clinic."

We wanted to change that mindset and make the HIP clinic respond effectively and efficiently to the needs of our community, so we organized to achieve our goals. As we expected, the HIP didn't want to pledge to make the needed changes. Fortunately, there are always people of conscience and good will in every institution, ready to help. The problem is always the boards of directors, which are made up of white racists.

The "inside person" at the HIP who was supporting us was Douglas Hiss, an excellent organizer who was committed to our struggles. One day, Douglas told me that his company was willing to invest in the clinic, but we had to show them that we could increase the enrollment of our people in the HIP within a reasonable period of time. We accepted the challenge. Douglas drew up a recruitment plan. Although I was interested in taking the lead in organizing, I couldn't do it because I was hip-deep in organizing the Puerto Rican Community Development Project. Others in the Congreso de Pueblos stepped in to move the HIP project forward. Rosina Rosinova, who was unparalleled as an organizer, was hired to work exclusively at the HIP recruiting desk. Rosina spoke English and Spanish perfectly and was extremely persuasive. She was joined by several members of the Congreso who volunteered their services. The campaign was so intense that in less than six months we had recruited ten thousand new members for the HIP clinic in the South Bronx.

Despite the successful campaign led by Douglas, several people inside the company were still opposed to making the clinic a decent place to provide our community with health services. One day I received an unexpected telephone call from Douglas, telling me that as part of an austerity plan the HIP board of directors was going to close the South Bronx clinic, suspend the recruitment campaign, and leave the workers whose salaries were paid by HIP without a job. The official decision was to be made that Thursday at a meeting called for that specific purpose.

The news hit us hard. We resented it profoundly, because we had invested an extraordinary amount of resources in our recruitment of thousands of members and in persuading the company to provide better services to the community. Now, overnight, and without consulting us, they were going to dismantle the whole enterprise. We were not going to allow it. We presented our demands to HIP's executive director, but he was deaf to our arguments. Now they were going to learn who they were dealing with. We organized to burst into the meeting room and set things straight. "Operation HIP" was well organized; it entailed, among other things, two workshops on logistics and discipline.

Before the day of the meeting, we sent one of our guys to meet with one of the directors, Mr. Mayer, I believe his name was. Our man was well dressed— coat and tie and briefcase. His mission was to prepare a map of the building, including entrances and exits, the number of telephones available, and how many workers remained in the building after 6 pm, which was the time set for our meeting. For his part, Douglas provided us with basic information on the personality of each of the members of the board, including who the most aggressive one was, who the most cowardly, and what each person's position was on the clinic.

At about 4 pm on the day of the meeting, the group that was going to carry out Operation HIP got together. We had decided to wait until the meeting started before we acted. Douglas was helping us from inside. When he gave us the signal that they were about to start, each of us proceeded to carry out our assignment. Five cars moved to 112th St. Two of them had picked up the young men and women of the Young Lords who were helping us. The other three left from the Bronx, from the clinic on 149th St. The idea was to set up a picket line while a group went in to negotiate with the HIP board of directors.

As soon as we arrived, two of our own people dressed as security guards stationed themselves at the entrance to the HIP offices on the second floor and at the building entrance while another group entered the building. We proceeded to disconnect all the telephones but one, which we would control. A member of the Lords stood guard over it.

We went into the office where the meeting was being held. In the room, everything seemed to be just hunky-dory. There was an enormous conference table, probably 15 feet long and 8 feet wide. And there sat the board members, many of them lawyers, all well dressed. There were twenty-five of us Puerto Ricans. Some of the women from the Young Lords were trained in karate; there were twelve Lords in all. Without beating around the bush, we delivered our demands to the board members, at the same time stationing an escort behind each one. Seeing strangers in the conference room, especially some of the Lords, who were big strong guys and girls wearing dashikis and Afros, the board members got a little nervous. Some of them said they wanted to go to the bathroom. The chairman of the board asked us very haughtily what this intrusion was all about. At that, I stepped forward and started telling him why we were there. I asked one of our group to take the chairman over to the window so he could see the demonstration out in front of the building. I explained that the next day there would be a picket line in front of every HIP clinic in New York City if the board didn't hear our demands. The demands were: that the clinic on 149th St. remain open, its finances supported if necessary by the profits from other clinics; that Douglas stay on as director of the recruitment campaign; and that the company carry out the improvements and provide the equipment and staff that the clinic needed—and that other clinics had. We informed them that no one would leave the room until our demands had been met.

Meanwhile, a policeman had arrived on the scene and was asking what was happening. The security guard, who was one of our own, tried to keep the cop from going upstairs. He told him the elevators weren't working. The idea of climbing eight flights of stairs dissuaded the cop from going into the building. Upstairs, the tensions were mounting. One of the board members, I think the one in charge of the clinic at 181st St. and Grand Concourse, told the chairman that he didn't want to have to face a picket line at his clinic. Apparently the idea of facing that situation at every clinic in the city caused the board to reconsider its decision. The chairman agreed to meet the next day, outside the office, with a smaller committee. We warned him that if he didn't agree to our just demands he would face further demonstrations. The tough guy turned out to be a pushover. Our demands were met. HIP continued to run the clinic. They remodeled it, brought in new equipment, and kept the recruitment campaign going.

Douglas, however, was so disgusted with those "gentlemen's" attitudes that he finally decided to resign. Rosina resigned, too, and found a job as an executive secretary in the Puerto Rican Community Development Project. I, of course, continued working as an organizer with the PRCDP.

47.
IT TAKES A SLEDGEHAMMER: OPENING DOORS IN THE CONSTRUCTION INDUSTRY

As it does now, during the sixties and seventies the construction industry in New York City paid very well. There are 144 trades in construction. Specialized laborers who are unionized—bricklayers, plumbers, electricians, drivers, carpenters, masons, and others—are paid better than workers in almost any other industry. The minimum salary is much higher than the federal minimum wage. Even back in the sixties, a guy just starting out, a "laborer" as they were called in the trade, even if he wasn't unionized, would earn ten dollars an hour. And these were non-specialized workers, the guys that prepared the ground for the foundations, carried cement blocks, pushed around wheelbarrows of cement, rocks, and sand, washed the vehicles, and ensured that the tools and equipment were in order. Those were the jobs we wanted, because it was easier to start there and work your way up—we had very few qualified skilled laborers. Once a man got on the job, in thirty days he could become a member of the union.

To protect their members' interests, unions limited their membership and worked in what were called "closed shops." That way they kept contractors from giving jobs to men who weren't union members. One of these unions was the Local No. 3 of the International Brotherhood of Electrical Workers. Its president was an Irishman named Harry van Arsdale, an influential man in New York politics and in other construction-industry unions. From the point of view of blacks and Puerto Ricans, the fundamental problem was that both the leaders and the membership of those unions were white, and they practiced segregation. Among their members, though, especially the apprentices, there were immigrants, many recently arrived from Italy. These new men could hardly speak English, but the minute they landed in New York the unions gave them a membership card, while Puerto Ricans, even those who came from Puerto Rico with loads of experience working in construction, couldn't get jobs even as water-boys. And the same thing happened with our Dominican brothers. When we went to apply for a job, the contractors would always tell us that we had to belong to the union. And the blacks were in the same boat we were.

Beginning in the early sixties, the Congreso de Pueblos worked closely with our black counterparts in Manhattan, Brooklyn, and the Bronx who were also trying to persuade the construction industry to give the people in their communities a chance. In fact, that was the first time that blacks and Puerto Ricans had worked together for a common goal. We concentrated our efforts on buildings constructed with public funds, especially in the large expansion projects of City College of the City University of New York (CUNY). It was this college, which was located at 139th St. and Convent Avenue, near Harlem, that most of the few Puerto Ricans who were going to college in the city attended.

In the early seventies, the Congreso took the initiative in forging a more permanent coalition with several black organizations. We met with a group in Brooklyn and later with a group in the Bronx. Our counterparts offered us valuable information on how they carried out their visits to construction sites. They also told us that on many sites, the employers would hire private security companies that specialized in dealing with people like us that went in to look for jobs. We reached a series of agreements, among them that we would meet each month to develop strategies and exchange information on jobs. We also agreed to coordinate certain tasks, including canvassing particular territories on certain dates and reporting on positions that we didn't have specialized workers to fill but that the other group might. Our common goal was to put an end to racism and to the companies' practice of excluding our workers. We were going to fight to get black and coffee-colored faces onto every construction project in the city.

The visits to construction sites were dangerous; you had to know how to walk in. In many places the water-boys were actually private security guards. They were big, muscular guys; you could see they lifted weights—they rolled up their sleeves to show off their biceps. These gorillas always carried a length of iron rebar, not the night stick that a security guard was supposed to carry.

We never sent just one person to visit these places; we went as a group. If the group from the Bronx or Brooklyn arrived, we'd include it in the brigade. The orders were clear: the men were to find the supervisor and ask for work. If they were turned away, they were supposed to just say thank you and leave the site. They were to try at all times to avoid confrontations with the workers or security guards. Whenever I went with a group, I was the one that spoke. From one site, we would move on to the next one on the list. The answer was always the same: "We've got no jobs; come back next week." When we'd go back the next week, we'd get the same answer. Once in a while a friend that worked on one site or another would call and tell us there was a job opening. By the next day, when we arrived at the project, there would already be a white worker on the job. The unions were always one step ahead of us.

In 1974 we decided to concentrate our efforts on a large building that was under construction at City College. At that time, City College was the main center of student activism in the city. In 1969, Puerto Rican and black students had occupied the institution, demanding racial and ethnic integration. The Congreso de Pueblos supported the students, and the students returned the favor by supporting our demand that blacks and Puerto Ricans be given jobs in the construction industry.

We went to City College on two different occasions. We presented our case first to the supervisor and later to the project manager, both of whom sent us away with the now-familiar phrase, "Come back next week." We tried to file a complaint with the Labor Department, but they referred us to the state Department of Education, alleging that that agency was in charge of the project. We went to the DE. There, they suggested that we speak to the respective unions. We spent two weeks going in circles. But we refused to give up, and we continued to pressure everyone we could think of.

In the early seventies the federal Department of Labor did a study on the state of black and other minority workers. As a result of that study, in 1972 Congress passed the Equal Employment Opportunity Act. We were certain that City College was in violation of federal law. The Labor Department pressured CUNY to comply with the law. City College, for its part, pressured by the unions, who threatened to go on strike if non-union workers were hired, didn't want to give in. For our part, we just kept pushing, trying to open the doors of employment to our community.

But our tactic of visiting construction sites was definitely not working. The doors remained closed. We decided, then, that each group would experiment with other approaches. Tired of all the excuses, we called a meeting to decide how we were going to counter the actions and attitudes of all these racists and liars. My group opted to do several things. We thought if we could get just two jobs, we could break the blockade. And if there were no jobs available, then we had to create some. We did a study of the site and its surroundings. We found that every morning, three big Italian-looking apprentice laborers that worked on the site came up out of the subway entrance on 137th St. and Broadway.

Early one Monday morning, a group of us, including a boxer named Pepito who hoped to find a job in construction, waited for the apprentices to come up out of the subway. As they made their way to the job site, Pepito "bumped into" one of them. There were words, and one of them started taking off his work gear, like he wanted to fight. But Pepito struck first, and floored him with one punch. The poor guy's hard hat went flying. The rest of us helped the guy up and saw him to the subway so he could go home and lick his wounds.

For the next three days, the apprentice missed work. On the third day, we showed up at the construction site with two workers. To fill the vacancy that had opened, the supervisor took one of them. The "new guy" was such a good worker that the foreman let him work the whole week. Not long afterward, they gave him the job on a regular basis, and a union card. It goes without saying that our comrade had promised to keep the existence of our secret organization a secret and to help us from the inside. Meanwhile, word spread of what had happened to the Italian apprentice, and several of his mates at work quit their jobs, saying they were too dangerous.

We had broken the ice, but came away with just a tiny cube. We had to put more pressure on these people. We concluded, however, that the strategy we had used was the wrong one. The idea of beating up a fellow-worker was wrong. We were acting like strikebreakers instead of honest day-laborers. Our comrades in Brooklyn gave us ideas for other tactics that had yielded results, including blocking vehicles' entrance to the site. This alternative, however, had its own drawbacks. We would be exposing ourselves to arrest and, in that case, would have to find lawyers, which was expensive, and also spend time—waste time, in my view—in court.

So we opted for another tactic: We decided to stop the delivery of concrete by sabotaging the mixers. We found out, first, that the mixers needed on the site—at least six or eight a day—cost the contractor thousands of dollars. Second, we learned that the mixers have to churn the cement constantly. If they stop for even half an hour, the concrete starts to harden and it sticks to the sides of the drum, which is a nightmare for the contractor because of the time that has to be spent scraping off the hardened concrete. And in the worst case, it could mean a total loss to the owner of the truck.

But there was a hitch. Nobody in our group knew how to stop a concrete mixer. Nobody had ever even gotten a close look at the machinery. But through our man who'd gotten a job at City College we found out that there was a black guy who operated a concrete mixer at another construction project in the city and could find his way around one blindfolded. He lived in Brooklyn. We got his address. Our comrades in Brooklyn talked to him. He gave us a sketch of several kinds of trucks and showed us the belt that turned the drum. He told us exactly how to cut it or run it off the pulley and put the mixer out of service. Actually, it was child's play. So that was that—we could bring the construction site to a halt. The real problem, though, was this: Since there would always be several mixers in line waiting to deliver their concrete, the drivers would sit up in the cabs waiting their turn, like taxi drivers in line at the airport, and there was no way to get to the trucks. We had to create a distraction. We saw that a lot of the drivers would read while they waited, and once in a while, one would leave to· buy something to eat. That was the moment when we could act.

The Friday we'd chosen for our sabotage arrived. We got a friend who had a hot-dog cart to give us a hand. His job was to show up at the job site around lunchtime, park his cart near the line of waiting concrete mixers, and ring his bell to attract the drivers. First one driver in the line of three mixers waiting stepped over to the hot-dog cart. A couple of minutes later, the other two drivers went over. When they returned, four mixers were out of order. Following our instructions, the hot-dog guy made himself scarce, as did everyone in on the plot. The two mixers in the middle couldn't get out because they were pinned in by the others, and that created havoc on the site. Out of concern for our safety, we closed the offices that were coordinating the operation for the next two days. Not long afterward, a couple of investigators paid me a visit, but they had no evidence whatsoever against me or anybody else. We always believed, though, that this incident brought us closer to our goal of ending the racism and exclusion that was rampant in the construction industry in New York City.

Finally, the City College administration sent us a message informing us that they were ready to sit down and talk to us. There were jobs for plumbers, masons, and carpenters available, and they wanted our people to have a chance at them. We said we'd be delighted to talk. We contacted our brothers in Brooklyn and the Bronx and told them to send some of their men to fill the vacancies. I think the administration thought that all we had were non-skilled workers, but they were surprised when we sent experienced men to fill the positions they had open. We took the occasion to demand that they also hire non-skilled workers. They gave us ten positions.

At that time, word had spread through the Puerto Rican community that the Congreso was recruiting people to work in construction. The list of people interested was long. City College couldn't absorb them all, but the ice had been broken, as I said, and later other projects began to give our men jobs. The federal government, in turn, put more pressure on the unions. I recall that one of them was fined for using undocumented workers, who were later deported. Given this new reality, the unions had to open themselves up and accept the Puerto Rican and African-American workers that were being hired.

One of our demands to City College was that they hire a person to monitor the labor force on the construction project and ensure that our agreements were being met. They offered me the job. Before accepting, I consulted first with the workers in my group and then with our comrades in Brooklyn and the Bronx. They all agreed that I was the ideal person for the job, since in addition to my union and leadership credentials, I had the advantage of speaking both languages.

City College set up one of those portable offices for me that engineers and architects use on construction sites. I made sure that the Equal Employment Opportunity Act was complied with: there had to be both black and coffee-colored faces in every trade. I also made sure that the law was applied not just to the apprentices, but also to the skilled laborers. We also encouraged the unions to open the doors of their educational programs to black and Puerto Rican apprentices so they could learn a trade and earn better pay. Within a year, we had made pretty good progress, and there was a climate of relative harmony.

48.
ONE GOOD TURN
DESERVES ANOTHER

As I said in the previous chapter, trying to open the construction industry to blacks and Puerto Ricans wasn't easy. You had to literally put your personal security at risk. During the picket lines and other demonstrations we carried out at the construction sites there were often confrontations with white workers, many of whom were racist and saw us as a threat to their dominance in the unions.

Another thing that couldn't be dismissed so easily was the presence of the Mafia in the construction industry. During this period, I was the object of assassination attempts on two separate occasions. Although I never officially learned who was behind them, I'm sure it was the hidden hand of the Mafia pulling the strings.

Those of us who took part in the actions to create jobs on construction sites knew what we were exposing ourselves to. That's why we kept our meetings secret. But it seems there was an informer in the group. On one occasion we called a meeting for Wednesday night. Out of nowhere, two or three armed thugs arrived, shot out the ceiling light, and sprayed the office with bullets. The two comrades that were in the office were unharmed, since they threw themselves to the floor as soon as they heard the first shot. I had not yet arrived, as a meeting I had been in took longer than expected. The shooters got into a car that was waiting for them and sped away.

With respect to the concrete mixers, it wasn't long before word got out that I had been the person responsible for that operation. I was advised to be careful and not leave the building by myself. Several guys I trusted always stayed with me. At night, a homeless man, some drug addicts, or one of the prostitutes I always gave a little money to would walk with me to the subway when I left work.

On one occasion, while I was in that portable office City College had set up for me, I received a visit from a policeman friend of mine. He was one of the ones that had helped us stretch Puerto Ricans so they could pass the Police Department's physical exam. It seems that his captain, a Captain Rivera, had sent him to tell me to watch my back, since there was a contract out on me.

When I asked my friend for more information, he told me they thought it was from some Mafia guys in Queens who were the bosses over parts of the Bronx and Manhattan. I thanked him for the tip, although it didn't exactly take me by surprise, since that shooting in the meeting room in the office had happened not long before.

When I went back to work the next day, four cops came to my office. I recall that my coworkers, who were outside on the site at the time, thought I was about to be arrested, and that the cops, knowing how stubborn I was and that I might put up resistance, had come in force. But it wasn't what my coworkers thought. It was my friend the police officer along with three others. After we'd shaken hands, he said, "I have orders to get you out of here immediately, no matter what." He explained that we were about to be attacked and that I had to get out at once. He handed me a Police Department shirt and hat to put on and we left.

We had hardly left the office when it caught fire. By the time the fire department arrived, it was too late. My desk, all the chairs, and a filing cabinet were destroyed, and the place was unusable. Fortunately, I didn't keep papers or records in that little office. Not long afterward, City College closed the monitoring office, since by then the quota for minority workers was fully filled. So, once again, I was out of a job.

The day after this incident, the police officers who had saved me came to the Congreso offices to pick up the hat and shirt they had loaned me. I asked them, jokingly, of course, why they hadn't given me a badge. Their only answer was that they were following orders from Capt. Rivera, who, it turned out, was one of the Puerto Ricans who had entered the New York City Police Department with my help. That year, during the Puerto Rican Day Parade, in which more Puerto Rican police officers were marching than ever before, a Puerto Rican cop approached me to say that Capt. Rivera sent his regards. I looked for his face in the crowd and I returned his greeting with thanks and real affection.

49.
SOLIDARITY WITH CULEBRA

The island of Culebra is part of the Puerto Rican archipelago. Its beaches are among the most beautiful in the world. That and its delightful tropical climate make Culebra an ideal place for a vacation. That, at least, is now. Before, when the United States Navy carried out military maneuvers on Culebra, life on the little island was hell.

A few years after it took over Puerto Rico, the government of the United States designated Culebra a naval reserve. It was not, however, until shortly before the United States entered the Second World War that the U.S. Navy began to use the island as its principal training ground in the Atlantic region for artillery fire and bombing runs. Even after the war was over, the Navy maintained a presence on Culebra. Toward the end of the 1960s, the naval practices intensified to such a degree that the deafening noise of the explosions became part of the island's inhabitants' everyday life. A strong movement developed on the island against the presence of the Navy there. Responding to this pressure, Congress requested a report on the situation from the Secretary of Defense. In April of that same year, the secretary tried to downplay the situation, reporting that in late 1972 the situation would be reviewed and a determination would be made as to whether to maintain military maneuvers on the island or relocate them.

As in Puerto Rico, in New York we developed a strong movement against the Navy presence on Culebra, and we created the Comité Pro-Rescate de Culebra, the Committee to Save Culebra. This committee launched an intense educational campaign in New York and neighboring states and initiated a lobbying effort with our congresspersons and senators, who in turn presented the case at the federal level. Among these legislators, I should especially mention Congresswoman Shirley Chisholm, representing the borough of Brooklyn, who played a central role in the "battle of Culebra." As part of our agenda, we decided to organize a mass march on Washington, D.C. Organizing that activity took us almost all of 1970 and part of 1971.

When we scheduled the March on Washington for November 19, 1971, we brought more than a hundred organizations into the organizing committee, including many town-clubs, among them the Culebra club. Sometimes there would be 100 to 125 delegates at our meetings. We met every Wednesday, without fail, at 7:30 pm at 2642 Broadway at 106th St. in Manhattan. We also held meetings outside New York, in New Jersey and Connecticut. As chairman of this broad front, it was my responsibility to preside over the meetings. It wasn't always easy to maintain order with such a heterogeneous group. In addition to the town-clubs, there were union members and representatives from political groups who knew parliamentary procedure very well, but parliamentary procedure only works effectively if *everyone* knows it. The problem was, one person or group might not know it and another person or group would use that to advance their own agenda, strategy, or priority. The person presiding, then, has to know it well and be flexible when the situation requires it, so that meetings run smoothly and everyone can be heard. As often happens in meetings with a lot of people, some people or groups tend to take up a little too much space.

On one occasion I had a run-in with the Puerto Rican Socialist Party, whose section in New York religiously sent three delegates to the meetings. For whatever reason, the PSP representatives always wanted to monopolize the meeting and set the agenda for the debate. At first, on behalf of unity, I was quite tolerant, but there came a moment when I had to put a stop to their domineering attitude. But watch out! They jumped on me like piranhas. In their infinite speechmaking, they argued that Gerena Valentín was not sufficiently politicizing the struggle, and they accused me, subtly, of being a bourgeois liberal. Their arrogance didn't go down too well with the other representatives, and the delegates from the unions and the town-clubs began to be resentful.

The situation became so critical that two PSP leaders—the president and secretary—were sent to New York from Puerto Rico to set down the "party line." They marched into the meeting like they owned the place and started to lecture us on patriotism, Marxism, and organizational theory. This was neither the time nor the place for that kind of intervention, which was not just arrogant but also patronizing. They had apparently been misinformed, because they didn't seem to know how we Puerto Ricans in New York worked. The delegates from the town-clubs and unions moved that the PSP delegates be expelled from the meeting. The delegates from the New York chapter left the room, but the leaders who'd flown in from Puerto Rico insisted on staying, calling a question of order. When they refused to comply with the will of the assembly, I had to call on the sergeant-at-arms to remove them.

The PSP delegation never came back to the meetings, but their members seemed to have been more mature than the officers, as happens in many organizations, and at the march we saw several members of the PSP New York chapter. Ironically, later some of the self-proclaimed leaders of the Socialist Party wound up opting for the American dream. You would see them in their three-piece suits, immaculately shined shoes, and designer ties. Some stayed in the belly of the beast that they pretended to despise, while others returned to Puerto Rico.

There were several attempts to sabotage the movement, and there were agents that infiltrated the organization. As always, the infiltrator presents himself as a person in total solidarity with the cause, so it isn't easy to detect him at the beginning. At first, you try to accept everybody and welcome the new arrival, but you always keep your eye open for signs that distinguish a new guy from the people who are truly acting in good faith. A first suspicious sign might be that no one knows the person. In one particular case, an infiltrator would work with us all day, supposedly because he was unemployed, and even stick around until we closed the office. One day, the secretary of the organization told me that this guy had asked to stay and sleep in the office. He had given her the story that he'd lost his room because some friends he was renting it from had moved, so she had let him stay. There were no important documents or information there that might have been used against us, since as a precaution we had stashed all that sort of thing in other places. The surprise came when the telephone bill arrived. It totaled almost two thousand dollars in long-distance calls. I asked the telephone company to investigate and they told us that the calls had been initiated by that person. We confronted him, but he denied everything, and he disappeared just as he had come. We found ourselves forced to borrow money to pay the telephone bill because our service was about to be cut off, which would have affected the work we had to do every day.

On November 18, the night before leaving for Washington, a saboteur cut the electric wires running to the office from the meter in the basement. The basement had a door with a lock that we had no access to, so we had to make do with candles and kerosene lanterns. And about four days earlier, two of the three bus companies we had hired had called, totally out of the blue, to cancel our contracts. We're talking about a hundred buses at $350 each. Our argument that we had signed contracts got nowhere with them—somebody else could put more pressure on them than we could. It seems the FBI had threatened to close them down if they didn't cancel our contract. The company that didn't cancel was the one the Congreso de Pueblos customarily used for its activities. With its help, we managed to find the other seventy-five buses we needed to transport our marchers. They weren't the best buses in the world, but they got us to Washington. However, contrary to the practice we had followed up till then, they demanded that we pay for all the buses in advance.

On November 19, almost five thousand people showed up to make the trip to Washington, D.C., to demand that the Navy withdraw from Culebra. It was raining until we reached Washington. The highways were wet and slippery, and there was a lot of fog. But as soon as we reached our destination, about 10:30 in the morning, we set up a very combative picket line in front of the Pentagon and another in front of the White House. The activity was covered by the national press and several international wire services. We organized a cultural and artistic demonstration, which was also very combative, in which several singers volunteered to entertain the demonstrators. Among these was "El Jíbaro," Andrés Jiménez, who had a huge Afro "so the people will remember me." The singers Pepe and Flora, who were still together at that time, accompanied Andrés in several of the songs in his repertoire.

I cannot fail to mention Joe Monserrat here. If not for Joe—who was always by our side, through thick and thin, and who took money out of his own pocket to complete the payment for the buses—we would have had many more problems than we did. The last time I saw him, he was in a wheelchair. His health was fragile, but his intellect, wisdom, and kindness were intact. He earned the admiration of every person he came in contact with. That was Joe Monserrat: a good man. May he rest in peace.

50.
SHAM CIVIL RIGHTS HEARINGS

It was late January of 1972.

"Mr. Gerena, two American gentlemen came in looking for you. They said they were from the FBI."

Though I tried and tried to get Mrs. Colón to describe them for me, all she could say was that one was tall, the other was short, and that the short one spoke to her in Spanish. I figured they'd come back later that day, but they didn't. I really didn't pay much attention to the matter, since the FBI was always spying on me, recording my speeches or taking pictures of me wherever I went. Even so, I gave doña Carmen instructions that if they did come back she was not to give them any information of any kind, and above all was not to let them engage her in any sort of conversation.

A week or so later I ran into José Monserrat, who was heading up the Commonwealth office in New York City. He told me that United States Civil Rights Commission was going to hold public hearings in New York City, supposedly to look into whether the civil rights of Puerto Ricans were being violated in the city, especially by the police. I had to laugh, because every so often some city, state, or federal agency named a commission to "study" what any fool could see was going on in broad daylight. Monserrat also told me that FBI agents were going around interviewing potential witnesses for the hearings, and he added, "I sent two of them over to interview you."

I thanked him for the favor, but I didn't tell him they'd already been to my office and hadn't come back. I knew they weren't going to invite me to testify— me or many other Puerto Rican civil-rights activists. Anyway, I wasn't interested in taking part in any more sham hearings. They were always a political charade, this time mounted by the Republican Party and President Richard Nixon in order to win over Puerto Rican votes and in the bargain make Mayor Lindsay's administration look bad. The fact that they pre-selected the witnesses that would testify and that the agency in charge of the vetting process was the FBI showed the bad faith behind the hearings and the lack of respect for our community. Just let me remind the reader that it was FBI agents who called the company I worked for in Long Island City to tell the management that a bomb had been planted in the factory by a terrorist, and FBI agents who always had a truck parked in front of my house "working" on the telephone lines because one of them was supposedly out of service, and FBI agents who, when I left my house, called their surveillance teams to tell them how I was dressed, whether I was alone or with someone, whether I was carrying a briefcase or not, and other details that would allow them to follow me. Sending FBI agents to protect civil rights was like giving the keys to the blood bank to Dracula.

The hearings were scheduled for February 14 through 16 at the headquarters of Brotherhood in Action, a non-profit organization that had worked with the police force for many years in an attempt to develop better relations with the black and Puerto Rican communities. We decided to pay the hearings a visit. Several groups, including the Congreso de Pueblos, the Puerto Rican Day Parade, the Puerto Rican National Civil Rights Association, and a Brooklyn businessmen's association, decided to denounce the farce publicly. We agreed that we would make our voices heard, and that we would speak out in Spanish. The first day of the hearings, we were there. The chairman of the commission, the Reverend Theodore Hesburgh, was at the microphone. Behind the commission's table was a curtain, and you could see that there was a whole squad of FBI agents with cameras back there. There were microphones scattered around the hearing room, and each committee-member had his or her own. The interpreter they'd hired could hardly speak Spanish.

Many of the witnesses were not even Puerto Rican, and among the Puerto Ricans, most were Uncle Toms who had never taken part in any of our community's activities. We were surprised to see Joe Monserrat on the list of those who were going to testify.

As we'd agreed, when the signal was given our own witnesses took over the microphones. Hesburgh refused to let us speak, and he ordered the federal marshals to remove us. And that started a ruckus. Those of us who were standing at the microphones on the floor threw the mikes in the trash, while another group rushed the dais, took the committee-members' microphones away and threw them in the trash, too.

Hesburgh stood up and rushed behind the curtains. Since there were lots of reporters in the room, the FBI agents didn't dare come out, for fear of being photographed. The next day, after receiving two anonymous bomb threats, Hesburgh decided to cancel the hearings.

About a dozen of us were arrested. We were accused of disturbing the peace, interfering with the work of a federal agency, and assault. The judge dismissed all the charges. Four weeks later, the members of the committee that had organized the "welcome" for the federal commission held our own hearings. We organized six committees, all of whose members truly belonged to our community: one committee on education, one on health, one on politics, one on the right to work, one on violations of our legal and civil rights, and one on violations of human rights. The hearings lasted six days. We recorded them and sent copies of the recordings to the federal commission for their information and attention. They never took any action.

51.
CULEBRA AND THE PUERTO RICAN INDEPENDENCE PARTY

The work we Puerto Ricans and our allies in the United States did to fight the presence of the U.S. Navy on the island-municipality of Culebra, in Puerto Rico, and especially a massive march on November 19, 1971, helped bring about its withdrawal. In the first week of January, 1972, John H. Chaffee, Secretary of the Navy, went to Culebra to sign the agreement that would end the naval maneuvers on the island.

The incident I'm about to narrate took place at about 11:00 am on January 11, 1972. It occurred in Culebra, inside a huge tent brought in by the Navy for the signing of the resolutions to end the naval maneuvers and other military operations on Culebra, and also to make sure that we protesters were kept at a good distance from the colonial officials attending the signing. (It was revealed during this ceremony that the Navy would be moving its operations to the nearby island of Vieques—same song, second verse.)

Secretary Chaffee represented President Richard M. Nixon, the same man who less then three years later, in August 1974, would resign in the wake of the Watergate scandal. Chaffee was accompanied by all his aides-de-camp, while the government of Puerto Rico was represented by Luis A. Ferré, the governor of the colony; Rafael Hernández Colón, the Senate president; and Ramón Feliciano, the mayor of Culebra. What resulted was a huge public-relations show—you'd have thought they were granting Culebra independence!

When I found out what they were doing, I was infuriated. I was ready to jump over the security guards standing between me and the signers, grab all that paper, tear it to shreds, and throw it in Chaffee's face. But then I heard a voice inside me saying, "This is not the moment; it's not worth it." I've never been superstitious, but that little voice had saved my life several times before. According to a friend of mine who's an *espiritista*, it could be the voice of my mother watching over me. I don't practice *espiritismo*, but I do respect it, as I respected my beloved mother, who was a believer in that religion.

Anyway, I now see that holding back was a wise decision. Had I let myself be carried away by my passionate dreams of freedom and my own innate rebelliousness, I'm sure the authorities would have punished me to the full repressive extent of every possible federal and colonial law—obstruction of the work of a federal agency, incitement to riot, assault, and attempt on the life of a federal official and a governor—and sentenced me to life in prison. I might still be in jail, or serving a long probation imposed by the empire, or in a grave under an almond tree in Lares.

The place was packed with law-enforcement officers of every stripe and color. There were agents from the colonial government's intelligence services, the Navy, the FBI, and the military police. And all armed to the teeth. Some looked nervous, never taking their hands off the butts of their pistols.

Attending the ceremony were also representatives of groups that had led the protests against the Navy presence on Culebra, including the leadership of the Puerto Rican Independence Party, the PIP, whose president was Rubén Berríos Martínez. The Committee for the Defense of Culebra, whose headquarters were in New York and of which I was a member, had brought in a good number of delegates, including the board of directors of the Culebra town-club and its president Juan Feliciano, the brother of the mayor of Culebra. There were also comrades of ours from New Jersey and Connecticut. In all, there were representatives from at least seventy-five organizations, among them the Puerto Rican Day Parade Committee, the Folklore Festival, the Congreso de Pueblos, the Puerto Rican National Association of Civil Rights, the Barceloneta town-club, and more, including several progressive American unions. Many of these organizations had passed resolutions calling for the Navy's withdrawal from Culebra and sent them to all the pertinent agencies in Washington, D.C.

When we arrived in Culebra we were subjected to a number of sad and painful situations. One I'll never forget was the arrogant attitude shown by Rubén Berríos. The day the agreement was to be signed, the PIP called a press conference outside the tent where the signing ceremony was to take place. Berríos went straight to the point and spoke eloquently in denunciation of what was happening. After the reporters had asked their questions, he stepped away from the microphones. At that moment, I approached him to ask that we be allowed to say a few words. Berríos got very upset; he treated us as though we were unwelcome, or were a nuisance. His response was sharp: "If you want to make a statement to the press, call your own press conference." The only thing we wanted to do was make clear our support for the PIP's statement. Maybe what upset Berríos was the irrefutable fact that the group from the States had more people there than the PIP did, and he wanted to give the press the impression that everyone there was a member of his own party.

At that very instant, Mayor Feliciano came out of the tent. Juan Feliciano and the Culebrans with him began berating the mayor, calling him a traitor and a Judas to the cause of demilitarization. We had to calm Juan down, because he wanted to make a public statement denouncing Berríos and calling on him to get off his high horse. Rubén realized the situation he'd created, and he proceeded to inform the press that there were two groups there: the PIP group and us. From my point of view, there was only one group in the struggle, fighting against a single enemy.

In the end, we didn't lose any sleep over Berríos' attitude. We knew that our work in solidarity with all the others was yielding positive results, and that its effect was being felt in congressional districts all over the United States, because it was the elected officials who were calling the Secretary of the Navy and other federal agencies, demanding action on the situation.

52.
HOW WE GOT HUMBERTO PAGÁN
RELEASED FROM PRISON IN CANADA

I think it was on a Wednesday. I'd just arrived at my office at the Congreso de Pueblos when my secretary told me that a man named Nelson had called, saying he needed urgently to meet with me. She'd told him she expected me around 3 pm, so he was supposed to come in at that time to see me.

I knew several people named Nelson. Around 3:15, the person in question came in, but it was none of the Nelsons I knew. This man said his name was Nelson Canals and that he'd come on behalf of comrades in Puerto Rico who were working to try to get a young man named Humberto Pagán out of prison in Canada. He was being held, Canals said, in Ottawa, Ontario.

Canals told me Humberto's story. He'd been a student at the University of Puerto Rico (UPR) and in the late sixties and early seventies he'd taken part in the fight to remove the ROTC (the Army's Reserve Officers Training Corps) from the campus. The presence of the ROTC on the UPR campus, which underscored the island's colonial status, had been the cause of violent conflict at the institution on and off for years. The struggle had intensified in the early seventies. In 1971, a police captain named Juan Birino Mercado had been mortally wounded in a confrontation with students when the police department's hated Fuerza de Choque, or SWAT team, entered the campus.

The authorities had needed a scapegoat, and they summarily suspended Humberto due to his militancy in the ROTC struggle. A short time later he was accused of first-degree murder and violation of the Weapons Act, and an arrest warrant was issued for him. An exorbitant bail was set, which he couldn't possibly have paid, but his defense team got it reduced. A short time after being released on bail, and fearing for his life,[26] Humberto fled the island. He flew to New York, where he hid out for several months, but then when he tried to cross the border into Canada he was arrested by the Canadian Royal Mounted Police and, on September 30, put into a maximum-security prison. The U.S. government was requesting extradition.

When Canals visited me, Humberto had been in prison for about three months. Just a few weeks later, the extradition hearing was to be held in Ottawa. He needed help. The first order of business was to find an attorney in Canada to represent him, since his legal counsel, attorney Roberto José Maldonado, was not licensed to practice in that country. The second thing Canals thought we should do was form a group in New York City to show solidarity with Pagán. And there needed to be supporters at the hearing.

We immediately called Bernard Mergler, a well-known labor lawyer and civil-rights activist, who agreed to take the case. We didn't have much time to organize a suitably impressive delegation from New York, so we started on that right away, too. We needed a bus to drive us to Canada; that was complicated because it was a long trip and winter was coming on. Fortunately, I had contacts with several charter-bus companies, so that was taken care of without too much trouble.

I called Frankie Gregory, a youngster I knew I could trust, to help me organize the activity. Frankie was a boxer, and he liked to play the conga drums and sing. He did a good job, and he recruited several of his friends. We also took several members of the Young Lords and of the Puerto Rican Socialist Party. El Comité,[27] which was located at 95th St. and Columbus, also sent a delegation. We filled the bus, which charged us $700 for the round trip. Some of the supporters didn't have the money to pay for their trips, so insofar as we could, we helped them out.

Before we left, we made the rules clear: We were going to Canada to defend a brother. We had to walk the straight and narrow and avoid giving the Canadian or U.S. government any ammunition against us or Humberto, or any reason to come down any harder on him than they already had. No one on probation would be allowed to go; there would be no alcohol, or even medicine containing alcohol, and no marijuana or other controlled substances. Two or three of the would-be travelers got off the bus.

Once that was all clear, we set off for Canada. Many of the men and women on the bus had never been outside New York except to visit their families in Puerto Rico. We left around 3:00 in the morning from 254 W. 72nd St. and headed directly for the turnpike to Buffalo. From there, we drove to Tonawanda and on to the Canadian border. We arrived at Niagara Falls around 9:30 that morning. The beauty of the falls was breathtaking. We went through border control without any major problems.

Frankie had brought his conga drums and some tambourines, and as soon as we entered the Canadian migration office, we started to play and sing. The Canadian officers didn't know what to make of us—nothing like that had ever happened before. They called their supervisors, but they decided not to take any action.

Not long afterward, the Canadian support group came and we followed them in our bus to the place where we'd be staying. That same day we organized a demonstration in downtown Ottawa. We handed out flyers with information on the case. The Ottawans greeted us enthusiastically and promised their support.

The next day the extradition hearing was to be held in the Queen's Court. We entered the courtroom and took our seats. We then proceeded to attach the flags of Puerto Rico and Lares to the walls. This action infuriated the prosecutors and the legal team from the U.S. government. After discussing the matter with our legal advisers, we decided to take the flags down.

The protocol in the thickly carpeted courtroom dated from the times of Henry VIII. When the hearing began, a figure entered all decked out in eighteenth-century regalia: a wig and a flowing robe with lace cuffs and collar. He moved ceremoniously toward the judge's chair and adjusted it. He then brought in a pitcher of water and poured a glass. He looked like he'd stepped out of a novel. After this strange figure left, another officer entered with a heavily decorated staff to announce the entrance of the magistrate who would hear the case. Finally, Humberto Pagán's turn came. He was brought in in handcuffs by two guards. As he entered, our group got to our feet, raised our left fists and started singing "La Borinqueña" with the revolutionary lyrics by Lola Rodríguez de Tió. The Canadian police were very upset, and the court officials told us that if we committed another act of that kind, they'd ask the judge to remove us.

Then the first figure came out again, stopped in the doorway, and exclaimed, "Hear ye, hear ye! All manner of person that have anything to do at this Court, let them give their attendance and they shall be heard. God save the Queen." Suddenly, someone yelled, *"Fuck the Queen!"* That wasn't part of our script, but since we'd been "acting up," we could easily be blamed for it. We weren't thrown out thanks to the intervention of the defense counsel, who argued eloquently that it was absurd to think that we'd come all the way from New York City just to do something stupid that would get us thrown out of the hearing. And several people had seen the shouter leave the courtroom immediately after he'd yelled. The bailiff corroborated this, saying the person had run out of the courtroom the minute he'd shouted. The judge looked down on us with his glasses halfway down his nose, as though we were some strange species of humans, but he did allow us to stay in the courtroom during the hearing.

The defense was brilliant. Humberto was exonerated. The government of the United States wasn't able to prove its case, and in June of that year the court found that there was no probable cause for thinking he was guilty of the crime he'd been accused of. The extradition request was denied.

Humberto lived in Canada for a time. When he returned to Puerto Rico, he was arrested, but his attorney presented a motion of *habeas corpus* and he was released. The case was not pursued. Humberto returned to the UPR, graduated, and entered law school. He graduated from law school, and according to the information I have, he's practicing his profession today.

53.
MY DEBUT ON PUBLIC TELEVISION

Since the thirties, Puerto Ricans in New York had had a pretty bad reputation. If not for the fact that we were American citizens, we'd probably have been deported back to Puerto Rico. Beginning in the fifties, and due in part to the tremendous number of immigrants from the island, the negative view of Puerto Ricans began to spread beyond the city: We Puerto Ricans were now problematic *everywhere*. We were seen as a plague. Wherever we moved to, things went to hell in a hand basket, or so people said. This image, created and propagated by the sensationalist, racist press, was fed by other mass media. In 1961, with the success of the movie *West Side Story*, which won ten Oscars and was the second-most profitable movie in the U.S. that year, the Puerto Rican "spic" became known to the entire nation. Over the next few decades we had to struggle against that image, which spread like a virus in the media. And to that, you might add the fact that the doors to the media were closed to Hispanics generally.

In 1972, a group of Puerto Rican activists, among them Diana Caballero, Esperanza Martel, Julio Rodríguez, and I, organized the Puerto Rican Education Action Media Council to combat that stereotypical image of Puerto Ricans in the media and to demand that they open their doors to us, in a gesture of "equal expression."

As was always our practice, we first tried to negotiate in good faith with the management of WNET, Channel 13, the main public-television broadcaster in the area, for a series of programs that would show the other face of our community, the face never shown by the media. As might have been expected, the management rejected our proposal. So we had no alternative but to convince them.

Every year, WNET held a marathon to raise funds for its operational expenses. Our operation was relatively simple. Several of us "volunteered" to answer the phones during the fund-raiser. Once inside, in the middle of the station's programming, we took over the main microphone, read a public proclamation, and held a sit-in, while outside more than 250 others picketed the station. WNET cut the signal and called the police, who arrested several of us. But Channel 13 realized that it had to negotiate, and finally the management agreed to give us our program. And that was the origin of

Realidades, the first bilingual program on public television in the United States and the first series in the United States to present us as we really are. In time, the series was syndicated and became a program produced by the most important and influential Puerto Ricans in U.S. television.

54.
FROM REPUBLICAN CADET
TO AIR PIRATE

My first contact with the Puerto Rican Nationalist Party came in 1932, when I helped plant that tamarind tree in the Plaza de la Revolución in Lares. Although I didn't become a "dues-paying, card-carrying" member of the Nationalist Party until 1993, I did take part in its activities while I lived in New York, and I served on its committees to defend the Nationalist political prisoners. Through his example and teachings, Pedro Albizu Campos taught me to love my country, to respect those who disagreed with me, to have no fear of the empire, and to defend my land no matter the cost. I met almost all the Nationalist leaders who were imprisoned at one time or another in our history, especially those who had lived for any period in New York City. I fought hard for their release from prison, and I cultivated the friendship of many of them, including Clemente Soto Vélez and Carmen Pérez.

In 1972, I organized a trip to Puerto Rico with the express purpose of taking a group of young Puerto Ricans, many of whom had never set foot on the island, to attend the commemoration of the Nationalist uprising on October 30, 1950. Although we were not members of the Nationalist Party, we dressed as Republican Cadets for our trip; it was our way of paying homage to the many Puerto Ricans who had been murdered or imprisoned by Yankee imperialism and its lackeys on the island.

All of us who took the trip were politically active in New York City. We knew that the FBI had us all under surveillance, and we suspected that there was an informant in the group, so before we left we steeled ourselves to avoid any confrontation, and we gave strict instructions to that effect. We were not going for a vacation, and we shouldn't expect the trip to be easy or fun. We were going to a political activity and to make a political statement on behalf of all the Puerto Ricans in the diaspora.

For many of the young men and women it was a very revealing adventure, and they were able to see the psychological effects that colonialism has caused on the island. When we reached the town of Jayuya to take part in the activities, many residents closed their doors when they saw us pass by. Several refused to give us water. Some businesses refused to sell us anything to eat, or even a box of chewing gum.

During the whole trip, the FBI dogged our heels. When we boarded the plane to fly back home, agents were waiting for us dressed in mechanics' and stewardesses' uniforms. We left late at night on the red-eye flight. We each took our seat. Mine was at the back. Fifteen minutes before takeoff, I heard a ruckus at the front of the plane. Then a stewardess came to my seat and asked if I was the leader of the group. I said I was. At that, she informed me that the captain was not going to take off until two members of our group, who were sitting up front, got off the plane. I asked her why that was and she told me that one of them had made a pass at a lady sitting beside him. The two youngsters, for their part, came back to complain that they wanted to throw them off the plane. I assured them that we'd fly back as we'd come: Together. They calmed down and returned to their seats. Just then, the captain came on the loudspeaker to announce in his heavily English-accented Spanish that the whole group had to leave the plane. We were prepared for any eventuality. I gave the order that no one was to leave the plane, that everyone was to stay calm, and I told the stewardess that to avoid confusion, I, as the group's spokesman, would be the only person to make statements for the group. The stewardess returned to the front of the plane and told the captain about our conversation.

The captain, a big, overweight, red-faced man with bags under his eyes, stormed back to me and started yelling at me in English and Spanish. He was accompanied by several men in mechanics' overalls. I noted that some of them were carrying not wrenches or other tools but some sort of cable, which reminded me nastily of garrotes. Very calmly, I told him that I spoke both languages, but that in his case I would speak only English. I then proceeded to tell him that they were trying to fabricate a case against us, since the young man they'd accused of making a pass at the lady was a very serious, respectful student.

By that time, we'd decided what action we were going to take: a group of us were going to stay on the plane. The rest, composed of anyone with a criminal record or on probation, were to leave the plane. We also agreed that one of the young women, who had experience with the press, was also going to leave the plane so she could inform the media what was happening. Around 12:30 am, the captain told us we had ten minutes to gather our things and leave. We took fifteen. The captain and stewardesses were waiting at the door of the plane. Twenty-four members of our group left. Eight of us stayed on board, and we sat in the last seats in the back.

Upset, the captain came back to where we were sitting and yelled: "*Everyone in your group has to leave this plane!*" I answered that the twenty-four who had left would sleep in the airport until the next day, but that we were going to stay on the plane, since we'd done nothing wrong, nothing that would justify throwing us off. If the plane couldn't take off because we were on board, then it wouldn't take off. "You're going to have to take us off in handcuffs," I told him.

Outside, the police were awaiting orders. In the meantime, another captain came on board—a police captain—with a squad of officers and said to me, "The captain said all of you have to leave. If you don't, we'll have to arrest you. You should be ashamed of yourselves, coming to Puerto Rico to create a riot and make all this fuss." I told him the one who ought to be ashamed of himself was him, who was discriminating against his Puerto Rican brothers and sisters— we'd done absolutely nothing wrong. "You, Captain González"—I knew his name because somebody had called him by it—"must know the procedure to follow when an accusation is made that's as despicable as the one the pilot has lodged." The captain told me to shut my mouth or he'd shut it for me, and that we were all under arrest.

While all this was going on, Rosalina Reilova, the young woman in charge of the group that had gotten off the plane, called the press and then called in two lawyers to represent us. It was now after 1:00 in the morning, and all the media— newspapers, radio, and television—had arrived at the airport, but they weren't allowed in to interview us. When we were taken out of the plane in handcuffs, we were loaded into police transport vehicles and taken before a magistrate.

The judge, who looked like he'd been waked up to hear the case, asked who was lodging the complaint against us. PanAm, which went bankrupt not long after, had sent one of its minions to lodge the complaint. The first thing the judge asked him was whether he had witnessed what happened. He said he hadn't; he was just repeating what the captain of the plane had told him. The judge immediately asked whether there were any eyewitnesses in the courtroom. When no one answered, the judge dismissed all the charges against us and set us free.

The fact is, that judge acted like Pontius Pilate—he washed his hands of us. We'd hardly left the courtroom when agents from the FBI identified themselves and informed us that we were being charged under such-and-such section of such-and-such federal law. We were being accused of attempting to hijack a Pan American plane and take it to Cuba! We were handcuffed again and taken to the FBI offices in Puerta de Tierra. They tried to interrogate us, but we demanded the right to have our attorneys present. So they threw us into holding cells. Not long afterward, an agent came in and told us they'd sent out for coffee for us. One of the girls yelled, "Nobody drink that coffee!" One of the guys said, "These guys take us for fools. We drink that coffee and we'll never shut up talking."

That night we slept in the FBI's holding cells. The next day, which was Saturday, we were transferred to La Princesa, the jail in Old San Juan where the Nationalist leaders had been imprisoned in the thirties. When we arrived, we found that a group of prisoners in the federal section were waiting for us, and they greeted us very respectfully. It turns out that by this time every newspaper and radio station and TV news program on the island had reported on our case, including the accusation that we'd tried to hijack a plane to Cuba. The reception committee had blankets, towels, toothpaste and toothbrushes, and razors for us. We stayed in La Princesa until Monday, since the federal court was closed during the weekend. On Monday, the judge the case had been assigned to was busy with another case. Finally, he heard the case on Tuesday.

The judge in our case was Hiram Cancio. Our defense was handled by attorneys William Abreu and Luis Estades. That morning when we arrived at court we found that our people had mounted a very combative picket line outside the courthouse, while other comrades packed the courtroom. The press, of course, was also present.

In federal court in Puerto Rico, only English is spoken. When I was called to testify, I began to explain in clear English what had happened. I guess I was going too fast because the judge stopped me in the middle of the story to ask me to speak more slowly, since he wasn't able to catch some of the things I said.

The FBI presented its case. After hearing the ridiculous accusations, and the obviously invented details, Judge Cancio found no probable cause and ordered us released. But before we returned to New York, we were locked up in La Princesa again while our names were stricken from the jail's register.

Finally, on Thursday, we were released. I had taken advantage of my stay in jail to record my radio program, Lucha. That Thursday all of New York heard the story of what happened to us that weekend.

When we returned to New York, a Puerto Rican attorney offered to represent me in a suit against Pan American Airlines. He sold out to Pan Am. Still, I feel I came out a winner—Pan Am went bankrupt, and the lawyer went to hell.

55.
BACK TO UNIONIZING

After my problems with Mayor Lindsay and the Human Rights Commission, I was unemployed for a while. Finally, a friend I had helped find a job as a wholesale liquor salesman with Peerless bought a liquor store and offered me his sales territory. Without a job and needing money, I accepted. Being bilingual was a definite advantage, but in fact most of my customers were Puerto Ricans, and they knew who Gilberto Gerena Valentín was. My sales were good, and since I was earning a commission, I was bringing home pretty good money. Still, the work was not satisfying to me.

In 1975, Dennis Silverman, president of Local 810 of the Teamsters Union, sent for me. He wanted to talk to me about several shops he wanted to organize and others that had contracts with the union but were causing problems. I agreed to go to work as an organizer again. The work included inspecting shops along the Hudson River and East River in Manhattan. Many of these factories employed only workers from Honduras, Ecuador, and other Central American countries, who could be more easily exploited than Puerto Ricans. The abuses became so blatant that in one of the factories, the management put up a sign in big letters (and bad spelling)—"*Si sabes ingles no te molestes en solicitor trabajo*": If you know English don't bother to aply. We reported the plant to the state Labor Department, but they did nothing about it.

It was rumored that the Mafia controlled many of these factories. People also said that in many cases the owners would pay the police to help them keep the unions out and ensure that no organizers infiltrated their plants. I think that was one of the reasons Silverman called me. In addition to the reputation I had as a defender of civil rights, everybody knew that I wasn't afraid of anything and that I'd go right out onto the floor to pass out preference cards for the workers to sign.

During this time I put together a group of Puerto Rican comrades who specialized in pickets. The number I used depended on the situation. I paid them $25 an hour, but it was money well spent. When that group was picketing, you had to watch out. I especially remember one printing plant in South Brooklyn. People said it belonged to the Gambino crime family. I set up a picket of 35 men, all with a great deal of experience in this kind of problem. By 5 am, the picket was in place. As always, my people came prepared for battle: combat boots, leather jackets, and ball-bearing-filled winter gloves that weighed about a half a pound apiece. You had to think about it twice before breaking that picket line. The trucks arriving with merchandise would turn around and leave, not just because a lot of the drivers were Teamsters and were supposed to respect the picket line, but also because of the elite picketers I'd brought in. That gave a little lift to the morale of the workers, and many of them refused to enter the factory.

After the third day of picketing, the owner threw in his cards and agreed to sit down and talk to the union. We signed the agreement. Silverman was very happy with my work at this and other plants, since I solved many of the problems he had, so I continued working as an organizer for him for a year. Many years later, after I'd moved back to Puerto Rico, I found out that Silverman had been fired for stealing several thousand dollars in union funds.

56.
CITY COUNCILMAN FOR
THE SOUTH BRONX

Until the 1950s, the Bronx was a borough of white people, mainly Jews, Italians, and Irish. In the early fifties, Puerto Ricans and, to a lesser extent, blacks began arriving in large numbers as housing costs in the Bronx began to fall. We Puerto Ricans concentrated in the South Bronx, the poorest area of the city, and the closest to Manhattan. You might say that the South Bronx was actually an extension of El Barrio. By 1960, most Puerto Ricans lived in that area. I myself started living there in 1976, after forty years in Manhattan. I left a pretty apartment I had on 76th St. and Riverside Drive and moved into a little three-room apartment at the back of the third floor of a building at 152nd St. and Cortland Avenue.

As it did in Manhattan, the Democratic machine controlled everything having to do with public service in the Bronx, including the courts. The machine leadership was almost entirely white, from the neighborhood leader to the borough president. If you weren't one of the boys, there was no way in. In order to be considered for any position, you had to have some political pull, and in order to be recognized as a leader you needed to be in a profession, preferably the law, had to belong to the neighborhood political club, and had to take part in what they called their "coffee klatches," which they almost always held outside the club. Every politician I knew—Herman Badillo, Bobby Garcia, Eugene Rodríguez, Ramón Vélez, Israel Ruiz, Salvador Almeida, Eugenio Álvarez, Armando Montano, Louis Nine, Manny Ramos, Irma Vidal Santaella, José Serrano, Felipe Torres and his sons, John Cordero, and William Martínez—put in their time with the Bronx Democratic Party machine.

A Puerto Rican would be admitted to the club because the machine let him in, and the machine let him in because it needed bait for the Puerto Rican voters' votes, not because we were considered equal. The men who ran the machine were racist to the bone. They referred to us as spics and made derogatory remarks such as "We don't want the spics to take over the town." Every one of the people whose names I mentioned were subjected to that treatment. Some of them even took part in such jokes. Don't misunderstand me—I'm not trying to diminish the political work done by those men and women, who in many cases made valuable contributions to the cause of our community. I'm just saying that's the way things were.

Even before I moved to the South Bronx, there had been a movement to create a coalition to end the corrupt machine's control in the borough. This coalition was made up of a broad range of organizations that included unions, churches, leftist political groups, and black and Puerto Rican community organizations such as the Congreso de Pueblos and the National Puerto Rican Association of Civil Rights.

When I moved, I started attending St. Ann's Episcopal Church,[28] where I met its pastor, the Reverend John Luce, with whom I developed a close friendship. John came from a very prominent Massachusetts family who were the owners of *Fortune* magazine and large shareholders in Con Edison, and very active in the community. In a conversation we had after the service one day, John suggested that I should consider running for the state assembly or the city council. At first, I resisted the idea. In the early sixties, I had run for city councilman-at-large, and those who had convinced me to do so, the reform wing of the Democratic Party, conspired at the last minute with the Democratic Party machinery and turned their back on me, so I lost the race. Plus, running for office meant investing a lot of money in campaign management and workers, lawyers, campaign offices, and all sorts of expenses that I just couldn't afford. "I'll have to think about it," I told John. While I was turning the idea over, a movement supporting my candidacy for city councilman for District 11 began to gather strength. My opponent would be the incumbent, Ramón Vélez.

Since his arrival in New York City in the early sixties, Ramón had taken part in the Puerto Rican community's struggles in the South Bronx. With money from the War on Poverty Program, he set up the Hunts Point Multiple Service Center, which became a kind of personal fiefdom in the community. In 1973, with the support of the Democratic machinery in the city, he was elected city councilman for that district. Ramón was an extremely astute politician. To keep his programs running, he needed to raise money. And he used the machine for that purpose, while the machine used him to keep its political control over the district.

Finally, the proponents of the idea of my candidacy invited me to a meeting at St. Ann's to try to convince me to run. Representatives from several groups were there, among them a church committee, a renters' committee, and a political organization known as the Community and Labor Alliance for

Change, whose headquarters were in Manhattan but which did community work in the Bronx. There was also a committee made up of gypsy-cab drivers. These were men I had helped years earlier in their struggle for the right to work. And last, there was a committee of parents from the district's elementary school. Attorney John Klotz was also there. I had known John for some time; he was an expert in election law. I told these groups that I would give them my answer at a subsequent meeting.

At that time I was single, but I had a girlfriend who was always a tremendous help to me. She convinced me to accept the challenge. I did accept, but under certain conditions, including the creation of a campaign fund. That same night the campaign committee was organized. Herman Badillo, who was a congressman at the time but was running for mayor in the Democratic primaries, promised to help me. We started from scratch. We set up a campaign headquarters at 391 E. 149th St. and ran the operation out of those offices. Our funds, almost always too little, barely stretched to pay the rent, two telephones, and our printing expenses. A lot of very well-known people joined us, along with several unions and many young people who wanted to change what was happening in the South Bronx. There were also those who would say, "Gerena, I'm with you," but I knew them, and I knew that was pure talk.

When the announcement was made that I was running for the city council, the Democratic machinery and its Puerto Rican allies started sharpening their knives. Seeking to discredit me, they announced that I was an *independentista* and a Nationalist. They repeated the old accusations that I was a Communist and a subversive, but then added that I was a terrorist and a "bomb thrower," as the racist Ed Koch called me. (Koch, by the way, won the primaries that year and went on to become mayor.) Other people accused me of being an opportunist, and of splitting the Puerto Rican vote.

From the beginning we knew that the race would be touch and go. Although gathering signatures is important, and not easy, validating them with the Elections Board was even more important, and considerably more difficult. The Democratic machine controlled the Elections Board, and on the machine's orders, the Board would invalidate enough signatures to keep a candidate from getting on the ballot. Officially, you needed 1,500 signatures from registered voters, but everyone knew you had to submit many, many more than that, because the nit-picking examiners would always "find" that most of the signatures were fraudulent. Then, in order to continue on, you had to go through a long, hard process of going through voter lists and sometimes knocking on doors to prove that the signatures you'd collected were legitimate. And the machine never admitted defeat. If you took your case to court, you'd be facing the borough president's battery of lawyers, including Stanley Schlein and Paul Bleifer, experts in political legerdemain who used every possible technicality to disqualify a candidate who hadn't been baptized in the Church of the Democratic Machine.

Our attorney, John Klotz, oversaw everything having to do with gathering signatures. We gathered 5,000, which was 3,500 more than the number required, and we were assured that they were all legitimate. And in fact, the city elections board accepted enough to certify my candidacy. But the state board revoked that decision, alleging that thousands of the signatures were invalid. We were left with 1,495 signatures, five fewer than needed. In the hearing to reconsider, we answered all the board's objections, but it still refused to certify me. Klotz took the case to court in the Bronx, whose judges were strongly influenced by Stanley Friedman, president of the Democratic Party in the borough. As we'd expected, the court ruled against me.

We decided to take the case to district court. The hearing was scheduled for Friday, September 9, 1977, at 4:00 pm, and the primaries were to be held the next Tuesday. Klotz's argument was brilliant. He argued that the board's action violated the civil rights of the 1,500 people who had endorsed my candidacy, as well as Section V of the Voting Rights Act of 1965. Federal judge Robert Ward accepted the argument and ordered that my name be included on the ballot. All parties, including the machine's lawyers and the representative of the elections board, left the courtroom like our coats were on fire.

The first thing we did after leaving the courtroom was call our headquarters, where our team of volunteers was anxiously awaiting the judge's decision. We were prepared for a judgment in our favor; we had prepared thousands of flyers in Spanish and English. The group in charge of the telephone bank called their contacts in the housing projects to come in and pick up the flyers and start distributing them in their communities. From that point on, for the next three days, we talked to people, shook hands, kissed babies, held rallies on street corners, and passed out thousands of flyers, while at headquarters more than twenty volunteers on the phone bank called voters day and night.

The judge's decision took the Democratic machine and Ramón's group by surprise—they'd given their people a vacation, since they thought I was out of the race. They'd even organized a dinner for that night at El Quijote, a restaurant on 116th St. in El Barrio, to celebrate their victory. You know what they say, though: Don't count your chickens. . . I still remember the faces of the people in the restaurant when I showed up to tell them that Gerena Valentín would be taking part in the primaries.

I won the primaries by 300 votes. That Friday we celebrated our victory as a city councilman, because whoever won the Democratic primaries was a virtual shoo-in for the elections in November. Even so, we didn't let our guard down. On election day, we posted volunteers near every voting place to ensure there was no campaigning going on and that the voting machines didn't break down (or "break down") and slow the voting and thereby discourage people, who would go home without voting. We won handily, with over 94% of the votes.

I took my seat on the city council on January 1, 1978. There, the Democratic machine's opposition and Mayor Ed Koch awaited me, and they made sure to do everything they could to hinder my work. Anything I tried to accomplish took a huge effort. Although there were two other Puerto Rican councilmen, Roberto Rodríguez, from El Barrio, and Luis Olmedo, from Brooklyn, their support was never assured, since in the last analysis they had to answer to the Democratic machine. It was a constant search for consensus, alliances, and coalitions, and many times it worked. Despite the machine, I was able to do a lot of good work for my district.

57.
SWANK

Newsstands in New York City sell not just newspapers but hundreds of magazines in every language and on the most diverse subjects, including the so-called "adult magazines." One of the most popular magazines of this last kind was called Swank. It was intended for middle-class white men. It was published monthly and sold for $2.25.

In its August, 1978, edition, *Swank* published a column titled "50 Puerto Rican Jokes." One day, around 8 am, I received a call from Luis Pérez, one of our community organizers in the South Bronx, who asked me if I had heard about the jokes. I told him I hadn't, but I bought the magazine when I went out to take the subway to the city council offices. When I read the article, I couldn't believe my eyes. I was so angry that my curses must have made the author's ears burn—some guy named Noel Joseph. Later I learned that earlier that year, Joseph had started publishing a regular column of ethnic jokes, and he'd already made fun of the Poles, the Italians, and the Jews. Now it was the Puerto Ricans' turn.

The jokes were totally racist, and they reflected the worst stereotypes about Puerto Ricans. We were portrayed as dirty, ignorant, criminal, and lazy. For example: "Why do Puerto Ricans wear pointed-toe shoes?" Answer: "To kill cockroaches."

Question: "How can you figure out how many Puerto Ricans there are in New York City?" Answer: "Count the number of basements and multiply by 15."

"Last night 115 Puerto Ricans died. The bed they were sleeping in collapsed."

"It's true that Puerto Ricans like to work. In fact, one opened a jewelry store not long ago. The problem is, he was captured by the police."

Nor did Puerto Rican women escape the insulting mockery. Question: "What are pretty women called in Puerto Rico?" "Foreigners."

"When a Puerto Rican woman says 'my man,' she means 'any man.'"

I was so enraged by these jokes that I couldn't go to work. When I came up out of the subway, I called in sick. I went back to the headquarters of the Congreso de Pueblos at 254 W. 72nd St. in Manhattan and called an emergency meeting for that night. About a hundred people came. After I explained the purpose of the meeting, we decided to launch a campaign to denounce *Swank*. Something that surprised us was the lack of support for the campaign by politicians. They refused to publicly denounce the magazine. It appears that they didn't want any trouble with the Fourth Estate.

Our plan to fight the magazine would unfold in stages. First, we created an organization called Puerto Ricans with Pride. Its director was the Reverend Ángel Luis Jaime Rivera. We went to the print media and later to radio and TV stations to denounce the magazine. Afterward, we requested a meeting with the magazine's board of directors to ask that they print a retraction. They refused to speak to us. So we decided to intensify our campaign. Among other things, members of the Congreso would go to newsstands and pour ketchup and other substances over the display of *Swanks*. The stuff would splatter other magazines and newspapers, and that would make the owners of the newsstands angry, since they wouldn't be able to sell those copies. The effect was that many newsstands stopped selling the magazine altogether.

Finally, on Thursday, October 26, we set up a picket line in front of the building where the magazine's offices were, at 56th St. and Seventh Avenue. There were about five hundred people on the picket line. Representatives from all walks of life took part: the labor movement, including the Hispanic Council of the AFL-CIO; show business; churches; and civic organizations. Thousands of Puerto Rican flags filled the street. If you know Manhattan, you know that this is a hub of vehicular traffic in the city. Traffic was paralyzed from 59th St. to 53rd St. We picketed for several days.

The editor of *Swank*, Herman Petras, called a press conference and made the following statement: "I am sitting in my office and I cannot believe that this is happening to me. We made Jewish jokes, Polish jokes, Greek jokes, Irish jokes, and black jokes, and nothing happened. We only got a few letters criticizing us. These jokes sell magazines. We made a few jokes about the Puerto Ricans and had no idea they were going to get so hot under the collar." Petras insisted that the magazine was just adding a little ethnic humor, and that there was no harm intended.

Our campaign was a complete success. The October number of the magazine, which I suppose was already in press when we mounted our picket line, contained the last 50-joke column. It was about "little people." From that point on, the magazine never published ethnic jokes again. In fact, I don't recall any case of a magazine distributed within New York City that ever published jokes about Puerto Ricans or any other group again.

58.
THE PEOPLES' PARLIAMENT FOR PEACE

In 1978, I got married for the third time. Her name was María Riquelme, a painter very active in the struggle for Puerto Rican independence. I had two daughters with her: Marielita and Gilmarí. We also raised Taita, María's daughter from her first marriage. I thought of Taita as my own child. Not long after getting married, we found a beautiful apartment at 800 Grand Concourse.

At that time, the international situation was very tense. The possibility of a nuclear war hung like a cloud over the world every day. I was invited to take part in the World Peace Council (WPC). I enthusiastically accepted the invitation, as I am a fervent believer in the need for a world-peace movement that will ensure that tensions between nations don't devolve into interminable wars in which innocent men, women, and children die unnecessarily. Even more important, at that time I was deeply involved in the struggle to remove the Navy from Vieques in Puerto Rico. The WPC provided me a forum in which to talk about that cause.

Bill Michelson, a veteran union organizer and tireless advocate for peace, was coordinating the Council's meetings. María and I regularly attended them, although occasionally one of us would go without the other. We were active at every level, in universities, schools, and union halls, organizing meetings and rallies everywhere, trying to present resolutions on behalf of world peace and against the Navy's presence in Puerto Rico. We would go anywhere we could.

At one of the Council meetings, it was announced that plans were under way for a Peoples' Parliament for Peace to be held in Bulgaria in 1980 and that the United States had the right to send fifty delegates. I said to myself, "Gosh, I'd love to be chosen for that."

At the next meeting, Michelson announced the names of the people who had been pre-selected to go to the Parliament, and he asked that in the next few days they inform him whether they were available for the trip. I was delighted when I heard him call my name. However, I didn't like the idea of leaving María alone with the girls. When I told her the news, she was very happy. I told her that although I was excited about the idea, I would feel better if she could go, too, as a delegate. If that were possible, I thought, we could find some way to care for the girls while we were away. We were excited to think about attending an activity of such magnitude. We would be able not only to plead the cause of Vieques on a world stage, but also to meet many people from different parts of the world, and we would be able to visit Sofia, a city of great historical interest. This would also be my first visit to a Communist-bloc country. It was, in a word, a once-in-a-lifetime opportunity.

When I told Bill that I couldn't go, since I couldn't leave María alone with the girls, he was crestfallen. I was an important delegate, since I would have been the only Puerto Rican in the group, and was also a government official. He told me to give him a couple of days to see if he could do something, since funds were pretty limited. Two days later, he called me to tell me that the Council had agreed that both María and I *and* the girls could go to Bulgaria. The whole family! Wow!

The journey from New York to Bulgaria was very interesting. We made stopovers in London and Warsaw. Once we arrived in Sofia, we were put up in a very comfortable apartment in a luxury hotel, with four restaurants to choose from, serving Chinese, Italian, Greek, and American food, all excellent. During the meals, a group of violins and accordion would play for the diners. The girls loved it. Marielita adapted quickly. I remember that during the meals she would go from table to table shaking hands and introducing herself, mixing words in English and Spanish. People thought she was a little dwarf. In the morning, we were awakened by music and the singing of birds. Breakfast was smorgasbord style, several dishes on a buffet table. The service was excellent, and the hotel first-class.

The parliament met for two weeks. We were assigned an interpreter, very sweet, very considerate, always trying to make us feel at ease, and she spoke Spanish perfectly. Between sessions she would take us to visit places of interest. The first time we took a trolley and I tried to pay, I was told that public transportation in Bulgaria was free. What a difference from New York!

Whenever the occasion allowed, I would expound on the case of Puerto Rico and Vieques. In the Parliament's plenary session, attended by over two thousand delegates from around the world, the resolution I presented on the matter was adopted. There I also offered, on behalf of the United States delegation, the farewell message. My speech went on a little longer than it was supposed to, but the chairman of the parliament, as a courtesy, allowed me to have my say.

We were very pleasantly surprised and delighted when we were told that the Bulgarian government had extended our visa and was granting us two weeks of vacation, all expenses paid, in the city of Varna, on the Black Sea. We learned that the government of Bulgaria sent all workers with their families for a month of vacation at that tourist complex. As part of the arrangement, all vacationers went through a rigorous health examination; all five of us passed with flying colors.

The hotel where we stayed was in a green, leafy forest. We were given an apartment with a view of the ocean. Marielita came down with a terrible cold and very high fever. As soon as the spa management learned of the situation, they provided her with all necessary medical attention, and within two days she was running and jumping again. We had a wonderful time in Bulgaria. When the time came for our return, we were given an official farewell.

On the return trip, we had a stopover in Warsaw. At that moment, the situation in Poland was very tense. Lech Walesa and his Solidarity group, with the support of the U.S. Central Intelligence Agency and the Catholic Church, was in the process of overthrowing the Polish Communist Party government. On our arrival, we were informed that all foreign flights had been canceled. Through the good offices of the Bulgarian government and the Peoples' Parliament for Peace, we found a room in a hotel. But the situation was critical. Due to the emergency situation in the country, everything was rationed. There was just one meal a day, and no diapers for Marielita.

The next day, I went to the travel agency to ask when the next plane would be leaving for New York. In perfect English, the agent said, "In a month. . . maybe." I almost fainted. I had piles of work waiting for me at the city council. I had taken two weeks' vacation to attend the Parliament, then extended our stay for two weeks more, and now they were telling me that I probably couldn't leave for another month! Fortunately, I had quite a few days of accumulated vacation with the city council. I decided, however, to call Bill Michelson, who, through his connections in Bulgaria, started trying to find a way to get me home. Thanks to Bill's intervention, our stay in Poland lasted only three more days. We took advantage of the situation to visit the Chopin Museum and see a little of the city.

On my return to New York, I was invited to speak at several places about my experiences. I continued working with the World Peace Council, until it finally dissolved. I understand that it was later reactivated. Wars, however, have continued. Optimist to the end, I hope to see the day when there will be no more war, or colonialism, or imperialist incursions.

59.
MY VISIT TO TEHRAN

In February of 1979, a revolution led by the Ayatollah Khomeini deposed the Shah of Iran, Mohammad Reza Pahlevi. In November of that year, angry over the United States' policies of intervention in Iran's internal affairs and by the U.S. government's decision to allow the Shah to enter the U.S., a group of radical students took all the occupants of the U.S. Embassy in Tehran, the Iranian capital, hostage. The students demanded that the Shah be returned to Iran, in exchange for the hostages. As a consequence of this action, a diplomatic crisis occurred, threatening a possible armed intervention by the United States in Iran. Across the United States, especially in universities, groups espousing solidarity with the Iranian revolution were formed. The students who had occupied the embassy asked Prof. Norman Forer of the University of Kansas to come to Iran with a delegation made up of representatives of various sectors of U.S. society, including a Puerto Rican. A spokesman for the organization Reconciliation with Iran, Forer had traveled to Iran in December 1979, hoping to mediate in the crisis. Since I was very active in New York, and was also an elected official, he invited me to take part in this new initiative.

On February 7, forty-nine representatives of various U.S. racial, ethnic, and political groups departed as a delegation to Tehran. As we approached the city we were to land in—I can't recall the name—we discovered that there was an internal struggle in the revolutionary movement with respect to the unilateral decision by the young student militants to invite a non-official U.S. delegation, and we were not being given permission to land. Our plane was forced to keep circling the airport until the Iranian government finally agreed to let us enter the country. Once on the ground, we had to wait for almost an hour, partly due to problems related to our visas, before we could board the flight that would take us to the capital.

We arrived shortly after midnight at the hotel where our delegation was to stay. The next day, we began to visit sites selected by the students. We visited the prison in Tehran, where we saw hundreds and hundreds of photos of young people tortured and murdered by the Shah. We were told that the Shah had recruited one member from each of 60,000 families to serve as a spy for the government. We were shown various prison cells and instruments of torture. One of these instruments had been manufactured in a factory on Long Island.

It was a plastic helmet with a radio, and it would be put on the prisoner and the sound turned up so high that the prisoner would be driven mad. They also explained to us how women were tortured: a hose would be inserted in the vagina and the water turned on. If the victim didn't talk, her torturers would turn up the water until all her internal organs were destroyed. We visited a cemetery where many of the previous government's victims were buried.

We also visited the Shah's palace in Tehran. We were shown photographs of his other eleven palaces in various cities throughout the country. He had one palace where he stayed one day a month. The palace in Tehran had a theater, a bowling alley, a swimming pool, doors with gold door handles, countless bedrooms, and several kitchens and dining rooms. And the other eleven palaces were just as absurdly, insultingly luxurious. On my return from Iran I submitted a report to the city council. As one might have expected, the council members ignored it.

The conflict with Iran was the most important crisis faced by the Jimmy Carter administration. After several failed attempts, including the use of force, Carter managed to negotiate the American hostages' liberation just as his term ended. However, his inability to resolve the situation more quickly was used against him by the Republican candidate, Ronald Reagan, during the campaign that led to Reagan's election.

With respect to Carter, it is important to recognize that during the 1979 Christmas season, in response to our campaign, he gave a presidential pardon to the five Puerto Rican Nationalists who had spent over twenty-five years in U.S. prisons. The prisoners released were Oscar Collazo, who had been jailed for taking part in the attack on Blair House in 1950, and Lolita Lebrón, Irvin Flores, Rafael Cancel Miranda, and Andrés Figueroa, who had been imprisoned in 1954 for attacking the U.S. Congress in order to call the world's attention to the colonial status of Puerto Rico.

60.
A SHORT-LIVED BRANCH OF THE INDEPENDENCE PARTY IN NEW YORK

In 1979, Professor José Antonio Irizarry, a comrade in the struggle of many years' standing who died a few months ago, invited a group of *independentistas*· in New York City to a meeting at the Cabo Rojo town-club headquarters in the Bronx. Among those invited were husband-and-wife Hipólito Rosado and Juanita Arocho, and I. Irizarry said he wanted to reactivate the New York committee of the Puerto Rican Independence Party. I accepted the invitation. At the meeting, a committee was organized made up of seasoned fighters for Puerto Rican independence. Irizarry was elected chairman. I was elected to the board of directors. We decided to publish a monthly newsletter, which we called *La Hora*, which was the same name as the newspaper published by the PIP in Puerto Rico in the early seventies. The committee worked pretty well, without much friction between members. At one point we had as many as fifty active members who paid dues and attended every meeting. We organized several activities, among them a talk at Hunter College (CUNY) by Rubén Berríos on Puerto Rico and the United Nations.

At one meeting, we agreed to raise funds to help the party in Puerto Rico. We also agreed to request that we be allowed to have a seat on the party board in Puerto Rico, so that we could coordinate activities between the island and New York City. Hiram Meléndez, one of the PIP's best-known leaders and shortly afterward named the party's electoral commissioner, attended one of our meetings and seemed receptive to the idea.

We sent a letter setting out a series of recommendations to the party in Puerto Rico. The reply from party president Rubén Berríos was that the best thing the New York City committee could do to help the party was raise money for the party in Puerto Rico. And that was that.

That response to our recommendations was like a pitcher of cold water on our members' enthusiasm. Little by little, they stopped attending meetings and supporting the committee's activities. The moment came when we couldn't scrape up quorum. We had to disband the committee.

61.
YELLOW CABS AND GYPSY CABS

Not long ago I went to La Vega, in the Dominican Republic, to visit my friend Gilberto Marmolejo, who had worked with me on the campaign supporting the rights of yellow cab drivers in New York City during the seventies and eighties. He asked me whether the situation had changed at all. "Of course," I replied, remembering those dust-ups he'd been in up on 149th St. and Third Avenue. During our conversation, he mentioned that in Hartford, Connecticut, where he often went to visit, there had been a similar problem, but it was worked out immediately when the community united. In New York, I thought to myself, it hadn't been so easy.

When I accepted Mayor John Lindsay's offer to become a member of the Human Rights Commission in 1965, one of the conditions was that he begin to take concrete steps to end the abuse by the yellow cabs,[29] who refused to pick up passengers in our communities. In fact, that had been one of Lindsay's campaign promises—one which, like any good politician, he immediately reneged on.

In every borough in the city, when yellow cabs entered our community they would turn off their roof light or turn on the "off duty" sign. They would also lock their doors and roll up their windows—according to them, to keep the "nigger muggers" and "dirty spics" from robbing them. Their phobia against our people was unbelievable. They were pure, dyed-in-the-wool racists. And if you hailed a cab in Manhattan and told the driver you wanted to go, for example, to El Barrio, many of them, without batting an eyelash, would say they didn't go there because of all the "dirty" Puerto Ricans. They'd tell you to get out of their cab, and if you didn't, they'd call the cops.

This was not a new problem. Ever since I'd arrived in New York in 1937, the situation with the yellow cabs had been the same, and it had gotten worse under the O'Dwyer, Impelliteri, and Wagner administrations. With the growth of the Puerto Rican and African-American communities in the city and the refusal of yellow cab drivers to serve them, a new player had entered the industry: the gypsy cabs. These drivers were not just willing to come pick us up and take us to other parts of the city, into our own neighborhoods, they would also pick us up on the street, which the yellow cabs, which supposedly had a monopoly on street pick-ups, refused to do.

Since Brooklyn was the borough with the highest number of poor black and Puerto Rican neighborhoods, it had the highest number of gypsy-cab bases. There were bases in the South Bronx, on Eastern Parkway, on Pitkin Avenue, and in Bedford-Stuyvesant. Depending on the neighborhood, the bases would be run by Haitians, blacks, or Puerto Ricans. They also flourished in the Bronx and in Queens. In Manhattan, the main ones were in Harlem and El Barrio.

In Manhattan, the police would not allow gypsy cabs in from other boroughs, and those that worked in Manhattan were constantly being watched. When a cop—white, black, or Puerto Rican—ordered a gypsy cab to pull over, which they did for any minor "infraction," you could be sure that when the cab pulled away the driver would be carrying a half-dozen tickets: the left turn signal wasn't working, the windshield was destroyed (even with a tiny nick), etc. And if the cop didn't find anything, he'd make something up. With a yellow cab, however, that stuff never happened. It was always the gypsy driver that paid the tickets. And who was the gypsy driver? A Puerto Rican, a black guy, a Dominican, or a Haitian. It seemed as though the orders were coming from above, though they were unwritten.

Being a gypsy cab driver wasn't easy. You had to pay to work from a base so you could receive calls to pick up passengers, and you had to buy or rent a cell phone—cell phones were terribly expensive in those days. Then there was the fact that insurance companies didn't like gypsy cab drivers because most of them were black or Puerto Rican, so the drivers had to pay higher premiums. They also had to deal with unscrupulous insurance agents and even base owners who sold fake insurance policies. When a driver reported an accident, it would sometimes turn out that he wasn't insured, because the person that sold him the policy had kept the money. That was precisely what happened to a friend of mine who worked out of a base on the east side of the Bronx. To his misfortune, he got into an accident, and when he filed his claim, the insurance didn't cover the damage to the other car. The poor man was in a jam. He was working six and sometimes seven days a week to cover all his expenses, and if he took home $300 a week it was a lot. Since he couldn't pay for the damage, he was forced to sell off everything. It broke your heart!

Once I was elected city councilman for the South Bronx I used my position, as I did when I was human-rights commissioner with Lindsay, to advance the cause of the gypsy cab drivers. My position was clear: denying a man or woman of color a seat in a taxi was exactly the same as denying that person a seat at a lunch counter. It was clearly a criminal act that should be punished to the full extent of the law.

And the abuse of gypsy cab drivers was absurd. One day, a driver showed up at my office and asked me to help him with a situation that had come up. He told me that a cop who'd stopped him had given him a ticket for nine "infractions," including one for having his hair too long. I called the Human Rights Commission to report the case and turn it over to them. The person who answered told me, "Councilman, you can send the gentleman over if you want, but these cases take six months or longer to resolve." The driver was in a real bind. He had been cited for traffic court, and he'd probably get the book thrown at him. He didn't have the money to hire an attorney to represent him, and if he did find one, he'd probably tell him to plead guilty and charge him $100, which would be deducted from his miserable wages. It all came down to either paying the fines or having his driver's license suspended.

The city's Taxi and Limousine Commission, which was the regulating agency involved, was controlled by the yellow cab owners. In the seventies, it had tried to keep gypsy cabs off the streets altogether, but the gypsy cab drivers wouldn't take that lying down, so they organized to fight back. The first to organize were the cabbies in the Bronx. Among the leaders of this movement were José Rivera,[30] who had a gypsy cab base in the north part of the borough; Bob Muñoz; and Gilberto Marmolejo, my good friend the Dominican. They were joined by most of the bases in Brooklyn and Queens and several in Manhattan. It was a question of life or death. The war that ensued was intense, sometimes violent, even fatal.

In the Bronx, the gypsy cabbies decided to run all the yellow cabs out of the borough. Suddenly there began to appear yellow cabs destroyed or burned. This practice, which began in the South Bronx, began to spread to other parts of the borough, and then into other boroughs around the city. It was an eye for an eye, a tooth for a tooth. I should make it absolutely clear, in the name of fairness, that not all yellow cabbies were racist or guilty of discrimination against the gypsy cabs or our communities. But in class warfare, unfortunately everybody pays.

In precincts 40, 41, 42, and 43 in the Bronx, the police declared all-out war on gypsy cabs. Although there were a few Puerto Rican cops on the force in the Bronx, many of them were worse than the whites, because they were ashamed of being Puerto Rican. Police brutality became the order of the day. On one occasion, police officers fired from the roof of a five-story building on a gypsy cabbie who was active in the movement. According to the neighbors, the guy pleaded with the cops not to shoot him. Despite the fact that their identities were an open secret, people were so intimidated that no one dared identify the cops responsible for killing the taxi driver.

In response to this abusive behavior, the gypsy cabbies held a rally to protest the murder of their coworker. The demonstration was held on Prospect Avenue, on the exact spot where the cabbie's body was found. The organizers of the activity asked me to speak to the crowd, since I had been one of the most constant defenders of their rights, and the rights of the community, to have access to taxis in order to move around the city.

On the day of the activity, the police started arresting all the gypsy cab drivers, to keep them from taking part in the demonstration. The mobilization was brutal. As soon as I finished speaking, several friends arrived to get me out of there, since they had been told by a trustworthy source that if I spoke at the demonstration I might suffer the same fate as the dead cab driver. They escorted me to a private car and took me to a secure place. I reported the incident to the authorities, but as one might expect, no action whatsoever was taken.

In my position as city councilman, I asked to be named to the Transportation Committee. There, I proposed that gypsy cab drivers be officially recognized. Of course, that would not be their official name. The recommendation was that they be treated the same as the yellow cabs, and that they be given their own color.

Finally, the Transportation Committee took action; they decided to treat the gypsy cabs fairly. From that point on, the taxi industry recognized that the gypsy cab is and must be an integral part of this enormous city. The Taxi and Limousine Commission recognizes them officially, so they can go wherever they are needed. But it should be clear that this was not the result of the commission's goodwill, but rather stemmed from our struggle and our commitment to justice.

62.
FIVE BILLION—NOT IN RUBLES, BUT IN DOLLARS

Isolina had been working as my secretary for almost two years. She'd been recommended by a social worker who told me that Isolina was on welfare. Later, Isolina confessed that she had gone on welfare, which was the last thing she ever wanted, after she left her husband because he beat her. She had to eat and support her daughter, whom she could lose to Family Services if she didn't, and she wasn't going to allow that.

She was very thin, but strong. She was dark skinned, tough, very proud, dedicated to her work and to me, always punctual, in control in the office, and sometimes, when there was a lot of work, she would stay until late to help me out. She was an excellent typist and took good dictation. To all these excellent qualities, she added perfect English and Spanish, and she knew everyone in the area around my office, which was located at 149th St. and Third Avenue, in the very center of my electoral district. Obviously, whenever she would ask for some time off for an emergency, I always gave her whatever she needed. She was very happy with her work, and she liked working with me.

One day Isolina said to me very seriously, "Mr. Gerena, I wonder if you could give me just ten minutes of your time to talk to you about something that worries me." Seeing the serious expression on her face, I thought she was thinking about going back to her husband and wanted me to give her some advice. I said to myself, "I'm screwed. I just lost an excellent secretary." I had had others, but none of them had been as efficient as Isolina. Some came in late, so the office wouldn't be open to deal with the people seeking our services. Others missed too many days of work. Some of them seemed to have a funeral to go to every other week. And although I don't have anything against animals, one of them took her dog to the veterinarian every Monday. When I asked her to change her appointments to Saturday, she got mad at me and accused me of discriminating against animals. She never came back to work. You see why I was worried when Isolina looked so serious and told me she wanted to talk to me.

We met that Wednesday at three in the afternoon. Outside, the noise was deafening. In front of the building, at any hour, there was always a convention of drug addicts, both men and women. Four-letter words flew around like pigeons. Sometimes I would shout out the window for them to keep it down a little, and there was always one person in the group who'd say, "Let's go, guys, we're bothering the old man." The "old man" part was usually affectionate, or so I like to think. Sometimes at night I would walk down those streets alone, and some of them would always walk with me to protect me. Once in a while I would give them a couple of dollars to get something to eat with, or if it was cold I would buy them a cup of hot coffee. I imagine that by now a lot of them are dead, or on the way there. Drugs do kill.

Isolina didn't know how to start. To break the ice, I asked her about her daughter. She said she had her in a kindergarten, where she was happy with her new little playmates. I can't believe I then asked her how long it had been since she had seen her husband James. She bristled like a cat and shot back, "Listen, don't mention that son of a bitch to me. If he thinks I'm going back to him, he's got another think coming. If he even *thinks* about coming close to me, they'll throw him in The Tombs for six months." That relieved me a bit, since my fears had been misplaced.

So then I asked whether she'd mailed the announcements for the meeting Monday night at St. Ann's Church. She said she had and that it was clear there was going to be quorum. Finally, she took a deep breath and came to the point.

"Listen, Mr. Gerena, you remember the letter you dictated and sent to the Soviet ambassador to the United Nations?" I said I did and asked whether there had been any response. She said there hadn't been any yet and then she asked her big question: "What would we do if the government of the Soviet Union accepted our request for five billion dollars to help reconstruct the South Bronx?"

In the late seventies, the South Bronx had become, to the embarrassment of the United States, a symbol to the world of the social and economic inequalities of the wealthiest country in the world. In 1977, a few months after being elected president, Jimmy Carter visited Charlotte St., and he proclaimed that he was going to bring a massive injection of federal aid to the city to reconstruct devastated neighborhoods such as the South Bronx in New York and Watts in Los Angles. Over the next few years, the Carter administration—and the Koch administration in the city—sat back and did nothing, despite the constant lobbying we representatives of the community did in Washington and downtown.

It was now 1980, a year of primaries and election promises. Senator Edward Kennedy, who was in the running for the presidency in the Democratic Party primaries, visited Charlotte St. and criticized Carter for failing to make good on his promises. It was then that I decided to call the world's attention once again to our situation, so I sent a letter to the Soviet government requesting funds to rebuild our community. Imagine, a city councilman in New York City, the center of U.S. capital, going to a socialist country and an archenemy of the United States to ask for money for a poor neighborhood!

Isolina, who was very committed to my agenda, hadn't been able to get it out of her head: What would we do if the Soviets agreed to see us and discuss my proposal? I explained that in that case, we'd invite a select group of men and women who have always been with us to be part of the negotiating committee, and I asked her to make up a list of ten people she thought ought to be on it.

Then she asked another question, which I figure was bothering her the most: "Well, suppose the Soviets tell you that they're prepared to accept your proposal. Do you know how many people are going to jump all over us? Some because they'll think that the program is like one of those run by the 'pimps of poverty,' as you call them. Others will come out of the woodwork to try to run it. By that I mean the politicians who've never supported you, always attacked you. I get nightmares just thinking about it.

"And what about the mayor, who hates you because you're supposedly a bomb-thrower, as he calls you? Miserable racist. I'll bet he doesn't call Badillo that. He won't be any too pleased, you know, and he's not going to take a back seat."

I explained that in politics, you have to expect that sort of behavior, and much worse, to which she replied in anguish, "I'll tell you, Mr. Gerena, I'll leave. In fact, I'm going to Puerto Rico."

When I heard that, I said, "So you're jumping ship? We don't even have the money yet, and you're talking about leaving me. Let me tell you—if the Soviets, for political or ideological reasons, decide to give that money to the South Bronx, I'll take it. I don't care about the pimps of poverty or the politicians and their politicking. Plus, nobody—*nobody*—is going to put one red cent into any project if there's not a serious commitment by serious people. You must know that the State Department would step in, because that would be news that would shake the world. Why, we'd have to register with the State Department as foreign agents! Everybody will want a piece of the pie. But they haven't answered our letter yet, so I suggest we cross that bridge when we come to it."

It was then that I got the idea of asking her when she'd sent the letter. When she told me last month, I asked her to call the Soviet embassy to be sure they'd received it. The next day, when she called, they told her they had received the letter and that they'd be in contact with our office soon.

The Soviet matter came up again two weeks later, one Wednesday in June 1980, while I was in a meeting of the city council's Transportation Committee discussing a motion presented by a councilman from Brooklyn and co-sponsored by me. The purpose of the proposal was to end discrimination by the yellow cabs,[29] who refused to take passengers to the South Bronx, South Brooklyn, Harlem, El Barrio, and other neighborhoods. In the middle of the meeting, while I was denouncing the racism and criminal actions of the owners of yellow cabs, one of the aides interrupted me to tell me that I should call my office in the Bronx right away. I had an idea what it was about, since I'd told Isolina that she should interrupt me in a meeting only in case of an urgent matter, like an invitation to meet the Soviets. I officially excused myself from the meeting and called my office. The phone was busy. I had to wait about five minutes before the line was free. I finally got through to Isolina. I asked her what had happened.

"Oh, Mr. Gerena," she said, "you have to come immediately. You have a visit from a delegation from the Soviet Union in your office."

I went out and flagged down the first cab I saw. Since I was going to the South Bronx and was used to taxis refusing to take me to that neighborhood, the first thing I did when I got in was take down the cab number and the cabbie's name. I asked him to take me as fast as he could to my office at 391 E. 149th St. in the South Bronx, near Third Avenue. Any cabbie in New York would know that that area was perfectly safe, but when I told him where I was going, he said he was sorry but he didn't go to the Bronx, since it was full of addicts and criminals, and it was outside his territory. I told him who I was, and his reply was, "I'm sorry, you might be the president of the United States, but this is my cab and I say where I go and where I don't go. So do me a favor and get out and find a nigger or spic taxi to take you."

I was so furious that I told him I wasn't getting out, that he could take me to the nearest police station, and that I was reporting him to the taxi commission. We didn't have to go far. On the corner of Broadway and Church St. I saw a patrol car. I called the cop over. When he got to us, I told him what had happened. The cop apparently couldn't believe his ears. "Well, buddy," he said in his deepest tough-cop voice, "if he doesn't want to take you where you want to go, that's his right. Get another taxi."

That was that, then. I took down the cop's badge number while I told him he was not doing his duty. All he said was, "So file a complaint," and he walked away. I had no alternative but to get out of the taxi, since I was already late for the meeting with the Soviets. Fortunately, I soon got another cab that took me to my destination. I gave that cabbie a good tip; the other one I reported to the taxi commission, but he apparently had some pull there, since to this day I'm waiting to be called to testify against him.

Meanwhile, Isolina, always efficient, had offered the Soviets coffee, soft drinks, and pastry. When I came in, the visitors seemed delighted to see me—I'm not sure whether because they were tired of waiting or because Isolina had made them feel welcome. They were a committee appointed by the Soviet Union's Peace Council, and they'd come to tell me that an official commission would be coming the next week to visit the South Bronx. I told them there were several points of interest I'd like them to see, but they insisted that they wanted to visit Charlotte St. The person in charge of the group wanted to prepare a detailed schedule for the visit, and he asked to meet some of the people that would be accompanying me. We also discussed matters relating to the security that would be provided. They were very insistent about this. Even though the New York police department would be providing security, the Soviets were bringing their own staff. For our part, I promised to bring in a group we always turned to when we needed extra security.

As was our custom when we held special activities in the district, we made up flyers with information on the Soviet delegation's visit and distributed them in the area around Charlotte St. The initiative met with enthusiasm in the neighborhood. Some residents asked us to invite the president of the Soviet Union to visit the street, as the president of the United States had done. (I figured they meant the Soviet premier. The president of the USSR had no power—or status—whatever.) We also sent press releases to the newspapers announcing the visit. We knew that the Soviet embassy would do their part, too, and mobilize the foreign press. To give the event a little more solemnity, we invited the members of the city council to join us that day. They all declined our invitation.

As per our agreement, the next Thursday we left my office on 149th St. at about 1:00 pm. When we arrived at the place we'd agreed on, the press was already set up. The chairman of the Soviet delegation, comrade Vakenti Matveev, introduced the members of his group. He explained that they were there in response to my invitation, and that I, a member of the New York city council, had made a request for economic aid to the Soviet Union in the amount of $5 billion for reconstruction of the South Bronx. As you'd expect, the news made headlines around the world.

It goes without saying that we didn't get any Soviet funds, but we did manage to call the world's attention to the problem of the South Bronx. Not long afterward, presidential candidate Ronald Reagan visited Charlotte St. as part of his campaign. It didn't go too well. People booed him and yelled at him to go home. Later, they made a bonfire on the spot where he and Carter had stood.

In the end, the government did very little to solve the problem. It was the residents in the neighborhood, those who refused to leave, that organized community associations and church groups and recruited truly committed people to help the community. And the urban renovation followed. Isolina didn't have to move out, or worry that the pimps of poverty, those who were licking their chops over the millions to be raked off the top, would take over the neighborhood.

After moving back to Puerto Rico, I visited Charlotte St. one more time. Once upon a time, the Bronx had been burning. Now the one-story ranch style residences were neat and well kept and the street looked like a suburban park. It has been called "the greatest real-estate turnaround ever."[31] I was very moved and proud to see the incredible results of a well-organized community movement.

63.
MY INITIATIVES ON THE CITY COUNCIL

During my term on the city council I presented countless resolutions. Since I wasn't "married to the mob," as I thought of the Democratic machine, many of my initiatives were rejected, shelved by some flunky, "lost," or filed in the circular file. The president of the council, an Irishman named Thomas Cuite who owed his job to the Democratic machine, controlled the calendar and decided if and when, and under what circumstances, my resolutions would be brought before the council. From the majority's point of view, there was no doubt that my proposals were out of place, embarrassing, shocking, or simply unacceptable.

For example, on one occasion I presented a resolution to the effect that the city of New York buy the Mets baseball franchise and give out contracts for the concessions that would benefit the city treasury. That one was tabled. I also suggested that a tax be levied on the tickets sold at OTB (Off Track Betting) parlors and at the horse races. That one, too. In the same spirit, I presented a proposal asking the state legislature to levy a five percent tax on the gross income generated by professional sports events. The fact was that the state and city granted professional sports teams—the Yankees and Mets in baseball, the Jets in football, the Knicks in basketball, and the Rangers in hockey—huge tax exemptions, in addition to free security and health services and publicity. My idea was to use the money to repair and maintain public parks, keep public gymnasiums and pools open until late, and hire personnel to teach sports in order to help reduce juvenile delinquency. I also submitted a bill to create a panel of sports and physical-education specialists who would submit a report to the mayor and city council within one year. Both those proposals were also tabled.

The city government couldn't have cared less about promoting sports among minorities if it were at the expense of the professional-sports magnates. It was only through the support of community organizations like Sports for the People, which had been created by professional athletes with a sense of social responsibility, that I was able to advance my agenda. Through my contacts with state and municipal community-service programs and foundations we managed, among other achievements, to establish the Roberto Clemente-Paul Robeson Park at 156th St. and Prospect Avenue in the South Bronx. Named in honor of the great Puerto Rican baseball player and that extraordinary black singer and political activist who suffered through the terrible period of McCarthyism in the United States, this community center for health and recreation was a successful model for the rest of the city and state. There, in a neighborhood abandoned by the city, the park offered exercise classes for seniors and boxing, gymnastics, dance, and martial arts for children and young people.

I also remember a resolution I presented in 1980 in which the council would censure the Time-Life Company for the way it presented the South Bronx, specifically through the stereotyping of Puerto Rican men and women in the movie *Fort Apache, the Bronx*, and would call for a boycott of that film. From the time the movie began filming, several community organizations expressed their opposition. I personally called a public hearing on the matter. My resolution generated a great deal of controversy. After several months of debate, the council voted it down. One of the results of our struggle against that racist film was the creation in 1981 of a new Puerto Rican civil rights organization, the National Congress for Puerto Rican Rights. I helped found the group, encouraging it to pass the torch in the civil-rights struggle to a new generation of young Puerto Rican activists born and raised in Puerto Rican communities in the States and tested in the struggles of the previous ten years.

I must say, however, that the council did pass several of the resolutions I presented, not because it thought they were fair or positive, but because it had no choice. In 1978, in the midst of the intense campaign we ran for the release of Puerto Rican political prisoners Oscar Collazo, Lolita Lebrón, Rafael Cancel Miranda, Andrés Cordero, and Irvin Flores, the council adopted the resolution I presented to ask President Jimmy Carter to free them. Councilmen Luis Olmedo and Roberto Rodríguez had to support it, as their respective constituencies were well aware of the issue. That same year the council adopted another resolution in support of the withdrawal of the U.S. Navy from Vieques. This time, Olmedo and Rodríguez actually co-sponsored the resolution.

In 1979, with the triumph of the Sandinista Revolution in Nicaragua and the fall of the Somoza dictatorship, I presented a resolution in support of the revolution. It passed. Not long afterward, I presented another one that asked the council to extend an invitation to the newly appointed Minister of Culture, famed poet Ernesto Cardenal, to come and talk to us about his cultural agenda for the new Nicaragua. By that time, relations between the United States and the Sandinista administration had begun to cool. Since my resolutions had been tabled so many times before, this time I stole a march on the council and told the media that the council was going to invite Cardenal to New York. When the press called the Public Relations Office for further information, the council had no choice but to recognize the existence of the resolution and say that it would probably be passed. And so it was. Cardenal was invited, and I had the honor of serving as his interpreter. Several liberal council members who spoke Spanish helped me with that job.

64.
DEFEATED BY GERRYMANDERING, BUT I SUED THEM AND WON

My victory in the municipal elections of 1977 weakened the Democratic machine's power in the Bronx. During my term I always acted as an independent, following the dictates of my conscience, and I always did everything I could to defend my constituents' rights and interests. I was, to all effects, one of the few dissident voices on the city council. Mayor Edward Koch, who was a tool of the Democratic machine that elected him, constantly put obstacles in the way of everything I tried to do, and he sometimes even excluded my district from the assignment of funds.

Not long before the end of my term, the grassroots coalition that was supporting me asked me to run again. I agreed, and I entered the primaries. The Democratic machine threw all their weight against me. Most of the elected officials who were Puerto Ricans, including Congressman Roberto (Bobby) Garcia, came out in support of the machine's candidate, Rafael Castaneira Colón, who was also supported by Ramón Vélez, whom I had defeated in 1977.

Koch, who was known as a racist, distributed a personal message around the district, written in Spanish and English, asking people to vote against me. He kept saying that I was a "bomb-throwing terrorist." One day I told him I was going to put a bomb in his pocket, to see how he felt when it actually went off. If what he said about me was a joke, then so was what I said—what was sauce for the goose was sauce for the gander.

In 1981, the Elections Board, which was, of course, controlled by the Democratic machine, carried out an electoral redistricting that I opposed because in my view it violated the rights of Puerto Ricans and other Hispanics. Although the official purpose of the redistricting was to reorganize the electoral districts on the basis of demographic growth or shrinkage within the various districts, the fact was that it was intended to maintain control of the city government by whites. As part of the initiative, the board drew a line that put my residence in another city council district.

Overnight, as though by magic, I was suddenly living in a district whose population was mainly African-American, and where there was already a leader highly respected by his constituents, Rev. Wendell Foster. He, like I, was a veteran fighter for civil rights and also had the distinction of being the first black city councilman from the Bronx. In other words, they were putting a progressive Puerto Rican and a progressive black man in the same district. One of us was bound to lose, and it was as clear as day that it would be me.

I filed a class action suit in court opposing the redistricting. Attorney César Perales from the Puerto Rican Legal Defense and Educational Fund represented me, arguing that the redistricting violated Section 5 of the Voting Rights Act of 1965. Meanwhile, I continued campaigning in the district's geographical area. Finally, with less than a week before the primaries, the federal court issued an injunction. The city council and Mayor Koch were ordered to redraw the district lines without violating the voters' rights. In May 1982, Mayor Koch signed a new law establishing the changes in the district boundaries. These boundaries favored 65 percent of the Puerto Rican population, while guaranteeing fair representation for the black community. This process had taken a year, all told, and it had given me the opportunity to cement my reputation on the city council as a fighter for my community.

The primaries were held and according to the official count I lost by 49 votes. It turned out that several of the results from precincts where I always won had "disappeared." They were found a week later in a church. Although I would have been within my rights, I decided not to ask for a recount. As I learned later, Koch boasted of having spent over $100,000 to defeat me in the primaries and elect another candidate—who, by the way, later wound up in jail on corruption charges.

The Democratic machine defeated me in those elections, but the moral victory was mine. As I was going through my files, I found a folder with information on the principle Democratic Party leaders in the Bronx who were opposed to the election of "Communist" Gerena Valentín as city councilman. During my campaign, I accused them of what they really were: thieves. And history vindicated me: In 1987, Stanley Friedman, Democratic Party chairman in the Bronx, was accused of corruption, found guilty, and sentenced to twelve years in prison. That same year, Stanley Simon had to resign as borough president and was sentenced to two years in jail. The next year, 1988, Congressman Mario Biaggi also resigned after being convicted and sentenced to prison. In 1989, Congressman Bobby Garcia was convicted of bribery and extortion in the Wedtech scandal and in January of 1990 was forced to resign his congressional seat. Finally, in 1994, Rafael Castaneira Colón, who was elected city councilman from my district in 1982, pleaded guilty to stealing almost $400,000 from the city treasury and was sentenced to two to four years in prison.

65.
THE NEW ALLIANCE PARTY AND I

One of the organizations that supported me in my campaign for city councilman for District 11 in the South Bronx was the Labor Community Alliance for Change. This group was closely associated with Dr. Fred Newman, a psychotherapist and philosopher who had founded the International Workers Party and was director of the Social Therapy Institute. The Committee, like the Party, had decidedly socialist leanings, and its program was profoundly anti-racist, anti-machista, defending the rights of racial and ethnic minorities and of women and homosexuals. Its members were deeply committed, disciplined, and dedicated.

The organization backed my campaign completely, putting at my disposal excellent organizers and financial aid. Working closely with me were Nancy Ross and Joyce Dattner, both of whom later, in the eighties, were candidates for the vice presidency of the United States for the New Alliance Party (NAP). Both were experts in mobilizing people, and they always took progressive stands, regardless of the consequences.

In 1976 and 1977 we began to discuss the idea of creating a new political party to compete with the traditional Big Two—the Democrats and Republicans. Our agenda would be clearly progressive, and aimed at attracting sectors marginalized by class, ethnicity, gender, and sexual orientation. In 1979, two years after I was elected city councilman, we officially created the NAP. At the founding meeting, I was elected president of the New York section.

The NAP headquarters were in Manhattan, but many of its members lived in the Bronx. Though a small group, the NAP reached out into many places in the city, allying with neighborhoods in their struggle against landlords, and against segregation and racism. I took an active part in those campaigns. During my term on the city council, the NAP supported my positions, and when I litigated my case against the Democratic machine, the party provided me with lawyers to defend my position.

There were people both inside and outside the Puerto Rican community who criticized my relationship with the NAP. Others, many well-intentioned, would tell me that the leadership of the New Alliance was using me. That was not the case. During all the time I worked with them, our relationship was one of mutual respect and support. I can also say with absolute certainty that many of my critics didn't contribute one red cent to help me in the electoral and legal process.

Years after my return to Puerto Rico, I read in a New York City newspaper that some of the NAP's main leaders had taken anti-Semitic positions, positions I had always completely rejected and that were totally opposed to the principles that guided the foundation of the party. But unfortunately, as often happens, time does strange things to people. Maybe they had changed. . .

66.
TAXI ORGANIZER IN MIAMI

In 1982, while I was working again as a union organizer for an independent industrial workers union in New York City, I was sent to Miami to look at the situation in the taxi industry and see how the drivers might be organized. In Miami, taxi drivers were at the mercy of the hotel industry and the government, which zealously protected the hotel industry's interests. Although not as large as New York City, Miami was and still is an enormous city, and equally or more complex, divided along racial and ethnic lines and extremely polarized over the Cuba question.

As soon as I arrived, I called my friend René, a Cuban who had been living in Miami since the Second World War. As the son of an organizer of cigar-industry workers in Tampa, René came from a long line of union fighters, and he was a socialist. Despite his support for the Cuban Revolution in a city where that was a moral stand, the workers respected him because he truly fought for their rights. Wherever he was needed, he would be there, making speeches and lifting spirits no matter whether his audience was white, black, or brown.

At this time there was a relatively large community of Haitians and Afghans in Miami in addition to the Cubans. Many of them worked in the taxi industry. The basic problem was that the three groups didn't talk to each other: the Haitians didn't talk to the Cubans or Afghans, and the Afghans didn't talk to the other two, all due to cultural and political reasons as well as the obvious linguistic ones. The idea that someone from outside would parachute in to organize them—especially someone from the North—was seen as a sacrilege. "That guy's gonna find himself in a heap of trouble," people said. Add to that the fact that most of the Cuban taxi drivers were rabid opponents of the Castro regime, so they saw me as a Puerto Rican Communist who didn't care about all the people Fidel had sent to the firing squad. But after several meetings, the Cuban taxi drivers started to feel a little better about the situation, as they realized that I wasn't there to organize another attack from the Sierra Maestra, but just to organize taxi drivers into a union that would be able to face down the big hotel cartels and the municipal government.

As a good organizer, the first thing I did was analyze the situation. I found, among other things, that the Cuban taxi drivers did favor some type of organization, while the Afghans and the Haitians were terrified of the idea of organizing due to their status as immigrants, often undocumented. Within their respective groups there were spies who reported their activities to the authorities, and the taxi drivers were always afraid of being deported. This was confirmed to me by my Haitian and Afghan contacts. After three months of intense work, I concluded that organizing this industry would take much more time than originally projected. In addition, in order to be effective, you would have to work from the inside, which meant that I would have to do as I'd done at the Emerson electronics factory in New Jersey almost 30 years earlier: go to work "on the floor." In Miami, that meant becoming a cab driver.

I returned to New York, but I left a task force working in Miami, made up of Cuban drivers. In later communications with them, they told me they had carried out some union-activist activities, and that their Haitian counterparts were beginning to work with them, overcoming to a certain extent the racism that had prevailed before. It seems that racism is one of the things that always rears its ugly head to keep workers divided. The task force also invited me to come back and work with them; they had housing and transportation arranged for me. I was tempted, I must say, but the union had another assignment for me. In the end, the taxi drivers in Miami did manage to organize. The project cost the union a small fortune, but it was worth the effort.

67.
THREE YEARS WITH
GOVERNOR CUOMO

Edward Koch wanted to be governor of New York. In 1982 he ran in the Democratic primaries against Mario Cuomo, a liberal Italian-American. After winning the primaries, Cuomo defeated the Republican candidate and in January 1983 he became governor. It goes without saying that I supported Cuomo in his campaign.

As a show of gratitude for having helped him win District 11, where I lived, by a large margin, Cuomo appointed me Special Under-Secretary for Migrant Workers. Attached to the Labor Department, this post was a political appointment with a glorified title. After several sessions of "consulting," it became clear to me that the work came down to supervising farms where hundreds and hundreds of agricultural workers picked tomatoes, onions, cabbages, and potatoes, and filing reports with my various recommendations.

My new office was on the 69th floor of Tower Two of the World Trade Center in lower Manhattan. I would take an express elevator to the 44th floor and from there, another elevator to 69. The view was incredible: you could see all of New York Harbor, and the people in the street below looked like tiny ants. My secretary, a career civil servant, told me that I was the fifth Puerto Rican she had worked with. Almost all, she said, had used the position as a springboard to better jobs. And with that same candor, I explained that any improvement in my position would be for my country, Puerto Rico, which I hoped to return to as soon as possible. At that time, I was trying to get the Labor Department's human resources office to recognize the years I had been in the Army so that in five years I would be eligible for a state pension.

In my work as special under-secretary, I had to travel constantly, so I lived most of the time in motels, which were comfortable enough but never the same as home. Usually, I would arrive where I was going on Wednesday and spend five days visiting the farms. I would go to Rochester, Albany, Syracuse, and all over Long Island to visit oyster farms and banks; to Buffalo for the dairies; and to Lockport for the cabbage farms.

Many of the workers who labored on these farms came from Puerto Rico. On the island, the government had abandoned agriculture and then, to deal with the problem of rural workers without jobs, it adopted a policy to encourage them to become contract laborers in the fields of New Jersey, Connecticut, Pennsylvania, Ohio, and New York. Facing joblessness in Puerto Rico, thousands of campesinos opted to emigrate. They simply walked away from their little farms in the hills and mountains, since there was no one to work them.

Although the workers were expected to return to Puerto Rico after the harvest, many of them saw the situation as an opportunity to make a new life in the United States. After working for a while on the farms, a laborer would find out where there were job opportunities in manufacturing nearby, and as soon as he could, he'd go there to find work. After a while, and with the security of a job, he would send for his family. He might already have a house in the little town of Glen Cove, New York, for example, and he and his family would put down roots there.

Puerto Rican workers were recognized for their excellent performance on the job. "They're one of the best workers there are; they are honest, good parents, good husbands and wives, responsible, and conscientious," Mr. James would say. He was a landowner who, year after year, would go down to Puerto Rico at Christmastime with gifts for Paco, his wife and children, who lived in Barrio Frontón in Ciales. He would also take Paco an airplane ticket so Paco would return to work in his oyster beds on Cape Cod. Paco, in turn, would say that Mr. James was like a father to him, and that he loved him.

But unfortunately not all farm owners were like Mr. James. On some farms in New Jersey and New York, workers were treated like slaves. They were made to live in rusty school buses with no facilities and with a miserable gas space heater for the cruel winters, and given cornflakes to eat for breakfast, lunch, and dinner. For many of these workers, the farm was where they lived their life, since in the nearby towns and villages they were considered undesirable. I recall the case of a bar whose owner required Puerto Ricans to wear a tie in order to come in and have a beer. His other clients, however, could come in as raggedy and badly dressed as they wanted and nothing would happen. In this case, the situation was resolved when the Puerto Ricans, fed up with the situation, made the bar owner change his discriminatory policy. . . and not because he wanted to!

During the time I occupied my new job, I was behind many improvements in working conditions on the farms. I recall that on one occasion I visited an enormous cabbage farm—over a thousand acres—where workers were required to cut and pick up heads of cabbage from dawn to dusk, and almost without rest. They looked like machines out in the fields, bobbing up and down mechanically. Although there was transportation, workers had to walk long distances for a drink of water and to go to the bathroom. After analyzing the situation, I showed that it was better for the workers and more economical for the owner to use a vehicle to transport the workers and to reduce the distances to the water cans and portable toilets. I also recommended that a second rest period be instituted in the afternoon on all farms that employed migrant workers.

One of the agricultural activities in which Puerto Ricans did not work was apple picking. For the apple harvest, the New York state government had a contract with the government of Jamaica. The owners of apple farms maintained that the Jamaican workers were better at picking that fruit. But then, in Georgia, a case came to court in which the owner of an apple farm refused to employ Puerto Rican workers. The farmer argued that although it was true that Puerto Rican workers were good, they tended to squeeze the fruit. The farmer lost his case; the court found that he had discriminated against Puerto Ricans. This case had important repercussions in New York, since it set a precedent for allowing Puerto Ricans to work on the state's apple farms.

Sometimes, Puerto Rican workers took action to improve their own working conditions. For example, there was a farm on which almost all the workers were from Ciales. One of them had brought his cousin up from Puerto Rico; the cousin sent for his wife as soon as he could, and pretty soon almost all the workers on the farm were related. The owner was done for, because if he mistreated one of them, the rest would make his life impossible. The Cialeños even sent for one family member who was a cook, so he could make Puerto Rican food for them. The food was so good that the owners of the farm would often have lunch with the workers.

After three years of working with Cuomo, I decided to retire. I wanted to spend more time with my family. Every day when I spoke on the phone with my two little daughters, who lived with their mother in Vieques, they asked when I was coming home. So in late 1985, I returned to Puerto Rico, after forty-eight years in New York. I arrived without the pension I'd have liked to have, but with a happiness that was priceless.

68.
FARMER

As soon as I retired in 1985, I moved back to my beloved Puerto Rico to be with my wife and two daughters. We lived in Vieques for about two years. With the help of Taso Zenón, one of the main leaders in the struggle to remove the U.S. Navy from Vieques, I had bought a house on a lot of about an acre and a half in Barrio Monte Santo. It was a beautiful place—a flat lot, with fertile land, on the road to the airport. The house had four bedrooms, one bathroom, and a large living room, dining room, and kitchen. A small creek ran behind the house, and when it rained it tended to overflow a little.

As soon as we moved there, I planted orange and lemon trees. There was also a breadfruit tree that bore fruit all year round. We had so much breadfruit that I would give it away to people living nearby. There were cashew, tamarind, and mango trees, two or three shade trees, and several coconut palms. When Hurricane Hugo hit in 1989, it tore the shade trees and the cashew tree out of the ground and destroyed the rest of the harvest. The breadfruit tree was split down the middle. The wooden house was also destroyed—the winds tore off the roof and drug addicts carried off the windows. A few years later, the same thing happened when Hurricane Georges hit.

Since I had family in Lares, I would often visit. In 1986, on one of those visits, my cousin Yaya asked me if I was interested in a little farm. My ears pricked up, because I had wanted to move back to Lares. She told me that she wanted to move back to New York City, and she offered to sell me the house, which was on a four-and-a-half acre piece of land. The house was made of concrete, with three bedrooms, a living room, a dining room, kitchen, and one bathroom. It had a carport and two porches. It was one of the houses that the government had built in Lares.

Yaya's offer was like a gift from heaven. It was on that farm that I had learned to work the land when I was just a boy. I'd also picked coffee, washed it, dried it, and ground it. The mango trees that I played under as a child were still standing. Now, I called it home again. We put the girls in a Catholic school, and then, a year later, we enrolled them in the public school in San Sebastián. Both schools gave them an excellent education.

The land on my little farm is very rich and fertile. There's a creek that's part of the watershed for Lake Guajataca, which supplies water to several towns in the vicinity. There's so much water underground that there's a spring on my property. I swear it's the sweetest water a man can drink. I'm sure the spring has enough water to supply several households. In fact, all the houses up on that mountain plain are blessed by water. The land lies 1200 feet above sea level, and it's so cold during the winter months that you have to wear a sweater, and at night sleep under blankets. In the spring, it's cool, usually between 60° and 65°. And the air, of course, is clean and pure.

This farm had been divided among the children of my uncle, Juan Cruz Valentín, when he died. I didn't inherit anything, although a relative told me that my uncle had left me a small piece of land, about an acre, that I've never seen. The relative who was in charge of dividing up the inheritance said that I had refused it, which was not true. Anyway, now I have my little plot of land. But as happens many times in these inheritance cases, I discovered that one cousin had illegally fenced off half an acre of the land I bought from Yaya. As I write this, we're in court over it, since I have the plot plan and the evidence that I bought four and a half acres. Although my cousin has died since I brought the suit, his children continue to claim that half acre.

I completely remodeled the house. On the ground floor I built a comfortable apartment, and beside it, I extended the house to make a library, a laundry room, and add about 12 more feet to the master bedroom. I put in new windows and built a studio and a terrace for entertaining. I planted all sorts of heliconias—birds of paradise, lobster claws, all that sort of thing—along with anthuriums, bromeliads, crotons, and medicinal plants. In front of the house I planted lots and lots of roses. I have one acre planted in plantains and another in beans and other vegetables. I planted a very pretty little cashew tree, and I have peaches, apples, figs, all sorts of citrus fruits, papayas, avocados, breadfruit nuts, the big variety of breadfruit, soursop and other kinds of tropical fruit, including a rambutan, a Southeast Asian tree with sweet fruit something like the lychee. I also grow eggplant, corn, and tomatoes. Not long ago I planted 300 plantain trees on an acre of land.

I still have my two mango trees. According to the oldest neighbors of mine, one of the trees is more than 120 years old. And the other one is no spring chicken. It takes four adults to put their arms around the older one. Beside it is a gourd tree, and two or three others. In 1993, I found some money to plant oranges. I bought a thousand small trees. They flourished, but Hurricane Georges destroyed almost all of them.

I farm for pleasure, and to raise food to eat. I never sell what I harvest. What Silita and I don't eat, we give to relatives, friends, and neighbors. I have a wonderful life on my little piece of land. I have Silita beside me—she is always with me and shares not only our daily life and my projects, but also the memories of a past of hard work, fighting the good fight, and respect. And I'm still writing. . .

69.
PUERTO RICAN CITIZENSHIP

Having lived so many years in the United States and having experienced so much prejudice and injustice there served to reaffirm my sense of being Puerto Rican. During the years of the great migration, when the government of Puerto Rico and many Puerto Ricans living in New York City, especially the elected officials and self-appointed "leaders" of the community, promoted integration through assimilation and tried in every way possible to maintain the view of Puerto Ricans as docile, I always insisted that our people should lose their fear and face reality. The United States was never, ever going to grant statehood to Puerto Rico, and that, for several reasons. First, economic: the Commonwealth sends a ton of money into the States. Second, because of the cultural issue, and especially the issue of language.

I consider myself Puerto Rican through and through. I'm a child of Puerto Rico and I have no stepfather. Statehood has nothing to add to my culture and particularity. On the contrary, it diminishes it. Several members of my family, including my uncle and my mother, were among the 288 Puerto Ricans who in 1917 rejected the American citizenship offered them by their colonial masters. As the story was told to me, many of them were farmers, who later accepted American citizenship grudgingly, since it was the only way to get banks to give them the loans they needed in order to maintain their land. In 1993, following the example of my mother and my uncle, I became a citizen of Puerto Rico. A certificate issued by the State Department recognized the existence of our national citizenship.

I have to give credit to José "Fufi" Santori, former basketball player, professor, columnist, and sports commentator, who in 1993 challenged the island's *independentistas* to renounce their American citizenship and demand that Puerto Rican citizenship be recognized. The idea was welcomed by thousands of Puerto Ricans who were disgusted by having to claim citizenship in a country that had abused, mistreated, and deceived them, and illegally kept the island under colonial conditions for almost a hundred years. Santori's proposal generated an intense debate within the ranks of Puerto Rican *inidependentismo*.

A few months afterward, during the celebration of the Grito de Lares, I used my moment on the speaker's box to publicly announce my renunciation of American citizenship and encourage everyone present at the ceremony to do the same. The idea was met with great applause. That same afternoon, attorney Luis Garrastegui, my dear childhood friend, notarized over two hundred renunciations, including, of course, mine. Attorney Juan Mari Bras, present as always at that sacred tribute to *independentismo*, hailed this initiative, and proposed a legal experiment that included renouncing American citizenship under the aegis of the U.S. Immigration Act, a tactic I had not thought about when I made my proposal.

Under Fufi's leadership, several of us decided to organize an ad hoc movement to promote Puerto Rican citizenship; we called it the Unión Nacional Pro Patria (UNA). I was elected secretary. The project included issuing a Puerto Rican passport to those who renounced their U.S. citizenship. In November of that same year, we called a meeting in the Liberty Theater in Quebradillas, where, in addition to collecting more renunciations, we issued over three hundred Puerto Rican passports.

From that point on, every year on September 23, in celebration of the Grito de Lares, on July 25 in Guánica, and at other UNA activities, we would gather renunciations. But over time, the enthusiasm waned. Fufi, who was the organization's spokesman, fell ill, which kept him from continuing to lead the movement. Today, it's more rhetoric than action. We need to revive the organization and the movement.

Let me take a moment to recognize the contribution of Juan Mari Bras to all this. It was he who developed the legal arguments for the existence of Puerto Rican citizenship and once again unmasked the colonial status of Puerto Rico when, following the procedure established by law, he formally renounced his American citizenship in Venezuela in 1995. When his renunciation was accepted, he was asked what country he wanted to be deported to, and he answered Barrio Salud in Mayagüez, which is where he lived. That action served to further strengthen our struggle for the American authorities' legal recognition of Puerto Rican citizenship. On trips they made outside Puerto Rico, many of those traveling as Puerto Rican citizens had their Puerto Rican passports stamped, further confirming the legality of our citizenship.

So far, over eleven hundred Puerto Ricans proudly display the Puerto Rican passport identifying us as Puerto Rican citizens. Although the campaign to renounce American citizenship is no longer in effect, it marked a significant step in our struggle, which was inspired by maestro Pedro Albizu Campos back in the early twentieth century.

Down through the years, many Puerto Ricans have been deceived into wanting something—statehood—that is simply not possible. I tell those people that Puerto Rican citizenship will be the only allegiance that will make us stronger. Those who pay homage to American citizenship actually, if unconsciously, seek to go on living in a welfare state.

70.
A SOLDIER IN THE
BATTLE OF VIEQUES

After the sham agreement the U.S. Navy signed with the colonial government over Culebra, we moved our meetings from 2642 Broadway to 173 E. 116th St., to the offices of the Folklore Festival, of which I was a member of the Board of Directors. That was where we undertook another struggle—the struggle to get the Navy out of Vieques and all of Puerto Rico. It was a hard fight, but we finally did get the Navy to withdraw, and the whole island of Puerto Rico was the winner.

In the 1940s, the U.S. Navy had taken over a large amount of land in Vieques. When it transferred its maneuvers from Culebra to Vieques, the island became a virtual hell—now, the same vultures that once flew over Culebra were bombarding Vieques. And to top it off, it wasn't just American ships, but also vessels from the English, Dutch, Argentine, and other countries' navies, which paid the United States $6000 an hour to make life even more miserable for the residents of Vieques. Finally, the opposition to the presence of the U.S. Navy was organized on the island and started to protest.

In 1978, while I was a New York City councilman, I was visited by Carlos "Taso" Zenón, president of the Vieques Fishermen's Association. Taso, who was a statehooder, was aware of the movement we had developed in New York in the early seventies to get the Navy out of Culebra, and also knew about the important lobbying and pressuring we had done at both the state and national level. He came to New York to ask us to do the same with Vieques; that is, create a support group in New York and take a clear, convincing message to Washington that the military maneuvers on Vieques had to stop.

And that's what we did. The 78 town-clubs, from Arecibo to Yabucoa, who had supported the struggle against the Navy in Culebra redirected their mission to get it out of Vieques now. The Vieques Support Committee met every Wednesday at 7:30 pm. In addition to the town-clubs, the Committee included labor leaders from textile unions, industrial unions, and Local 1199 of the hospital union, which was led by Denis Rivera, as well as several political groups, including the Puerto Rican Socialist Party. It was clear from the beginning that this would be a broad-based movement of solidarity with Vieques, not one concerned with promoting Puerto Rican independence.

We saturated businesses with flyers and passed out flyers at the entrances to the subway. Between 1982 and 1984, there was not a wall in New York City that we didn't cover with bills saying "Get the Navy out of Vieques." We organized art exhibits on the subject of Vieques in several places, including the Museo del Barrio. We visited schools, held radio debates, and prepared a petition in Spanish, English, and French in support of Vieques. We gathered over ten thousand signatures. In 1984 we organized a march on Washington, D.C., in which over five thousand Puerto Ricans took part demanding that Congress get the Navy out of Vieques. It was at that activity that we delivered the signatures we had collected to our congressional representatives. In addition to our support activities, we organized several fund-raising events, including dances at the Vieques town-club headquarters, and we sent the money to the Fishermen's Crusade led by Zenón. We also donated a photocopying machine to him. As a city councilman, in March of 1979 I persuaded the city council to pass a resolution—Resolution 109—in support of the withdrawal of the Navy from Vieques.

In 1983, not long before my return to Puerto Rico, the Navy, responding to growing pressure, signed an agreement with Gov. Carlos Romero Barceló in which it promised to be a good neighbor and encourage industrial development on Vieques. This had the effect of weakening our movement. In 1985, when I returned to Puerto Rico, the struggle had cooled down a bit. My commitment to Vieques, however, never ebbed. I moved to Vieques to live, and continued to take part in events and activities there.

In the late nineties, and specifically in 1999, after an errant bomb exploded near an observation post and killed a guard named David Sanes, the struggle once again caught fire. Immediately, groups began invading land that "belonged" to the Navy, while the fishermen sailed out into open waters to defy the Navy's heavy artillery. I, in turn, went back to work full time in the struggle, and among other things would travel almost every weekend from Lares, up in the mountains, to Vieques, taking food, water, and soft drinks to comrades who were doing civil disobedience at what we were calling Camp David, in honor of David Sanes. Lino Hernández, owner of the Econo supermarket chain in Puerto Rico, always sent a big shipment of food and water with me.

In the year 2000, I was arrested, as was my dear friend from New York City, Chegüi Torres,[32] who had also joined the struggle, for entering Navy lands. We were taken before a judge who spent his free time playing golf with one of the Navy admirals. We were held for three days on Roosevelt Roads Naval Base and then set free. I had told my attorney, Elías Abreu, not to take me in front of some kangaroo court, and if they found me in contempt of court and ordered my arrest, they'd have to come for me in Lares and cut the chains that I'd used to chain myself to the tamarind tree I helped plant with Albizu Campos.

In February 2000 I helped organize a large delegation, representing all the groups fighting against the Navy presence in Vieques, to go to Washington to lobby the members of Congress still supposedly "neutral" in the debate. I received donations from friends to help pay for airline tickets and lodging for the delegates. We set up a picket line outside the White House. I think they remembered what had happened in 1950 and 1954 so they mobilized a line of cops to surround the demonstration. We did a good job. We met with several members of Congress, and as a result of our lobbying, the Defense Department started looking for an alternative site for their maneuvers.

Around this time, Ramón Vélez and I had smoked the peace pipe. He was still in charge of the Puerto Rican Day Parade. In a meeting in his apartment, with his wife Cary present, Ramón promised to dedicate the parade that year to Vieques. He also told me, "I think we should dedicate the Parade to Pedro Albizu Campos, too." And Ramón kept his promise. A big delegation flew in from Puerto Rico; I had made all the arrangements for them. In that edition of the Parade over a thousand people marched in the Vieques contingent. We saw thousands of the town's flags flying among the participants. Among those attending the parade was the First Lady, Hillary Clinton, who danced on the dais when the Vieques contingent passed by. Over a million people lined up on the sidewalks of Fifth Avenue to cheer, while millions more television viewers across the United States witnessed this mass repudiation of the Navy's presence in Vieques. In the end, we persuaded the New York state legislature to adopt a resolution denouncing the Navy's presence in Vieques. There was practically no organization in New York City that did not join our struggle. And although New York was the center of the struggle, it spread to many other parts of the country.

Camp García looked like a Lego town beside the tremendous activity that took place in front of Camp David. Even dogs wandered in and out of the Navy land. I recall that a mutt we called Negro came into the camp one day, trotted over to one of the Navy men, lifted his leg, and peed on the sailor's boots. The sailor tried to kick Negro away, but Negro was quicker—he bit the sailor on left calf, and with that, the dog became the whole camp's mascot overnight. Everyone wanted to adopt him.

There was so much pressure that the Navy finally had to give in. They started looking for other islands to bomb. They even played with the idea of building a floating island similar to Vieques in the middle of the ocean. (I imagine they demoted the genius who came up with that one!) Finally, after thirty-nine years, the Navy pulled out of Vieques and, not long after, Roosevelt Roads. When they withdrew from Vieques they left behind God only knew how much contamination from the bombs and munitions, a tremendous number of people with hearing problems, cancer, skin diseases, and blood poisoning as the Navy's payment to the people of the little island for having used their land for training sailors and mercenaries to kill human beings in distant lands. At least the population of Vieques no longer has to live every day with the hell the Navy created. And one social good came out of all this: The young people of Puerto Rico learned to fight for a free, sovereign land governed by justice and freedom. We set an example for men and women not just in the United States, but around the world—we showed that you can fight the navy of the most powerful country on the planet and win.

71.
RAMÓN VÉLEZ AND I

In early 2000, I learned that the board of directors of the Hunts Point Multiple Services Center (HPMSC) had thrown Ramón Vélez off the board without due process. I immediately sent a press release to Gerson Borrero, who at that time was editor-in-chief of the newspaper *El Diario-La Prensa*. My title was "In Defense of Ramón S. Vélez." I can imagine Gerson's face when he saw that title.

And he had every right to be surprised. For over twenty years, Ramón Vélez and I were political adversaries. Our battles were legendary—perhaps bloodier than any other Puerto Rican leaders in the history of the Puerto Rican community in the Unites States. Why, on one occasion there was a rumor that Ramón had put a price on my head. But I repeat: Ramón Vélez and I were adversaries; we weren't enemies. I, at least, saw it that way. The fight between us was essentially a struggle between people with different ideas as to the means for achieving a single end: improving the conditions of Puerto Ricans living in New York City. In addition, Ramón, like me, was always proud of being a Puerto Rican, and he was a patriot.

Ramón was an extremely astute, hardworking politician with a gift for organizing people. But he had no scruples, politically speaking. You never knew where he stood: one day he might be on the right, the next day on the left, and the day after that somewhere in the middle. He arrived in New Jersey in 1962, where I've been told he organized migrant workers, and he lived in the South Bronx. There, he found the support of Luis Gigante, an Italian priest very active in that community, who helped Ramón found the United Organizations of the Bronx. In his thirst for power, and to undermine my political base in the city, mainly within the Congreso de Pueblos, Ramón joined the Democratic Party—in the Bronx, Puerto Ricans voted Democratic. In my first campaign for the city council, in 1965, the Congreso de Pueblos campaigned against me fiercely within the Puerto Rican community.

There was also a move to take the leadership of the Puerto Rican Day Parade away from me, since I didn't play according to the Democratic machine's rules. In that, Ramón also played a part, and with the support given him by the machine, he took over the Parade, in the process redefining its purpose.

It was also the support of the Democratic Party machine that in large part allowed Ramón to receive funds from the War Against Poverty and thereby to lay the foundations of what came to be his personal political empire. And that was what led to the Puerto Rican Community Development Project, which eventually he came to control. He was accused of nepotism, favoritism, and misappropriation of funds.

But in the world of New York politics, Ramón was hardly an exception, and his legacy was a positive one. In an abandoned community like the South Bronx, he set up a series of service programs that helped mitigate the miserable conditions of life. He supported, among other initiatives, the creation of Lincoln Hospital and the Eugenio María de Hostos Community College of the City University of New York. Of course, he could have done much more. No one will dispute that, much less me. But others who enriched themselves on the poor—the pimps of poverty, as I call them—left nothing for anybody else. Ramón did quite a bit of good.

Years after my return to Puerto Rico, Ramón and I met one more time. He was sick, diagnosed with Alzheimer's. On one of his visits to the island, he called me to make peace. It was a very emotional meeting, in which he showed regret for some of the things he'd done to me. After that, our relationship was a good one.

In the late nineties, Ramón began to show real integrity with respect to several very controversial issues. I'll always remember that in 2000, it was Ramón, as president of the Puerto Rican Day Parade, who dedicated the event to the people of Vieques in their struggle against the U.S. Navy, and to Pedro Albizu Campos, the martyr of our people. This action earned him a ferocious denunciation from the anti-sovereign Puerto Rican mob in Puerto Rico and New York City, but Ramón was unfazed, and he went on, in his position as president of the Parade, to demand the release of Puerto Rican political prisoners from federal prison, bringing with him tremendous support from the community.

That same year, then, the board of directors fired him from the HPMSC and put him on permanent "sick leave." They also took the Parade away from him. What they did to Ramón is unforgivable. He was betrayed by the same people that he lifted up and supported. I'm sure that the same people who criticized him for his stand on Vieques and Albizu Campos were behind the firing.

Ramón died in early December 2008, in Manhattan. He asked to be buried in Hormigueros, where he was born. I attended the funeral and the burial. The casket was closed, but I asked that it be opened so I could bid him one last farewell. The family was kind enough to do so. Rest in peace, Ramón.

72.
ORGANIZING THE DIASPORA
ON THE ISLAND

Many Puerto Ricans who left Puerto Rico seeking a better life for themselves and their families never forgot their native land, and they always dreamed of returning. I know of many who never did return, but others, like myself, were able to come back. There is no doubt, though, that our stay in the U.S. marked us and defined our lives.

One of the first things I did when I returned, after kissing the ground, was start making a list with the names and addresses of everyone who had taken part in the struggles in the States, and especially in New York. The idea was to create an organization of what I called "pioneers." The project was interrupted, though, as new battles like the fight for Vieques claimed my attention. Finally, in the late nineties, I went back to my project. The notebook I was using to compile my list wasn't big enough. In 1998, I had over a hundred names. A year later, there were two hundred, and the list kept getting longer. Finally, I decided to call everyone together.

In April 2002, a hundred and twenty-five men and women came to Lares. We met at a little mountain inn, La Paragua. Some people thought the organization was founded in order to organize parties, tours, and other recreational activities. But what I had in mind was that and more. . . . My proposal was well received, and out of that meeting emerged the Asociación de Pioneros Unidos—the United Pioneers Association. Our mission was to work as volunteers to help other Puerto Ricans who had been living in the United States to come home again and make their contribution to our patria. I was elected president of the group. We agreed to launch a recruitment campaign in every municipality on the island. As part of this campaign, we held meetings in San Germán, Lares, Yauco, Mayagüez, Guayama, Luquillo, Vieques, Cidra, Cabo Rojo, and Ponce.

In Ponce we agreed to hold a parade, like the one in New York, and we incorporated that organization in June 2002 under the name Desfile de los Pueblos, Inc. We were more than prepared for this project, as three of the members of this new organization had been president of the Puerto Rican Day Parade in New York City. We agreed from the beginning that the activity would be a cultural event, and completely apolitical. Political parties divide; culture unites. The objective was to present the best of the entire spectrum of participating towns and cities: baton-twirlers, bands, floats, paso fino horses, the queens of each town and city, the folklore ballet of San Germán, San Sebastián's hammocks and yearling heifers, Lares' bananas, and many other cultural expressions of the island.

We adopted by-laws similar to those of the Puerto Rican Day Parade and created a board of directors composed of twenty-six members, plus an executive committee. I was chosen to preside over the parade the first year. We were united by a very strong sense of camaraderie. We didn't have any money, but we did have the most important things: enthusiasm, commitment, and the conviction that people would come out in droves, as they did in New York City, to support us and take part in the event.

In 2005, we held the first parade in San Juan, with the aid and support of the mayor's office. The second parade, which was held in Carolina, was not so great, since the person the municipality appointed as liaison wouldn't work with the organizers. When we took the event to Aguadilla and Yauco, though, we got tremendous support from those cities' mayors, Carlos Méndez and Abel Nazario, respectively.

In 2010, our cultural review *Grito Cultural* and the Parade committee organized a Festival de los Pueblos dedicated to the Puerto Rican flag. The idea was to pave the way for the unification of all Puerto Ricans, so that we could develop a national movement to create a new Puerto Rico. As part of this initiative, we invited our brothers and sisters living in the United States and other parts of the world to come to the island in July of that year to celebrate with us. We created an organizing committee that included people from both Puerto Rico and the United States. The festival would close with a grand concert, to be held on July 11. The mayor of Hormigueros, where the event was to be held, promised us all the help we needed. Unfortunately, the weather was against us and we had to suspend many activities, including the concert, due to thunderstorms and wind. Since then, we have not held another parade.

There were many problems we had to deal with, including a lack of financial support. Almost all the cities and towns of Puerto Rico hold cultural activities such as their patron saint's festivals and other celebrations. The smaller municipalities have very few funds available for these activities, especially one as ambitious as ours was. Another thing is that Puerto Rico is divided into warring tribes of many kinds—political parties, mainly—and there are municipal jealousies and other causes of division. So many flags, so little recognition of the one that might unite us all—the red, white, and blue of Puerto Rico with its single star. In New York it's not that way; it's easier to bring everybody together, because over and above all the political flags, the Puerto Rican flag flies highest.

Another problem we had to face was that some people thought that everybody living in New York would come to the island for the festival. That didn't happen. One of the leaders of the Puerto Rican Day Parade in New York turned against me, and even sent an infiltrator to derail our plans. Fortunately we found him out in time and could control the damage. It turns out that this former president of the Puerto Rican Day Parade in New York City belonged to Ramón Vélez' bunch, but he was such a rat that he'd turned his back on Ramón when Ramón needed him most.

I've always been an optimist. Despite all the obstacles, I'm sure that in due time this parade in Puerto Rico will come together and take off. I also firmly believe that if the Pioneers Association is reorganized and functions as it should, it will provide much-needed services to people returning to their native land.

73.
GRITO CULTURAL AND
THE LITERARY CONTEST

After we returned to Lares, my wife at the time, María Riquelme, and I actively joined in the town's cultural life. In 1988, María became director of the Lares Cultural Center. As we talked one day about what we could do to help make our culture better known, the idea occurred to us to create a publication. We requested a grant from the Institute of Puerto Rican Culture (ICP) and it was approved. And thus *Grito Cultural* was born.

We formed an editorial board, which I chaired, since I had had some newspaper experience in New York. I was also the editor and advertising man. I'm still wearing those hats today, and I'm helped by my current wife, Sila Tirado. In 1988, the first number of our review was published. We started with four pages, and we're now publishing 48. It comes out six times a year and is maintained financially through donations from businesses in towns in the center of the island.

Down through the years, many people have offered their services free of charge, including artists, professors, medical doctors, psychologists, psychiatrists, writers, and musicians—people aware of the value of a review of this kind in today's Puerto Rico. Among the contributors I might mention Eduardo Seda Bonilla, Ricardo Alegría, José Collazo, Raquel Seda Rodríguez, Héctor Bermúdez Zenón, Carlos Zenón, Ketty Maldonado, Peter Vargas, Juan Linares, Laura Escorioza, Luis Morales, Ferdinand Rivera Ortega, Awilda Palau, Carlos Delgado, Rafael Cancel Miranda, Juan Mari Bras, Eduardo Villanueva, Diómedes Avilés, Carmen Alers, and Luis Garrastegui.

Grito Cultural is a non-profit enterprise. We publish everything submitted to us, only reserving the right to edit and copyedit the articles. All the corrections are checked back with the author. Although we publish in Lares, we also distribute the review in Aguada, Quebradillas, Camuy, Mayagüez, Hormigueros, Cabo Rojo, Trujillo Alto, Aguadilla, San Sebastián, Hatillo, and Arecibo—all through the central and western parts of the island. We also send copies to libraries in schools in Puerto Rico and abroad, including New York, Chicago, Los Angeles, and Hartford in the United States, Barcelona and La Coruña in Spain, and Canada.

In the last analysis, the review is an instrument of patriotic education. Each edition presents the symbols and icons of our culture. For example, in one edition we ran articles on cockfighting arenas, how the cocks are raised, the spurs they use, and we identified the good and bad cockfight managers, all thanks to Peter Vargas. In one edition we discussed the fauna of Puerto Rico, including coquís, bats, paso fino horses, and our flora. The section on medicinal plants is terrific. Our contributors send in short articles on the use of these plants.

We created a dictionary of jíbaro expressions, a section on the Taíno culture, a legal dictionary that helps the neophyte understand a little about law and justice, and a section of sayings that's very popular. Often, our readers send in information on other sayings, and we publish it. Our poetry section is very special. Sometimes we dedicate an entire section to one poet. Since each edition of the review deals with a specific theme or subject, the poetry has to fit the theme. For example, in the edition on violence against children, all the poetry was on that subject. We did the same with the numbers devoted to Negritude and racism. We have a section called "Cheo's Page," in which we publish common linguistic errors and the crazy things people say.

One project associated with *Grito Cultural* is the Literary Contest, a competition involving poetry, short stories, and *décimas*. We started the contest in 2003, and have held it every year since then, thanks to the financial support of the Shellie and Donald Rubin Foundation. So far, we've held ten contests. A group of teachers coordinates the contest in their schools and schools near them; we focus the contest on clear and critical thinking and writing ability. Over twelve hundred students and public-school teachers have taken part in our contest, which awards prizes of $200 and $250.

74.
THE "DON" FREE SCHOOL

The "Don" of the Free School might be Don Vicente or Don Ramiro, but it has nothing to do with Donald Rubin, the president of the foundation that is helping us. Donald Rubin doesn't want his name associated with the projects he sponsors. He isn't that kind of person.

When I spoke to Don about the magnitude of the problem of drop-outs in the island's public schools—over forty percent of the students who start out in the first grade never graduate—he couldn't believe it. He suggested that I submit a proposal for preparing drop-outs to take the high-school equivalency exam. The Foundation approved my request for funding.

The project began in 2005. In *Grito Cultural* we made a plea for five classrooms, and a high school in Lares responded. In addition to the classrooms, the principal put all the school's facilities at our disposal.

The original program lasted 150 hours: five hours over thirty Saturdays. Later we reduced that to fifteen Saturdays, with the last five for review. We paid for the participants' lunches and gave them other financial incentives. If the student passed the exam, he or she was given a bonus.

Our first series of classes ended very successfully. For the second series, we decided to do an experiment and include youngsters addicted to drugs. The first of these was Germán, a kid who had dropped out of school to work but couldn't find a job, so he got involved with drugs. We explained what sort of school this was, and he agreed to take part in the program. One day Germán took me to the corner where he bought his drugs, and I met his friend Pito, a youngster born in the United States and who also joined our program. We saved them from becoming permanent citizens of the Lares cemetery.

We began the second series of classes with 25 students, of which only 7 dropped out. Of the 18 who stayed, several passed the exam, among them Germán and Pito, who applied to and were accepted in a college. Others decided to go to a vocational school.

Like the literary contest, the Free School is still going on, thanks in part to the unconditional support that Donald, through his Foundation, has given us.

75.
MY BELOVED SON JOEY

When I was told that my son had died, I couldn't control my tears. I wanted to be with him when he passed on to another life, but I couldn't, as I was in bed with pneumonia. Even when I was a bit better, I could hardly stand. Donald called my doctor to ask about me. Dr. Rodríguez told him I could walk, but only with help. Silita also had pneumonia, so she couldn't go with me. When Joey died, on Monday morning, January 7, 2012, I wasn't there. It was a very traumatic moment for me.

Joey was born one December 25 in New York City. He was a Christmas gift in one of the country's worst periods. The government was imprisoning everyone accused of being a Communist. And if people weren't imprisoned, they lost their jobs and found their lives turned into a hell. I lived through all that, and I had no alternative but to go to another state to find work in a factory, always worrying that if they found out who I was I'd lose my job. Francia, Joey's mother, was also nervous about her job, because she, like I, was involved in the struggle for social justice and was being investigated. Joey was raised in that atmosphere of uncertainty, but he was never unsure about the love that surrounded him.

The anti-Communist hysteria passed and things returned to normal.

Joey was a brilliant student. After graduating from high school, he studied musicology. He wrote music and played instruments. He had an art gallery on 86th St. on the East Side. He traveled throughout the East, visiting Nepal, Hong Kong, India, Australia, Indonesia, and Vietnam. With his death, the world lost a grand promoter of the culture of those peoples. I love you, my son.

76.
THE TAMARIND TREE

Over the course of my life, I've planted hundreds of trees. Many of them have died due to old age or the forces of nature or the actions of men. Others have shown a singular strength that has enabled them to overcome the vicissitudes of life. And some will survive forever.

In 1990, the tamarind tree I helped to plant when I was just a boy began to sicken. Its branches were drying out. Around it there was a wall and several benches where people sometimes sat down to drink, and they'd throw their empty rum bottles, beer cans, and soda bottles on the ground. There were rumors that the mayor, Héctor Hernández Arana (1989–1996), wanted to cut it down and in its place plant another palm tree, the symbol of his political party, the New Progressive Party.

Concerned about the tree's health, a group of us created an organization called Collective 23, whose mission was to rescue the tree. Through our efforts, an agronomist diagnosed what was killing it. A professor at the University of Puerto Rico's Mayagüez campus, Eugenio Toro, offered a series of recommendations that we immediately put into practice. We planted grass around the tree, pruned off its sick branches, painted the trunk with a special paint, and cut the branches off several trees that were cutting off sunlight and "crowding" it.

Professor Toro also sent a letter to the mayor recommending that a fence be built around the tree. The mayor completely ignored the letter. We decided to raise the money needed for the fence ourselves, and we canvassed the countryside in search of donors. We raised $1,300.

Meanwhile, we posted a guard 24 hours a day to be sure that nothing happened to the tree. We hired a welder to build a beautiful wrought-iron fence. We put in two gates with locks to protect the tree from its enemies, including those who littered. We painted the obelisk on the plaza, retouched the coats of arms, and put down paving stones. The tamarind started to get better.

On November 19, 1991, the day the discovery of Puerto Rico is celebrated, the mayor made his move. Since it was a holiday and all the municipal offices were supposed to be closed, we didn't post our guard. Taking advantage of that omission, the mayor sent several city workers to tear down the fence, which also tore up the paving stones—I guess we were lucky they didn't dig up the grass! When we protested and denounced the attempted arboricide, the mayor argued that the Independence Party had protested the erection of the fence and its executive committee had demanded that it be torn down.

We took the case to court. But we met nothing but postponements, so finally it all came to nothing. In 1992, the case was postponed indefinitely, probably due to pressure from the mayor's party. In 1996, the Plaza de la Revolución was rebuilt. But we maintained our vigilance and they didn't touch the tamarind or the obelisk. In 1997, a new Popular Democratic Party administration was elected, and in a show of greater awareness of the historic importance of the tamarind tree, they began giving the area regular maintenance. The New Progressive Party eventually retook the mayor's office, but they haven't touched the tree—yet. For our part, we have kept up our watch over the tree, because the mayor has decided, on his own initiative, to change the name and motto of the town from Lares, The City of the Cry for Freedom, to Lares, The City of Open Skies, so anything might happen.

Every week I go to visit the tamarind tree. It is still robust and strong. I will look after it and defend it until the day I die because I grew up believing in our patria. And when my time comes, I will go out of this world as I came into it: naked, but with the serene conviction that the tamarind tree will survive the passing of the years, for its roots are profoundly intertwined with the collective conscience of my people, and its seeds have been scattered over all of my beloved island.

NOTES

1   Until relatively recently (1956, with the naming of Hurricane Betsy, still known on the island as Santa Clara), hurricanes that struck Puerto Rico were given the names of the saint's day on which they struck. Thus, if a hurricane should strike on the same day in different years, the two or more storms would have the same name. This is the case of San Felipe I and II, which struck on September 13, 1876 and 1928, respectively.

2   The Rhoads incident shook Puerto Rican society in the early 1930s. Cornelius "Dusty" Rhoads (1898–1951) was an American pathologist, and later oncologist, who in 1931 went to Puerto Rico as part of the Rockefeller Institute anemia research commission. In a letter he wrote to a colleague in Boston, which was picked up from his desk by a Puerto Rican assistant, Rhoads made derogatory racist comments about Puerto Ricans, saying further that they should be exterminated from the earth. He also boasted that he had personally helped in the extermination process by transplanting cancer cells and killing off 8 patients. Pedro Albizu Campos and the Nationalist Party of Puerto Rico used the letter as proof of the genocidal plans of the American colonial administration. Subsequently, Rhoads made a half-hearted apology, saying the letter was intended as a joke between friends, and denied that he had intentionally killed patients. Separate investigations of records at Presbyterian Hospital, where Rhoads had been working, undertaken by the Rockefeller Foundation and the government of Puerto Rico, revealed that no patients under his care had died. The investigations were also unable to confirm that Rhoads had injected cancer cells into patients. Rhoads went on to become one of the leading cancer researchers in the United States and the first director of the Memorial Sloan-Kettering Cancer Center in New York. The controversy over Rhoads's letter was revived when in 2002 Edwin Vásquez, a University of Puerto Rico biologist, pressured the American Association for Cancer Research (AARC) to remove Dr. Rhoads's name from the most prestigious award for cancer research given by the organization. An independent investigation launched in 2003 by Dr. Jay Katz, a leading Yale University law and medical professor, confirmed the results of the 1931 investigations, but recommended that the letter itself was reprehensible enough to warrant removing Rhoads's name from the award. The AACR accepted the report, gave the award a new name, and removed Dr. Rhoads's name from the plaques of all previous recipients.

3   A *cuerda*, which is the unit of surface area used in Puerto Rico for surveying and real-estate purposes, is equivalent to .97 acre.

4   The Grito de Lares was an uprising against Spanish rule on the island, a blow struck for the island's independence. It was, as its name in Spanish notes, a "cry for freedom." Led by Ramón Emeterio Betances and Segundo Ruiz Belvis, it began in Lares and spread to various revolutionary cells on the island. Protesting Spain's treatment of the island and its citizens, Betances wrote the "Ten Commandments of Free Men," which was based on the Declaration of the Rights of Man that inspired the French Revolution, and this document lit the fuse for

the revolt. The uprising lasted just a day; it was put down by an overwhelming force of Spanish troops. The movement still inspires, however, and every September 23, independentistas and other patriots of Puerto Rican sovereignty make a pilgrimage to Lares to celebrate Puerto Rico's first attempt at securing its political self-determination in the post-Columbus world.

5   *Gofio* in its Puerto Rican incarnation is a candy made of ground starch—wheat, cassava, corn—mixed with sugar. Originally a food ingredient from the Canary Islands, it emigrated with the Canary Islanders to the Caribbean and other parts of the New World bordering the Caribbean, where in some places it took on its sweetened form. Unsweetened, it is used as a thickener in a myriad of dishes, including soups, porridges, desserts, ice creams, sauces, etc. Historically it was also sometimes eaten mixed with a small amount of milk or water and carried in a goatskin bag, as a kind of convenience-food *avant la lettre*.

6   Browder's tactic, known as "Browderism," consisted of dissolving the party and encouraging cadres of Communists to join various political and civic organizations in order to continue the party's mission of transforming capitalism through peaceful means. This strategy, a continuation of the Democratic Front, and which arose out of the agreement signed in 1943 at the Tehran Conference between the United States, the United Kingdom, and the Soviet Union, stressed that it was cooperation between the classes, not the class struggle, that was needed in the postwar world, and that could work as a peaceful vehicle for change. Browder thought that the Communist Party of the United States (CPUSA), as it was constituted at that time, was an obstacle to the transformation he felt was needed. Thus, in 1944 he dissolved the party to create the Communist Political Association.

7   Henry Wallace (1888–1965) served as secretary of agriculture (1933–1940), vice president of the United States (1941–1945), and secretary of commerce in several of President Franklin Roosevelt's administrations. In 1948, he was the Progressive Party's candidate for president. The party's platform called for the establishment of friendly relations with the Soviet Union, an end to racial segregation, the extension of the right to vote to African American, an end to discrimination against blacks and women, an increase in the minimum wage, the establishment of universal health care underwritten by the government, the strict regulation of corporations, and an end to the House Un-American Activities Committee's investigations of the "Communist threat." Wallace came in fourth, with just 2.37% of the vote.

8   See http://www.ebmarks.com/about/ for information on Marks Music.

9   The revolts began on October 30, 1950, upon the orders of Pedro Albizu Campos, president of the Nationalist Party. Uprisings occurred in Peñuelas, Mayagüez, Naranjito, Arecibo, and Ponce. The most notable uprisings occurred in Utuado, Jayuya, and San Juan. These were suppressed by strong military force, including the use of planes.

10   District Leader is an unpaid volunteer elected official. All formal parties in New York State are required to have at least one District Leader (DL) per Assembly District (AD). These positions are subject to primary elections every two years. This ostensibly guarantees that any party with formal status in New York State (e.g., a permanent ballot line) is democratically governed by its members. In essence, the District Leader is the representative of the party members in their district to that political party's apparatus.

11   Yiddish for a person from the same town or village, implying ties of friendship and community.

12 The Manhattan Center is located at 311 W. 34th St. in midtown Manhattan.

13 O[scar] Roy Chalk (June 7, 1907–December 1, 1995) was a colorful and often innovative American entrepreneur who owned real estate, airlines, bus companies, newspapers, and a rail line that hauled bananas in Central American. His diverse holdings included D.C. Transit, Trans Caribbean Airways, the Houdon bust of Thomas Jefferson now at Monticello, the Chalk Emerald, and the Spanish-language newspapers *El Diario de Nueva York* and *La Prensa*, merging them into *El Diario La Prensa*. Chalk was chairman of the United Nations finance committee for several years and was a prominent fundraiser for the Democratic Party in the 1960s. He also helped raise money for the United Negro College Fund and served on the Georgetown University Board of Regents.

14 Evelina López Antonetty (1922–1984) came to New York City in 1933 on the *SS Ponce*. Early on she distinguished herself as an activist, organizer, and leader of the Puerto Rican community. From 1946 to 1956 she worked as a union organizer, and in 1965, along with the parents of Puerto Rican children in the Bronx schools, she founded the United Bronx Parents organization, which was dedicated to educational reform, offering bilingual and bicultural childcare and adult-education services and leadership training for young people.

15 Antonia Denis (1892–1983), a social and political activist, arrived in Brooklyn, New York, from Vega Vega, Puerto Rico, during World War I. She soon became a major figure in several Brooklyn-based organizations, including La Casa de Puerto Rico, the Puerto Rican Pioneers Parade, and the Betances Democratic Club. These organizations advocated for political and social equality, celebrated Puerto Rican history and culture, and administered anti-poverty, cultural, and educational programs for Brooklyn's Puerto Rican community.

16 The Reverent Milton Galamison (1923–1998), of the Siloam Presbyterian Church in Bedford-Stuyvesant, was one of the main leaders in New York City's struggle for civil rights, equality in the workplace, and the desegregation and decentralization of the city's schools. He played a central role in the school boycotts in 1964 and 1965.

17 Ewart Guinier (1910–1990) was born in Panama to Jamaican parents. He attended high school in Boston, and in 1929 he entered Harvard University. He was the only black student in the university, the result perhaps of not having included a photograph with his application papers. During his early life he was a trade unionist, and he ran for office in New York City under the banner of the American Labor Party. He returned to Harvard as a full professor when Harvard, in response to the demands of black students, established the Department of Afro-American Studies.

18 Irma Vidal Santaella (1924–2009) was born in New York City and took part in the creation of the Puerto Rican National Civil Rights Association, the National Federation of Puerto Rican Women, and the Puerto Rican Day Parade, in which she served as chair of the board of directors. In 1961 she became the first Puerto Rican woman admitted to the New York bar association, and in 1983, the first Puerto Rican woman elected to the New York State Supreme Court.

19 Juan Antonio Corretjer (1908–1985) might be considered the poet-laureate of Puerto Rican independence. Even as a boy in school, Corretjer showed his *independentista* leanings, joining the Nationalist Youth, organizing a protest against the American colonial rule, and finally, organizing a strike at his high school to have it renamed for José de Diego. (For this, he was expelled and sent to school in another town.) As a young man he worked as a journalist while at the same

time laboring actively to secure Puerto Rico's independence. In 1936, as secretary-general of the Nationalist Party, he was part of the leadership of the Party that was tried for sedition by Federal authorities in Puerto Rico. He was sentenced to six to ten years to be served at the Federal Penitentiary in Atlanta. Upon his release from prison in 1942 he settled in New York City and would later join the Communist Party. In the early 1960s, in Puerto Rico, he founded, and became secretary-general, of the Liga Socialista Puertorriqueña. Later in his life, he became perhaps best known for his poetry, which always revolved around nationalist sentiments.

[20] Antonia (Tony) Pantoja (1922–2002) was a well-respected educator, social worker, feminist, and civil rights activist who founded many community, self-help, and educational organizations, among them ASPIRA, the Puerto Rican Forum, Boricua University, and Producir. Her memoirs, titled *Memoir of a Visionary*, were published in 2002.

[21] Meredith recovered from his gunshot wound and rejoined the march before it reached its end in Jackson. The dramatic photograph of Meredith wounded and lying in the highway, grimacing in pain, won the Pulitzer Prize for Photography in 1967.

[22] Stokely Carmichael (1921–2005) was born in Port of Spain, Trinidad, and grew up in the barrios in Harlem and the East Bronx. During the sixties he was a leader of the civil rights and Black Power movements. Carmichael was one of the six Freedom Riders who in 1961 rode the train from New Orleans to Jackson, Mississippi, in order to desegregate the train cars. He was elected head of the Student Non-Violent Coordinating Committee (SNCC) in 1966, taking over from John Lewis, one of the great leaders of the black civil rights movement. In 1969 Carmichael moved to Guinea and under his new name, Kwame Ture, became one of the main exponents of Pan-Africanism and socialism.

[23] Joseph Monserrat (1921–2005) was an important public official who from 1951 to 1969 held high positions in the New York office of the Puerto Rican Labor Department's Migration Division. Monserrat later was a member, and then president, of the New York City Board of Education.

[24] Mariana Bracetti (1825–1903) was a leader of the Puerto Rican independence movement in the 1860s and is reputed to have made the flag flown during the Grito de Lares revolt against the Spanish colonial government. Blanca Canales (1906–1996) was an educator and Nationalist leader. In 1950, she led the "Jayuya uprising," in which Nationalists took control of that town for three days. José de Diego (1866–1918) is known as the father of the Puerto Rican independence movement. He founded the Unionist Party and in 1904 was elected to the House of Delegates, the only elected governmental body allowed by the U.S. colonial administration, and chaired that body from 1904 to 1917. De Diego opposed the Jones Act, which imposed U.S. citizenship on Puerto Ricans, as he believed this action would hinder Puerto Rican independence. De Diego was also a fervent advocate of higher education, and he founded the Colegio de Agricultura y Artes Mecánicas de Mayagüez, which later became the Mayagüez campus of the University of Puerto Rico.

[25] A *tortilla española* is a Spanish omelet, made of eggs, onions, and diced potatoes.

[26] Not without reason, it turns out, did Pagán fear for his life. In 1978, two young students and pro-independence activists, Arnaldo Darío Rosado and Carlos Enrique Soto Arriví, were entrapped in a police operation, carried to the top of Cerro Maravilla in the center of the island, where their undercover police abductors said they were going to blow up a communications tower, and murdered as they pleaded for their lives. Although it took years to get to the bottom

of the plot—many elements of the government conspired to cover up the truth—eventually
ten police officers were convicted of various crimes, including murder. Even today the insular
Police Department is responding to a federal Justice Department review, and a court-ordered
restructuring, that has accused the department of rampant civil-rights abuses and police brutality.
27 El Comité–MINP (Movimiento de Izquierda Nacional Puertorriqueño—Puerto Rican
National Left Movement) was one of the main Puerto Rican radical organizations that
developed in the late 1960s and early 1970s. El Comité came out of the housing struggles that
engulfed the Upper West Side of Manhattan during the Urban Renewal/Model Cities programs.
It was formed by groups of squatters, Vietnam veterans, factory workers, the unemployed,
former gang members, and students who organized to fight what they considered to be "urban
removal," rather than urban renewal, programs being implemented in poor urban communities.
Unlike other Puerto Rican leftist organizations of the time (i.e., the Young Lords Party, the
Puerto Rican Socialist Party), El Comité was characterized by its focus on local community
issues, its rejection of the "divided nation theory" (privileging the struggle for Puerto Rican
independence over civil rights issues in the U.S.), and the view that Puerto Ricans in the U.S.
were a "national minority," that is, a minority within the American working class.
28 St. Ann's is located at 295 St. Ann's Avenue and 140th St. in the South Bronx.
29 At this time, yellow cabs were the only vehicle authorized to pick up passengers on the
street. They operate on the basis of a fixed fare and tend to concentrate in Manhattan, south
of 96th St., which creates a scarcity of taxis in other parts of the city. The need for taxis in the
other boroughs is met by gypsy cabs.
30 José Rivera, state assemblyman for the Bronx from 1983 to 1987 and from 2000 to the
present, began his career as a union organizer for construction workers and gypsy-cab drivers.
Rivera was a city councilman in New York City from 1987 to 2000, and he was president of the
Democratic Party in the Bronx from 2000 to 2008.
31 CNN on-line (http://money.cnn.com/2009/11/09/real_estate/greatest_neighborhood_
turnaround/), accessed August 5, 2013.
32 José "Chegüi" Torres (1936–2009) won a silver medal for boxing in the Melbourne Olympics
in 1956; he was world light-heavyweight champion from 1965 to 1967 and was elected to the
International Boxing Hall of Fame. He served as commissioner of the New York State Athletic
Association and was president of the World Boxing Organization. Torres was also a columnist
for El Diario La Prensa and The Village Voice and author of several books, including biographies
of Muhammad Ali and Mike Tyson.

INDEX

10736407R00179

Made in the USA
San Bernardino, CA
24 April 2014